Geopolitical and Economic Changes in the Balkan Countries

Geopolitical and *Economic Changes* *in the* *Balkan Countries*

NICHOLAS V. GIANARIS

Westport, Connecticut
London

Library of Congress Cataloging-in-Publication Data

Gianaris, Nicholas V.
    Geopolitical and economic changes in the Balkan countries
/ Nicholas V. Gianaris.
       p.   cm.
    Includes bibliographical references (p.) and index.
    ISBN 0–275–95541–9 (alk. paper)
    1. Balkan Peninsula—Economic conditions. 2. Balkan Peninsula—
Ethnic relations. 3. Balkan Peninsula—Social conditions.
4. Balkan Peninsula—Politics and government. 5. Balkan Peninsula—
Relations—European Union countries. 6. European Union countries—
Relations—Balkan Peninsula. I. Title.
HC401.G49   1996
330.94′4—dc20   95–52997

British Library Cataloguing in Publication Data is available.

Library of Congress Catalog Card Number: 95–52997
ISBN: 0–275–95541–9

First published in 1996

Praeger Publishers, 88 Post Road West, Westport, CT 06881
An imprint of Greenwood Publishing Group, Inc.

Printed in the United States of America

The paper used in this book complies with the
Permanent Paper Standard issued by the National
Information Standards Organization (Z39.48–1984).

10 9 8 7 6 5 4 3 2

To the suffering peoples of the Balkans

Contents

Illustrations

TABLES

FIGURES

Preface

The Balkan Peninsula, which is known as the powder keg of Europe, has been the battleground of different cultures, ethnicities, religions, economic institutions, and peoples, mainly because of its location at the crossroads of Europe, Asia, and Africa. As a natural bridge between Europe and the Middle East, it has had great economic and geopolitical importance from antiquity to the present time.

Throughout history, the Balkan countries, that is, Albania, Bulgaria, Greece, Romania, Turkey, and the former Yugoslavia, have largely been influenced by many ethnic, economic, religious, and political elements of the big neighboring countries and other nations. From the ancient times, the Hellenes (or Greeks), the Romans, the Byzantines, the Ottomans, and currently the European Union, the Russians, the Arab countries, and the Americans exercise a strong influence on the Balkan countries that may affect developments in Europe and, perhaps, in the whole world.

Although many efforts have been made for closer cooperation among themselves, nationalistic and religious differences frequently lead the Balkan peoples to severe conflicts, also drawing other nations into wars at times. Recent economic and political reforms and the problems created from the split of the former Yugoslavia led again to ethnic and religious disturbances and the involvement of other countries and the United Nations.

There are all kinds of economic, sociocultural, and ethnic varieties and diversities in the Balkan countries, and it is difficult for a book to encompass all of them. However, this book will concentrate on the main economic and geopolitical developments as related to ethnic, religious, and other social elements involved. Nevertheless, the weakness of comparative analysis of these countries with such diversities remains a challenge to economic and political theories and measurements.

The purpose of this book is to examine the historical background and the recent economic and political changes in the troubled Balkan countries from the standpoint of ethnic conflicts, developmental trends, and potential cooperation among themselves, as well as with the European Union. After a brief introduction in chapter 1, a historical review is presented in chapter 2. Chapters 3, 4, 5, and 6 deal with Hellas (Greece), Turkey, the former Yugoslavia, and other Balkan countries (Albania, Bulgaria, and Romania), respectively. Chapter 7 deals with economic growth, foreign trade, and international relations; whereas chapter 8 reviews the possibilities of closer cooperation and eventual integration with the European Union.

I wish to acknowledge my indebtedness to professors George Bitros, Ernest Bloch, Theodore Lianos, Kostas Papulias, John Roche, Dominick Salvatore, Robert Wolf, Paul Vouras, and Xenophon Zolotas for their stimulating comments during the earlier stages of preparation of this book. I gained significant insights from valuable discussions with professors John Kenneth Galbraith and Arthur Schlessinger, Jr., on matters of trade expansion and the possibility of "convergence" in the Balkans. Harry Gianaris, Andreas Hrysanthopoulos, Anastasios Kokaliaris, Takis Papaioannou, and Christos G. Tzelios provided useful criticism in related discussion. Many thanks to all my colleagues, especially Janis Barry-Figueroa, Clive Daniel, and Shapoor Vali, for their valuable suggestions for the improvement of the manuscript. My final debt goes to Deirdre Cogger, Tania Garrido, Pauline Hamme, Mun Suk Lee, Jaqueline Rosario, Aravella Simotas, and Telly C. Tzelios for their assistance in typing, photocopying, and related technical services.

Introduction

A BRIEF RETROSPECT

The Balkan Peninsula is located at the crossroads of three continents (Europe, Asia, and Africa). As such, it has been the battleground of rival cultures, economic institutions, and peoples (Illyrians, Thracians, Hellenes (or Greeks), Persians, Romans, Slavs, and Turks). Frequently, big powers have found fertile ground for their influence and conflicts, but as the saying goes, "When elephants quarrel, the grass is destroyed." The term *Balkanization* is used for similar conflicts around the world, whereas the Balkan Peninsula is known as the "power keg of Europe."

Historically, the inhabitants of the Balkan Peninsula were thought to be descendants of the Indo-European race to which Romans, Germans, Slavs, and other Europeans also belong. They moved primarily from central Europe during the fifth millennium B.C. In the second millennium B.C., the Greek-speaking Achaeans and Ionians, Aeolians, and Makednoi can be distinguished in the south.

Although the Hellenes were not considered the original inhabitants of the peninsula, they were the first to leave a record of themselves and their neighbors. The Illyrians were probably the first inhabitants of the peninsula. They settled mainly on the western coast, opposite the heel of Italy, where the Albanians (who are considered their descendants) live today. In the eastern part of the peninsula were the light-haired and gray-eyed Thracians.[1]

The Thracians (Thrake, in Greek mythology, was the daughter of Oceanus and Parthenope and the sister of Europa), an Indo-European people having common roots with Hellenes, were kin to the Illyrians and the Phrygians (a Thraco-Macedonian people related to Trojans). They had the same religion and the same gods as the Hellenes. They worshipped Zeus, Hera, Apollo, Ares, Artemis, Dionysus, and other divinities. According to Herodotus (V, 3), the Thracians were "the biggest nation in the world, next to the Indians." They were unreliable and belligerent and extremely hard to fight. However, Homer describes them as noble and virtuous. They lived mainly between Ypsaltai (eastern Thrace) and Edoni (between the Strymon and the Nestos rivers), Artakii and Tribali (between Haimos and the Danube).[2]

In the southwestern part of the peninsula—mainland Hellas or Greece—were the Achaeans, an Alpine people who had migrated from central Europe. They were descendants of Achaeus, grandson of Hellene, the legendary ancestor of the Hellenes.

The Achaeans, descendants of the Hellenes, moved to Peloponnesus, and by 1400 B.C. they had developed into a powerful maritime nation and overran Crete. Around 1200 B.C., they started the long Trojan expedition in Asia Minor (recounted by Homer in his *Iliad* and *Odyssey*).

The Makednoi (Macedonians) split into three groups. One group moved into central Greece and the Peloponnesus, one to Thessaly and Doris (and together with the local populations acquired the name "Dorians"), and another group to Macedonia. In 1100 B.C., the Dorians moved south and colonized central Greece, Crete, Sicily, and parts of Asia Minor. Pelasgians and other tribes living in the area were largely assimilated. In the seventh century B.C., and later, the Macedonians, under the dynasty of Argeads and the Temenids, moved eastward from the area of Kastoria to Mount Vermion, Pieria, and crossed the river Axios to east Macedonia. The Macedonian rulers claimed to be the descendants of Heracles and therefore, genuine Hellenes. At the same time, the Hellenes, primarily Ionians, developed trade and founded colonies in the Black Sea and other places up to the Danube, including the colonies of Vachia near Belgrade, Histria, Callatis, and Byzantium (later renamed Constantinople).[3] During the sixth century B.C., the Achaean League, which resembled the present European Union, was created and the first silver coins appeared in Aegina. In the fifth century B.C., the Athenian democracy reached its acme in trade, shipping, and the arts.

Rapid economic and cultural developments occurred during the reigns of Kings Amyntas, Philip II (395–336 B.C.) and his son, Alexander the Great

(336–323 B.C.). Philip overran the divided Greek city-states while Alexander marched northward to Danube to subjugate the unruly Thracian tribes and then eastward to conquer Asia Minor, Egypt, Persia, and Punjab. Under Alexander the Great, who was a student of Aristotle (a Greek philosopher born in Stagira of Macedonia), a remarkable diffusion of Greek culture occurred not only in the Balkan peninsula but throughout the Asiatic domains.[4]

Under the Romans (31 B.C. to A.D. 326), the Illyrian lands flourished, but the rest of the Balkans, especially Greece, suffered a steady decline. The construction of the Egnatia highway from the Adriatic coast to Salonika or Thessaloniki and Constantinople and other roads facilitated trade and the transfer of slaves, including Spartacus.

During the Byzantine period (326–1453), the introduction of the Christian religion and the spread of the Hellenic language generated unity and economic development in the area. From the fourth century onward, the Slavs moved southward and slowly settled into Balkan areas. Later, the Slavs became permanent settlers and formed different ethnic groups (Slovenes, Croatians, and Serbs). In the seventh century, a Finno-Tatar race, known as Bulgarians, moved from the Volga Valley to the south of the Danube and were assimilated into the Slavic majority. In a number of ways, the Slavic economic and political system was a form of village cooperative.[5] During the Ottoman period (1453–1913), almost all the Balkan regions came under the occupation of the Turks.

THE PROBLEM OF MINORITIES

Among the minorities (nationalities) in the Balkans are the Albanians in the former Yugoslavia, about 1.7 million in 1981, mainly in Kosovo (about 85 percent of the population are primarily Muslim but without high esteem for Islam). Muslims in Yugoslavia are considered as Slavs converted to Islam during the period of the Ottoman rule. Kosovo is the focus of ethnic conflict because for the Serbs it is the heartland (holy land) of the medieval Serbian kingdom. Many monuments of the Serbian Christian Orthodox church are located in Kosovo, where thousands of Serbs were massacred by Turkish invaders 500 years ago. For the Albanian ethnic majority, it is the place where the national revival began (the League of Prizren) in 1878. Also, there were 377,726 Albanians (or 19.8 percent of the population) of the Former Yugoslav Republic of Macedonia (FYROM) according to the 1981 census and 13.4 percent Muslims in Montenegro.[6]

Although there are not official statistics, sources based on historical accounts, schools, and Greek Orthodox churches estimate that some 400,000 ethnic Greeks live in Albania. However, the government ordered name changes for the citizens and the villages (Administrative Decree 5339, 1975, and other decrees) to "pure Albanian names" (e.g., from Saint Nicholas to Drita), and it is difficult to have reliable figures. As a result of liberalization, the Democratic Union Party of the Greek minority (which the Albanian president Sali Berisha estimated at 80,000) known as Omonia, was registered in 1991, but later six members of the party, including elected deputies, were imprisoned. Although they were released, mainly because some 250,000 Albanians were working in Greece and sent back valuable convertible currency, fears of minorities regarding human rights violations exist.[7]

FYROM has a mosaic of minorities. The largest minority is the Albanians followed by the Serbs, Greeks, Bulgarians, Gypsies, and others. In many cases, religion is a more unifying factor than ethnicity. Kiro Gligorov, the first president of FYROM (1991–95), was arguing that he was using the name of the new state "Macedonia," which Tito introduced in 1945 for the territory of South Serbia, for expansionary reasons, as a glue to keep these diverse minorities together. However, the split of the former Yugoslavia and the conflicts thereafter proved how difficult it is to keep this mosaic of ethnicities together no matter how many years they are under occupation or oppression. Perhaps the incorporation of this territory and the other Balkan states into a united Europe, with allowances for people to freely express different national identities, appears to be the best long-run solution.

The majority of the population of Greece (95 percent) is ethnically Greek. Large-scale changes were due to ethnic migrations from 1913 to 1926. Some 25,000 Greeks left Bulgaria for Greece, and 52,000 Slavs left Greece for Bulgaria. Following the Greco-Turkish war of 1920–22 and as a result of the peace treaty of July 1924, the Greek and Turkish populations of Turkey and Greece, respectively, were to be exchanged, except for the Greeks of Istanbul and the Turks of western Thrace. About 1.5 million Greeks left Turkey and settled in Greece (540,000 in Greek Macedonia) and 390,000 Muslims, mostly Turks and smaller minorities like the Pomaks (Muslim Greeks) immigrated to Turkey. According to the 1981 census, there are 60,000 Muslims in western Thrace, 30,000 Pomaks, 20,000 Athingani or Roma (Gypsies), and smaller populations of Gagauz, Sarakatsani, and Circassians.[8] After the Turkish atrocities in September 1955, of 180,000 Greeks living in Istanbul, only a few thousand remained. (More details are provided in chapter 4.) Other sizable minorities are the Muslims in Bulgaria (about 10 percent) and the Hungarians in Romania (about one-third of the population of Transylvania) and in Vojvodina (under 19 percent in 1981). The Serbs of Croatia and Bosnia and Herzegovina (about one-third of the population in each) are fighting because they do not want to be under the control of these two states, as explained in more detail in chapters 5 and 7.

The friction among Balkan states or, rather, nations, parts of which are minorities, is a frequent phenomenon in the peninsula and leads to the Balkanization of the region. In addition to recognized minorities in almost all Balkan countries, there are those that are scattered throughout the region, such as Roma or Vlachs, who have no states of their own and may in the future organize and create further conflicts.

COMMON PROBLEMS

Geographically, the Balkan Peninsula is located southeast of the Alps and the Carpathian Mountains. It is a mountainous area (the term *Balkans* means *mountains* in Turkish) that includes Albania, Bulgaria, Greece, Romania, the former Yugoslavia, and part of Turkey. Although all six countries are included in most Balkan studies, at times Turkey is excluded as an Asian country, and Romania is excluded as a country depending heavily on central Europe.

It is usually argued that the geographical complexity of the area has been a significant factor in the disunity and polyethnicity of the Balkan peoples, who throughout history have repeatedly found themselves in the midst of powerful cultural and economic crosscurrents. In a region with such great diversity, it is difficult to find a unifying force, a center around which a strong state could be created.

The economies of the former Socialist Balkan countries face the problems of low production incentives, inadequate consumer choices, and, in many cases, inefficient resource allocation, mainly because of remaining controls on their economies. Production incentives seem to be higher under private ownership than under state or public controls, especially in agriculture and small-scale industries. As Aristotle said in criticizing Plato's ideal Communist state, common ownership means common neglect.[9] The establishment of middle-level corporations, the encouragement of private farm markets, and vertical and regional decentralization of decision making, practiced to some extent in recent years, are measures intended to stimulate incentives and increase productivity. However, better results can be achieved by the free market mechanism, not by more government controls, because the government is best that governs least, as Thomas Jefferson said.

Such concurrent trends and reforms bring the Balkan nations closer to each other and prepare the ground for more cooperation and, possibly, common developmental policies. The rapid growth of mutual trade in recent years, and the numerous bilateral and multilateral agreements for joint investment projects, tend to submerge religious and nationalistic differences and to lead these countries toward eventual convergence by adopting the best of each other's traits. There is always the possibility of recurrence of regional or political disputes and frictions that these nations have experienced so frequently in the past. However, such frictions would most likely lead to greater economic isolation, restrictions on resource movements, and less socioeconomic development.

The need for hard currencies, the recent inflationary pressures, and the gradual transformation from agriculture to industry and services, as well as the need for resource utilization and environmental protection, are common problems that require similar and coordinated policies. Moreover, the fact that the Balkan Peninsula stands as a bridge between Europe and the Middle East makes common efforts for the improvement of the transportation network necessary.

At present, common problems facing the Balkan region that are expected to continue in the future are those of reducing inflation, raising labor productivity, and eliminating ethnic and religious disturbances.

Other major problems of the Balkans are those of satisfying growing demand, cutting down on raw material and energy consumption, and correcting adverse foreign trade balances. To avoid extensive use of raw materials and increased imports, plans with somewhat lower overall and industrial growth targets have been implemented. To increase productivity, reforms have been introduced that will stimulate capital investments.

These countries have introduced tax incentives and other benefits to encourage investments, particularly in backward regions. Their governments make great efforts to manipulate aggregate demand through public spending and tax programs, so that they can achieve the happy, but perhaps elusive, combination of high employment and low inflation. However, as similar programs in other market economies indicate, the problems of inflation and unemployment require long-term policies committed to greater and more efficient production through capital investment and incentives for higher rates of labor productivity. To fight inflation and reduce unemployment the Balkan governments are trying to reduce bureaucracy, implement fiscal restraints, and boost productive investment.

Bulgaria and Romania have effected a number of measures designed to give greater latitude to large enterprises, which remain under state control, to maintain their own activities. Such measures include greater work participation in decision making, profit sharing, and higher rewards to the workers and managers of efficient enterprises, as well as bringing management closer to production operations. Moreover, reorganizations in industry and agriculture include the creation of larger production units and delegating more power to middle management on matters of self-financing.

Such reforms, which have been introduced in almost all Balkan countries, emphasize more autonomy and a competitive spirit among enterprises. Reforms in Yugoslavia incorporate the novel concept of workers' self-management as an evolutionary process of "withering away the state." It would seem that a similar principle is contemplated, and is slowly creeping into, the economic reforms practiced by other countries in the area, in the form of easing statism and decentralizing decision making. The dilemma in such reforms is how to stimulate efficiency through decentralization and, at the same time, avoid inflationary tendencies.

In all Balkan countries inflation has become a serious problem. Each group or class in these countries seeks a bigger share of the national income that is based on aspirations and expectations about inflation. In the previously controlled Balkan economies, inflation, which officially was not recognized, was attributed primarily to structural emphasis on investment and the resulting shortages in consumer goods relative to incomes. Continuous emphasis on the capital producing sector, at the neglect of the consumer sector, in these countries led to periodic shortages in needed commodities. This was a form of concealed inflation.

Because of regional economic differences inherited from the past, all Balkan governments have emphasized policies of development of backward areas, which include establishment of infrastructural facilities, subsidies, and tax incentives for new investment. However, such policies of lessening regional inequities, have had only limited success, and per capita income disparities remain a serious problem for the policy makers.

A common problem for the Balkan countries is the negative balance of trade. Year after year they face sizable trade deficits and rapidly growing foreign debts. The ratio of debt service to exports has increased, particularly for Greece and Turkey. More exports are required to pay for servicing the debt, the value of the currency declines, and the credit position deteriorates. That is why all Balkan countries have changed their laws to encourage foreign investment. They hope to attract foreign firms that will do business on their soil, thereby acquiring new technology, improving their terms of trade, and earning hard currency needed to service their growing debt.

Heavy dependence on foreign trade requires flexibility in foreign trans-actions and, eventually, structural innovations in the economy. However, bilateral negotiations should remain; otherwise, many opportunities may be lost, since some countries want to make greater concessions than others. Nevertheless, concessions between the European Union (EU), of which Greece is a full member and Turkey is an associate member, and the other Balkan countries come in packages and affect all countries involved.

Gradually, Balkan countries are laying aside ideology and making efforts to generate practical solutions to problems concerning a better livelihood for their peoples through a growing foreign trade and improved relations with other countries. In the past, Western discrimination and a monolithic foreign trade system in the East held back expansion of trade in the area. However, growing dependence on money, both domestically and interna-tionally, an increase in multilateral transactions, and the growing role of interest and prices in the Balkan economies support the free market mecha-nism. Such a development and the growing cooperation make the economic systems of the Balkan countries increasingly similar and indicate that some arguments of the convergence thesis may prove to be correct.

Economically, there are still state monopolies, national price systems (that fail to reflect relative scarcities), and arbitrary exchange rates and inconvertible currencies that lead to domestic and foreign imbalances. Although power is scarce for most persons in the Balkan economies, politically it is abundant for the few, and this gives politics great control over economics. At the same time it is difficult to accept a trade-off between freedom and equality in these economies, despite arguments of support of an egalitarian society.

It should be recognized that country comparisons on economic perform-ance and factor productivity are difficult in practice because of differences in the process of price determination, consumer tastes, and data gathering and interpretation. Sector-by-sector or industry-by-industry comparisons probably are more reliable.

SCOPE

Historically, various peoples have inhabited the Balkan Peninsula. Even the present composition of the population of each of its nations is not homogeneous. Furthermore, each of these countries follows its own socio-economic policy. Perhaps, the Balkan Peninsula is the only area in the world that incorporates such a variety of ethnicities and problems.

Long occupations, religious and ethnic conflicts, and constant involvement of "big powers" have been common experiences of the Balkan nations throughout history. The area is strategically vital to the world's power centers, but the people who live in the region are not responsible for others' sensitivity and interests. Like the rest of us, they prefer to put their own needs and aspirations first. They do not like to have their own interests subordinated to those of other countries and to remain under the constant uneasiness of the superpowers' rivalries. Thus, it is of great interest to examine the possibilities of closer cooperation among the people of this region.

With respect to natural and human resources of the peninsula, the question may arise as to their effective use to achieve high rates of economic growth (compared with other countries at the same or higher stages of development). Comparisons of labor and capital productivities, differences in inflation rates, and deviations in economic policies will indicate areas of further cooperation and possible joint ventures.

An important question related to the structure and organization of production and distribution in the Balkan countries is which economic policies can be more effective in achieving the highest rates of growth with the least sacrifice in terms of consumer choice, workers' advantages, pollution, and the like. To what extent and in which sectors of the economy can the price mechanism bring about better results than government controls? Is development planning a proper instrument to coordinate all the sectors of the economy so as to achieve the highest levels of output, while avoiding the traps of bureaucracy? Are the Balkan countries in the process of economic convergence by adopting the best of each other's traits?

Economic development, which refers to material improvement and the dissemination of knowledge and technology, is identified with structural transformation of the economy from predominantly subsistence agriculture to industry and services. To what extent has this sectoral transformation been achieved by the Balkan economies?

Increase in intra-Balkan and foreign trade would spread the benefits of development to all the countries concerned through division of labor and specialization. However, questions may be raised about sectoral and regional inequalities that may appear in each country and within the region. Moreover, while the rapid spread of multinational corporations in the area is conducive to the dissemination of the technological transformation and managerial know-how, it has also created a fear of foreign domination in some segments of the population.

More economic growth means increased production, which may lead to resource depletion, urbanization, and environmental deterioration. Economic progress eases some problems, such as health, education, and material well-being, but it creates others that affect the quality of life. Thus, closer cooperation among the Balkan nations is desirable not only on economic but also on sociocultural and environmental grounds. The following chapters review all the aforementioned issues associated with the economic and geopolitical conditions and trends in the Balkan countries.

This study presents a brief historical review of the Balkan countries and attempts to shed light on the underlying geopolitical factors that have affected the process of development in the area. It also points out that the complex terrain, the struggle against invasions, and the political and economic instability within the region have hindered regional cooperation and racial assimilation of the Balkan peoples, in a way similar to what no other countries have experienced throughout history. The strategic position of the peninsula has attracted the intrusion and repeated involvement of the great powers in affairs of these countries, for the promotion of their own geopolitical and economic interests.

From ancient times to the Roman period, then through Byzantium, the Ottoman occupation, and primarily during the postliberation and interwar years, the Balkan Peninsula had such a turbulent history that some specialists argued that peace in the West could be assured if the Balkans could be sunk beneath the sea. Events there were usually reported to the rest of the world in times of trouble and terror; otherwise they were ignored.

The following review of such a broad topic is admittedly brief and selective, but it was considered necessary for an objective evaluation of the socioeconomic and political complexities of the countries involved.

It is our hope that this survey will suggest, and lead to, more detailed studies of the various phases of the Balkan economies and institutions. Such studies might be of major practical value in the coming years, since the Balkan Peninsula is expected to play an important role in facilitating transportation and trade between Europe and the Middle East. Moreover, the trends toward closer cooperation among Balkan nations present new areas for further research and exploration not only in economics but also in sociocultural and political developments. However, the weakness of comparative analysis of countries with different problems, such as the Balkans, remains a major difficulty and a challenge.

Although a considerable number of studies have been made on the individual Balkan countries, little or no attention has been given to the Balkan countries as a group. This work attempts to fill this lacuna and to furnish a comprehensive examination of the socioeconomic and geopolitical developments of this region. Recent visits and personal contacts in all Balkan countries have reinforced the belief of the author that the Balkan peoples desire closer economic and sociocultural cooperation for the improvement of their standard of living, although under severe conflicts for some of them.

The purpose of this study is to reveal the main characteristics of the Balkan countries and to review developmental trends toward closer cooperation among them. Such trends may affect the nature of development in larger blocs of countries, particularly the Common Market group in Western Europe and the Commonwealth of Independent States (SIC) of the former Soviet Union. From that point of view, portions of the book can be used as supplementary material to related graduate or undergraduate courses in comparative economic and political systems, public policy, and international relations.

$$2$$

A Historical Perspective

ANCIENT TIMES

In ancient times (from 3400 B.C. to 1100 B.C.), the first culture in the area flourished on Crete, a Mediterranean island south of the Balkan Peninsula. Gradually the Cretan (Minoan) culture, radiating over the neighboring areas, influenced the mainlanders of the southern Balkan Peninsula, the Achaeans, from the Hellenic race, who came in successive waves from the Alps and central Europe. The Achaeans, with Mycenae (in Peloponnesus) as their center, adopted the Cretan culture and developed their own civilization, which in turn spread to the Aegean islands, Syria, Asia Minor, and other Mediterranean lands.

At about 1100 B.C., the Dorians, from the same Hellenic race as the Achaeans, appeared. They were considered to be the descendants of Dorus, the son of Hellene. Under pressure from the Thracians and Illyrian barbarians, they infiltrated and finally colonized central Greece, the Aegean islands, southwestern Asia Minor, Sicily, and Crete, gradually replacing the civilizations of the Minoans and the Mycenaeans. Finally the Achaeans were restricted to the northern coast of Peloponnesus, mostly to the area presently known as the province of Achaea. The southern coast of Peloponnesus (Laconia) was considered an important center of the Dorians. The Spartans, a military and disciplined people, were always looked upon as the descendants of the Dorians.

The Makednoi (or Macedonians), also from the same Hellenic race as the Dorians, inhabited northern Hellas (Greece), known as Macedonia.

During the sixth century B.C., the Achaeans established a league of ten or twelve towns, which survived until the fourth century B.C., when the area was conquered by the Macedonians. Following the death of Alexander the Great (323 B.C.), the Achaean League was reestablished (in 280 B.C.); between 251 and 229 B.C. it was expanded by the addition of the non-Achaean states of Sicyon, Corinth, Megalopolis, and Argos. Each member of the confederacy retained its independence, but all members participated in a council that met twice a year to formulate a common economic and foreign policy and to enact legislation involving common coinage and related matters. Aratus of Sicyon and Philopoemen of Megalopolis were among the prominent statesmen of this Achaean League, which resembled modern federal systems and economic unions similar to the present economic communities (EU, NAFTA).

From the Homeric Age (around 1200 B.C.) to the Classical Age (beginning in the fifth century B.C.), the society of the early Hellenes was primarily agricultural and pastoral. By this time the city-state (polis) as an independent political and economic unit had been created. Athens was the main center of civilization at the time. The expansion of city-states brought about the development of trade and commerce in the coastal areas of the Balkan Peninsula and the eastern Mediterranean. It was during that time that the first silver coins appeared in Lydia and Aegina. Banking services, shipbuilding, and agriculture flourished and markets expanded. Trade and commerce not only were carried out in the coastal areas of the Aegean, Adriatic, and Black Seas but also were expanded to Phoenicia, Egypt, Sicily, and other Mediterranean lands.[1] All this was accomplished despite opposition from the Greek philosophers and writers (mainly Plato, Aristotle, and Xenophon) who regarded trade as a dishonest occupation and the charging of interest as immoral and unnatural.[2]

As early as the seventh century B.C., the Ionians, from the western islands of Greece, moved eastward and established a number of colonies, including Byzantium (later renamed Constantinople).

During the Golden Age (fifth century B.C.) Athens reached its acme not only in terms of economic prosperity but also in terms of theories and philosophies that are still part of basic scientific concepts. Together with its nearby port of Piraeus, and under the leadership of Themistocles and Pericles, the area thrived in trade, shipping, industry, and the arts. A number of arcades, the most famous called Degma, were used for exhibitions and exchanges of commodities from all the commercial centers of the Balkan

Peninsula and the eastern Mediterranean. Merchants and adventurers sailed eastward to the Indian Ocean and westward to Gibraltar, which ancient Greeks called the Pillars of Hercules, to explore new markets and sources of supply. These adventurers were the first to support the notion of a direct canal in the Suez for the purpose of facilitating the flow of trade from the Indian Ocean, through Aden, to the Mediterranean ports, and vice versa.[3]

Despite arguments presented by Plato, Herodotus, and Aristotle against tariffs and in favor of direct taxes, ad valorem taxes of 1 to 2 percent were imposed on imports and exports. Later, however, a tax system similar to the modern progressive system, referred to as "contribution," was introduced to finance shipbuilding and other state expenditures. Regulations similar to antitrust laws were enacted to prevent price fixing and to discourage monopolization of the market. Monopolies were permitted only when they supported state policies or offered free meals to the poor. At that time the systematic study of economics or *oikonomia* (estate management and public administration) was introduced. Much later, prominent economists and theoreticians such as Thomas Aquinas, Adam Smith, Karl Marx, and Joseph Schumpeter based their theories of just prices, division of labor, and welfarism ("the good life"), and their economic ideologies upon such philosophies.[4]

However, the non-Hellenic people who inhabited the interior of the Balkan Peninsula did not share very much in the stimulating experience of the commercial and seafaring Greeks, and remained mostly agricultural and pastoral. The penetration of Greek civilization to the interior plateau and the Hellenization of the Balkan Peninsula were difficult, mainly because of mountainous and rough terrain. Nevertheless, Greek colonies were established along the coasts of Dalmatia and the Black Sea and along the banks of the Danube (for instance, Vachia, ten miles from Belgrade, and Histria and Callatis on the Lower Danube).

In the colonies of Dalmatia, metallurgical and other craft works were established, and manufactured goods were exchanged for raw materials produced in the interior by the Illyrian tribes. Similar colonies along the eastern section of the peninsula, where the more tolerant and less ferocious Thracians lived, were more successful in trade and shipping.

The independent and jealous Greek city-states, which once had fought each other, were forced to form alliances and leagues in order to defend their land and civilization from Persian invaders (mainly Kings Cyrus, Darius, and Xerxes) at Marathon, Salamis, and Plataea. It was Philip II, king of Macedonia (395–336 B.C.) and his son Alexander the Great (a student of Aristotle) who subdued and unified the Greek city-states to finally dispel the Persian danger once and for all. The Macedonians who claimed to be descendants of Heracles, marched northward to the Danube and southward to the rest of Greece. Under the command of Alexander, they marched eastward through Asia Minor and the Middle East, up to Persia and the Far East. After the death of Alexander, a Greco-Macedonian state, incorporating the Balkans as well as other eastern Mediterranean regions, survived until the area fell under the control of Roman conquerors. Throughout this Hellenistic period (395–106 B.C.), the Hellenic culture was extended within the interior of the Balkan Peninsula. It was also diffused along the eastern Mediterranean coast and even into Asia. As a consequence, the Balkan Peninsula lost its economic and social supremacy to other commercial centers of the eastern Mediterranean.[5]

THE ROMAN PERIOD

The Romans first conquered the Adriatic coast, then Macedonia and its environs, and finally southern Greece, when the Achaean League was defeated during the second century B.C. As a result, the whole Balkan Peninsula was brought under a single rule. The Illyrian lands flourished under the Romans, but the rest of the Balkans, especially Hellas, suffered a steady economic decline. However, the construction of a well-organized network of paved highways, particularly the one stretching from the Adriatic coast at Dyrrhachium (Duzazzo) to Salonika, via Egnatia, provided the basis for the development of trade to the interior. This brought into existence local industries: weaving, marble quarrying, mining, lumbering, production of wine and table delicacies, and the like. Also, military camps in Singidinum (Belgrade), Naissus (Nis), Sardica (Sofia), Philippopolis (Plovdiv), and Adrianople (Edivne) were swiftly expanded into trade centers.

The Latin language was spread throughout Balkania, especially among the Illyrians, to the extent that many people thought that they belonged to the same Roman race, the Romiosine. This name was later used as a unifying force against the Ottoman yoke, and was used even in more recent times. However, Greek culture and civilization also exerted a great influence over the Romans, particularly the upper classes, to the extent that many historians and social scientists call this era the Greco-Roman period.[6]

In the north the Romans used the Danube River as their frontier. However, in A.D. 106, Emperor Trajan crossed the river and conquered the area known as Dacia. Although little is known about the first inhabitants of Romania, it is generally accepted that at that time Dacia was inhabited by Thracians, who engaged mainly in agriculture, cattle raising, mining (gold and silver), and domestic and foreign trade. The Romans, with their efficient administration of justice and the security of life and property under the Roman system, stimulated the permanent establishment of peddlers, soldiers, and workers from Italy and other Mediterranean areas in Balkania, especially in Romania.

When the Romans withdrew under pressure from the Goths, they left behind the name of the state as well as the fundamentals for the Romanian language. They managed to Latinize the country to a considerable extent. (Even present-day Romanians take pride in the fact that they are the offspring of the ancient Dacians and Romans. Recently they even changed the spelling of the country's name from Rumania to Romania.) After the Romans, a number of invaders—the Avars, Slavs, Getae, Huns, Bulgarians, Hungarians, Kumans, and Tatars—succeeded one another. To secure protection, most of the native inhabitants fled to the Carpathian Mountains. After the string of invasions and disturbances, which lasted for about 1,000 years, the Romanian population settled (around the thirteenth century) in the provinces of Moldavia, Wallachia, Transylvania, Bukovina, Bessarabia, and the Banat of Temesvar.

In the south, Roman merchants used the Aegean islands for their shipping and trading activities. During that period the island of Delos became an important junction for the transport and exchange of commodities and slaves from east to west. One authority states that some 10,000 slaves were sold in a single day in this market.[7] A similarly prosperous market was developed on the Adriatic coast, where thousands of slaves from the Balkan countries were sold. At that time the term *Slav* meant *slave*. More than a million slaves from Macedonia, Thrace, and the rest of Hellas were sold to Italy and Sicily at a relatively high price, because of the variety in their skills.

The Romans were efficient administrators and organizers. They managed to bring together the diverse Balkans and other Mediterranean peoples, and keep them under their control for centuries. Emperor Augustus is credited with bringing the whole Balkan Peninsula within the Mediterranean civilization. However, it was the Roman Emperor Constantine who broke with Western tradition by enthroning himself in the Greek trading post of Byzantium. This was where merchants from the Aegean and Black Seas met with those from Asia and the Balkan interior, developing the city into an important economic and cultural center.

Although wealth was concentrated with limited numbers of people and the breach between the classes widened, commerce and cottage industries flourished in Balkan cities during the Roman period. The Illyrian lands provided valuable raw materials used by the growing commercial cities. Illyrian peasants provided brave soldiers for the Roman legions, and some became famous emperors, such as Claudius II, Aurelian, and Diocletian. The excellent administration of justice, the good roads, the comforts of the towns (with their theaters and baths), and the granting of Roman citizenship to all free men of the empire by Emperor Caracalla in 212, facilitated business travel and enhanced the economic and cultural development of the area. However, a number of tribes, mainly of German and Slavic origin, started to move toward the south, using the Danube River as their main route, and gradually weakened the Roman military and administrative structure in the Balkan Peninsula.

BYZANTIUM

The overexpansion of the Roman Empire and the pressures of invaders from the north, mainly Goths, weakened its administration, paralyzed the processes of production and exchange, and led to the rivalries of emperors and armies. At that time (326) Emperor Constantine moved the capital of the empire to New Rome (Constantinople as of A.D. 330). Because of destructive raids carried out by the Goths, the western section of the empire collapsed, and Rome came under the control of Alaric I in 410. However, the eastern part of the empire, known as Byzantium, held its ground for about ten centuries, despite raids by Goths, Slavs, and Mongolians.

Administrative reforms, stimulation of trade (by reducing taxes on commerce), the strengthening of a common Hellenic language, and the introduction of the Christian religion through the efforts of the emperors of Byzantium were primarily responsible for the unity maintained in the East. Moreover, the geographical position of the Balkan Peninsula, with its mountainous area and the protection given by the Danube to the north, enhanced the prospects for the survival of Byzantium. As a result, the reputation of Constantinople as a commercial and industrial center was furthered. Jewelry, pottery, weaponry, shipping, and textiles (mainly silk goods) were its main industries.

Nevertheless, attacks from the north continued against the Byzantine Empire. During the fourth century, hordes of Slavs crossed the Danube and pushed the native Illyrians and Thracians southward. The influx of the Slavs into the Balkan Peninsula began as a gradual infiltration. Although other peoples, primarily Mongolian Huns (with Attila as their main leader) and Avars from Asia, crossed the area, they did not settle, as the Slavs did. By the seventh century, the Slavs were recognized by Byzantium (mainly by

Emperor Heraclius I) as permanent settlers, and started forming the different ethnic groups of later times (Slovenes, Croatians, Serbs, and the groups
in Bulgaria). At times, Avars attacked the Slavs, and Slav tribes began
fighting among themselves. While the Mongolians were nomads, dropping
no roots in Balkania, the Slavs kept advancing slowly to the south, creating
agricultural settlements.

Near the end of the seventh century a Finno-Tatar race, related to the
Huns from Asia and later known as Bulgarians, moved from the Volga valley
to the south of the Danube, where they settled. Soon they were assimilated
into the Slavic majority, which was primarily engaged in agricultural and
pastoral pursuits.[8] During the ninth and tenth centuries this population mix
created its own (Bulgarian) ethnicity, and once even threatened to overrun
Constantinople. In the ninth and tenth centuries, under Khan Boris and his
son Simeon, the Bulgarians reached the peak of their political and economic
power. At that time they accepted Christianity from Constantinople and
were influenced by Greek culture. In 1054 the Roman Catholic and Eastern
Orthodox churches split over doctrine, ritual, and the infallibility of the
pope. The main agents associated with this religious and cultural transformation were the brothers Methodius and Cyril; Methodius introduced what
is known as the Cyrillic alphabet which is based on the Greek. With the
decline of the Bulgarian state, the development and expansion of the Serbian
state occurred in the central Balkans, mainly during the reigns of Ivan II
(Ivan Asen) and Stephen Dushan in the thirteenth and fourteenth centuries.

On the western side of the peninsula, the Slavs, coming mainly from the
northwestern parts of the Carpathian Mountains during the great migration
of the sixth century, pushed the Illyrians southward. Occasionally, Slav
tribes penetrated and settled in Thessaly and even Peloponnesus. However,
the coastal cities and the islands remained Greek and kept their traditional
Hellenic character.

In a number of ways the Slavic economic and political system could be
characterized as a close partnership of goods, some early form of village
cooperative, or an early type of communism. Each member of the village
was assigned a task, and for performing it would share equally in the total
labor product with all the other community members.[9] As late as the
nineteenth century, this type of institution (the *zadruga*) was still found in
various parts of the peninsula.

Under pressure from the Slavs coming into western Balkania, the native
Illyrians were pushed into the mountainous area of present-day Albania.
Despite the Slavic admixture and the influence exerted by the Greeks,
Romans, Venetians, and Turks, the Albanian people retained their predomi-

nantly pastoral activities and their language. They called their land Skipetars (children of the eagles). It seems that modern Albanians are the descendants of the ancient Illyrians.

In addition to the pressures from the north, the west, and especially the east, the economy of Byzantium experienced a continuous decline. Commercially minded Venetians, who were better organized in shipping and foreign trade, managed to settle in a number of ports and other strategic areas around the Balkan Peninsula. With the Crusaders they captured Constantinople in 1204 and annexed many islands and coastal areas, where they established a feudal system. Although they fled from Constantinople in 1261 under pressure from Michael VIII Palaeologus, the Nicaean emperor, they continued to drain the financial resources of Byzantium by collecting customs revenues and controlling banking activities. Being relieved of imperial taxes, the Venetians could undersell the Greek and other merchants in the lucrative Balkan and Mediterranean markets. Moreover, the Genoese, another commercial people, competed with the Venetians for the possession of the Golden Horn and the lucrative trade of the Black Sea.

In the southern part of the peninsula, the land of Hellas was divided up and distributed, mostly to the Latin barons. These fiefs, the largest of which were the duchy of Athens and the principality of Achaea (Morea), were established after the Fourth Crusade (1202–1204), and existed for many years.

With domains under their control, the emperors debased the currencies, increased taxes, spent on luxurious living, and pawned their crown jewels with Venetian financiers. This economic mismanagement, on top of social and religious strife and military weakness, led the empire to the point of bankruptcy, and finally it collapsed.[10] However, the spread of Byzantine religious concepts and educational and legal ideas throughout the Balkan countries influenced all the peoples of the peninsula's interior, who until then had been considered barbarians.

In later periods, the East Roman, or Byzantine, Empire faced a still more serious and untiring enemy from the east, the Mongols. Roaming the plateau of western Asia, they approached and finally swept through the Balkan Peninsula, like waves from an inrushing sea. The struggle went on until the last of the medieval invaders, the Ottoman Turks, occupied Constantinople in 1453.

OTTOMAN OCCUPATION

From the eighth century on, Turkish tribes, mainly Mongolians, moved westward and overwhelmed the Islamic and Byzantine empires. While the Byzantine rulers were preoccupied with political, economic, and religious matters at home, they neglected the incursions of the Turkish horsemen into Asia Minor. Emperor Romanus IV finally decided to come to grips with the Seljuk Turks, but it was too late. He was badly defeated at Manzikert, in distant Armenia, in 1071. Asia Minor, except for the coastal areas, gradually fell into the hands of the Turks.

As mentioned earlier, other factors that weakened the aging state of Byzantium were the advances of the Crusades and economic pressures exerted by the Venetians. While the Byzantines lamented the losses and prayed for the recapture of occupied territories, they failed to pay proper attention to their defense. In 1354 the Turks advanced on the Dardanelles and gradually moved into the Balkan Peninsula. Following their usual practice, they distributed conquered lands to their warriors. This policy helped them establish Islam in the Christian Balkans. In 1393, Bulgaria came under the heel of the oppressor, as did other Balkan areas during the following years. In 1453, Constantinople, the political and economic center of Byzantium and the symbol of Christianity in Balkania, fell to Muslims under Sultan Mohammed II.

After the bitter struggle (1444–66) Albania was conquered by the Turks. George Castriota, better known as Scanderbeg under the Turk designation, was an Albanian hero during the struggle against the Ottoman occupation. Young Castriota, who escaped from Turkish Bondage, organized the Albanians and used guerrilla tactics to defeat the Ottoman armies of Murad II and his son Mohammed II. Because of his successes Scanderbeg was acclaimed as the prince of his tribe and hailed by Balkania and the West as the "athlete of Christendom." After his death in 1468, Albania, along with other Balkan states, came under the control of the Turks.

In order to promote the economic well-being of the Balkans, Mohammed recognized the value of trade and industry, and even wanted to repopulate the peninsula with merchants, preferably Greeks. Also, trading privileges that Venice enjoyed under Byzantium were renewed.

Within a few decades after the fall of Constantinople, the whole Balkan Peninsula and its assortment of ethnic groups (Albanians, Bulgarians, Greeks, Romanians, and Slavs) were under the Ottoman yoke.[11]

Administratively, the Turkish government called Porte, was concentrated in the *serai* (the sultan's palace), while the counselors (*viziers*) operated as civil chiefs and army heads. *Pashas* and *sadjakbegs* were the main regional or provincial chiefs, while *cadis* and *muftis* acted as judges and jurists. The *spahis* (landlords and warriors) and *janissaries* (Christian boys violently recruited and converted to Islam) were part of the Ottoman troops. The sultans rewarded their followers (mainly the *spahis*) with gifts of land (*ziamets* or smaller *timars*) after each military victory, and trained the most promising *janissaries* for high positions in administration. The empire was ruled by the sultan and his family for the benefit of Muslims, who monopolized the professions and exploited their Balkan Christian subjects (the *rayahs*). Under the laws of Islam, polygamy was permitted and harems (where women were treated as inferior beings) were common.

The establishment of a common Ottoman system put an end to internal Balkan strife, and perhaps brought the peninsula and the lands of the east Mediterranean some economic improvement; but, if so, it was most likely accomplished with sacrifice of the liberty of the people and their cultural improvement. Periodically outside powers such as Spain, Venice, Hungary, Poland, Austria, and Russia engaged the Turks in wars but with limited success.

The Venetian fleet attacked Turkish army and naval forces and established a number of colonies in Dalmatia and other coastal areas of the Balkan peninsula, as well as on a number of islands, where the Venetian-style buildings and fortresses can still be seen. One of the more serious attacks by the Venetians occurred in 1687, when an army commanded by General Francesco Morosini marched from Morea and captured Athens. During the siege of Athens, the Venetians bombarded the Acropolis, which was used as a powder magazine by the Muslims, causing a partial destruction of the Parthenon.[12] Morea was recaptured by the Turks in 1715–18. However, the Ionian Islands remained under the control of Venice (from 1386 to 1797) and, for a few years (1797–99 and 1804–14), of France.

In Romania, after a short period of independence for Walachia in the thirteenth century and Moldavia in the fourteenth century, the area came under Ottoman domination in the fifteenth century. Prince Vlad III of Walachia, otherwise known as Dracula, strongly resisted the Ottoman occupation, in his peculiar way, by nailing his victims to the ground after the battles in the Romanian plains or nailing the fezzes of Turkish envoys to their heads in order to demonstrate his disdain for the sultan. Around 1600, Prince Michael the Brave managed to assert the independence of Walachia, Moldavia, and Transylvania, but for only a short period.

Economically, before the establishment of the independent principalities of Walachia and Moldavia with a central authority, the Romanian peasants had common ownership of the land in each village (similar to the present cooperatives), giving one-tenth of their produce and three days of labor per year to the village heads (*boyars*).

During the Ottoman occupation all these principalities were vassal states with some degree of independence. The Turks were more interested in economic exploitation and shipments of grain and sheep to Constantinople than in political domination. As a result, the Romanians enjoyed some degree of autonomy, and the boyars elected their own princes (the *hospodars*). Later, the country was split between the main neighboring powers. Austria acquired Transylvania (1699) and Bukovina (1775), Russia obtained Bessarabia (1812), and the rest of Romania remained under Ottoman control. In 1848, Romania and the other subject Balkan states rebelled, seeking national independence.

Toward the end of the Turkish occupation, the boyars and the monasteries controlled a large proportion of land while the peasants worked as serfs. The Greek Phanariots moved into the area as merchants and money lenders, and even achieved political power. The Mavrokordatos family, for instance, furnished five hospodars to Moldavia and two to Walachia, where they abolished serfdom in the 1740s.[13] By that time the agricultural sector had been largely commercialized, productivity had increased, and large amounts of grain produced on the plains of Romania were being exported via the Danube and the Black Sea to Austria, Turkey, and Russia. After the introduction of the "Organic Statutes" (1831–32) and the land reforms, large estates were distributed among the poor farmers. Two-thirds of each large estate was given to the tilling peasants and one-third to the local boyar. The boyar also had the authority to distribute the land after the death of the peasant owners. However, he imposed heavy labor obligations in return, or kept the land for himself. The result was the creation in Romania of large *latifundia* owned mainly by the boyars. In addition to large payments in kind, every Walachian peasant owed the boyar some fourteen days of labor a year.

The border wars and the heavy taxation and oppression practiced by Muslims and *janissaries* helped the Balkan rayahs to rise and to start a long and difficult war of liberation. Moreover, separate authorities, independent of the sultan, were created by Pasvan Oglu in a large part of Bulgaria and by Ali Pasha in Epirus and Albania during the early 1800s. About that time the Greeks of the Morea and archipelago, influenced by the promise of support from Empress Catherine of Russia, rose up against their Ottoman masters. Although the revolts of the rayahs in Morea and other Balkan areas were put down with massacres, the stubbornness of the Greek *klefts* and Serbian *heyduks*, supported by popular ballad literature praising them, gave new impetus to the struggle against the Turkish rule. George Petrovich, called Karageorge (*Black George*), proved to be a magnetic leader of the Serbian heyduks. After Karageorge, having suffered a nervous breakdown, deserted to Austria, Milosh Obrenovich, combined revolution and diplomacy to achieve autonomy for Serbia during 1830–34. The insurrection of the Greeks in 1821, combined with Russian pressures, helped speed autonomy for the Serbians.

The rebellion of the rayahs was not supported by the behavior of the high Christian clergy and the educated Greek elite in the Phanar quarter of Constantinople. On many occasions Phanariots collaborated with the sultan and were called upon to serve as administrators and civil servants, especially in Romania, where they appeared as the new masters. They even reached such high positions as *dragomans* of the Porte and of the fleet. A number of them, however, played an important role in supporting the resistance of Christian rayahs by organizing a revolutionary society, the Philike Hetairia (Society of Friends), in 1810, although it was carried out at a price of demoralizing servility to their Ottoman masters. Alexander Ypsilanti, a Russian officer of Hellenic parentage, was the head of this society, which, as a conspiratorial group with idealistic aims, began to spread through the Balkan Peninsula, primarily in Greece. This movement preached liberty and equality, ideals that sprang from the French Revolution.

The Greeks of Morea raised the banner of revolution at Aghia Lavra Kalavryta on March 21, 1821, beginning their struggle for liberation, gradually wiping out the regional Turkish garrisons. On March 23, the city of Kalamata was liberated. Under Theodore Kolokotrones, an experienced and clever leader (born of *kleft* [revolutionary] parents and a former officer in the British army in the Ionian Islands), the Greeks managed to besiege and take Tripolis, Navarino, and other towns of Morea. The fighting quickly spread to Sterea Hellas, Thessaly, Epirus, and the islands, despite massacres on the island of Chios (by Sultan Mahmud II), in Missolonghi, and in Morea (by Imbrahim Pasha with his Turco-Egyptian forces). With the help of the philhellenic societies in Europe and the romantic supporters of the Greek liberation struggle, such as Lord Byron, the Greeks achieved their independence.[14] The pressure by the Russians against the Ottomans in the Caucasus and in Balkania, and the help of the European fleet at Navarino in 1827, were additional factors affecting the progress of liberation in

Greece and the establishment of a free Greek state with its borders at Thessaly, the Arta-Volos line. From then on, Greece remained under Western influence.[15]

Throughout the Ottoman years, trade among the Balkan countries was conducted primarily by Greek merchants and, to a lesser extent, by Armenians, Jews, and Slavs.[16] The Aegean merchants, mainly from the islands of Hydra, Psara, and Spetsai, as well as Macedonian and Vlachian merchants living in northern Greece and Thessaly, became the main traders and artisans of the Balkans. Hellenic culture, which was influenced by the West, and the Hellenic language had gradually diffused throughout the commercial centers of the area, especially in the ports of the Black Sea. Other nationalities, primarily Bulgarians, sent their children to Greek schools in Athens, Salonika, Ioannina, Smyrna, and the islands. Greek merchants were regarded as the elite class of the Danube principalities, and they were instrumental in the wars of liberation against the Ottoman Empire. However, within Bulgaria, Serbia, Bosnia, and Vlachia, where people of mainly Slavic extraction lived, trade and entrepreneurial leadership had not expanded very much because of the autocratic family system (the zadruga) and the production of primarily competitive goods that were mostly consumed by the producers.[17] This may explain the accumulation of less wealth and the existence of less inequality in the northern Balkan countries compared with Greece and Turkey.

Raw materials from the Balkans were transported to central Europe and shipped from the ports of the Black Sea, mostly by Greeks who had established prosperous communities in Vienna, Bucharest, Trieste, Odessa, and Taganrog. After permission was granted to have Greek ships fly the Russian flag, in accordance with the terms of the Russo-Turkish treaty of Jassy (1792), and also as a result of the French Revolution (1789) and the Anglo-French wars, Greek merchants and mariners were able to expand their operations to the ports of Spain and France. Some 615 Greek ships carrying 5,878 cannons (useful during the struggle for liberation) were, by 1813, plying the Mediterranean.[18] This expansion of trade helped to develop handicraft industries and to create production cooperatives, such as the Ambelakia enterprise in Thessaly (1795), which manufactured and distributed dyed cotton thread, despite growing English competition.[19]

Toward the end of the Ottoman Empire, the influence of the industrial revolution in western Europe was felt in the Balkans, particularly in Romania and Yugoslavia. New handicraft and manufacturing units were created with the help of capital and know-how from capitalist Europe, and even the educational system was affected. This trend of modernization also spread in agriculture and finance, despite the Turkish bureaucracy. Exports of cotton and thread increased considerably during the second half of the eighteenth century, in spite of the existence of export tariffs.[20]

As a result of Europeanization, the administrative structure of the Porte changed and the units of janissaries were dissolved in 1826. Extensive training of army officers and civil servants took place domestically and abroad, and the bureaucratic centralism of the Ottoman Empire started to change. Even high-ranking administrators and army generals suggested that "Either we follow the European trend, or we have to return to Asia."

THE POSTLIBERATION YEARS

Having been under long periods of occupation and economic exploitation, the newly liberated rayahs of Balkania were by and large uneducated, not anxious to establish their own governments, and managed their own economic affairs. Thus, during the struggle for liberation and afterward, the Greek ex-rayahs appeared as courageous individualists with characteristics similar to those of their ancestors. However, the violent and fatal quarrels among the Greek klefts and among the sea captains over personal or territorial interests (similar to the ones among the ancient city-states) reappeared. With the economic and educational improvement of the newly created Greek state came the mystic fervor to expand the state to engulf the Greek "brothers" of Crete, Thessaly, Epirus, Macedonia, and the coast of Asia Minor.

In the meantime, Great Britain, in alliance with France, Austria, and Prussia, supported the preservation of the Ottoman Empire in order to oppose Russian expansion. Russia was forced to recross the Prut and give up Moldavia, Walachia, and Bessarabia in 1854–56, while the Ottomans were strengthening their hold on large portions of Balkania. In 1859 the assemblies of Moldavia and Walachia jointly elected Prince Alexander Cuza (as native boyar) as their common leader. With his minister Michael Kogalniceanu, Cuza introduced laws to confiscate the property of monasteries (which controlled about one-third of the arable land), and implemented agricultural reforms favoring the poverty-stricken peasants. However, Cuza was opposed by the great landlords, and since he was not effectively supported by the uneducated peasants, he was forced to abdicate in 1866. In the meantime many schools, from the elementary to the university level, were established, the judicial system was modified, and tax collection was improved.

Then, Charles Hohenzollern, a member of the ruling dynasty of Prussia, was offered the throne of Romania, which he occupied until 1914. This long period of sociopolitical stability provided the proper conditions for the modernization and economic development of the country. The construction of railways, roads, and ports, and the use of the Danubian waterway, increased the volume of mercantile traffic and stimulated domestic and foreign trade. Bucharest grew rapidly and became an intellectual and artistic center, while Braila, Galati, and Sulina developed as important ports facilitating the steadily growing exports and imports. The fertile plains of the country helped to increase productivity in wheat and corn, and Romania became a great grain-producing and grain-exporting country. Toward the end of the nineteenth century, petroleum was discovered in the foothills of the Carpathians, and this new source of wealth increased the industrial and commercial potential of the country.

However, the bulk of the rich Romanian lands belonged to a few landlords, while the peasant masses owned small pieces of land burdened with heavy debts that forced them to work as laborers on the large estates, barely earning a living. This undesirable situation led to economic unrest among the peasants.[21] Five peasant uprisings took place, the most severe occurring in 1907 (some 10,000 peasants were killed); all of them were suppressed by troops, and resulted in unfulfilled promises. Most severely repressed were the Romanian peasants of Transylvania, by the *magyars* (Hungarian landlords). As a result some 77,000 of them had immigrated to the United States by 1910.

Roughly the same condition prevailed in many other Balkan areas, especially Serbia, where the peasants cultivated the fields for a bare livelihood while the mainly Muslim lords (*beys*) extracted a large share of crops as well as personal services from the working peasants. The heavily taxed peasants were pressed to the point of revolt in 1875, particularly in Bosnia and Herzegovina.[22]

On the other hand, the rayah group living between the Danube and the Rhodope Mountains—the Bulgarians—were gradually absorbed into the Ottoman system after the occupation of their lands in 1393, and were more completely subjugated by the Turks than the other Balkan people. Only after 1835, when they heard about the Serb and Greek rebellions, did they begin organizing for their own resistance, which lasted until their liberation was achieved in 1878. A Bulgarian uprising in 1876 was crushed by the Turkish militia, who were well known for their terror tactics, and more than 10,000 Bulgarians were slaughtered. The Albanians, on the other side of the peninsula, were the only people in Balkania who did not revolt against the sultan, mainly because the Turks were unable to keep these mountain people under their domination. Also, many of them had turned to Islam by the time of their liberation in 1912.

After the victory of Russia over the Turks in 1877–78, when the Russians reached Adrianople and supported the creation of an enlarged Bulgaria with an outlet to the Aegean Sea, in accordance with the terms of the treaty of San Stefano, the west European powers, especially Great Britain, were jealous and suspicious of the expansion of control by the "northern bear," and wanted to revise the Treaty of Paris (1856). The Treaty of Berlin was concluded in June 1878. It permitted Russia to retake southern Bessarabia from Romania (lost in 1856) and allowed Austria to take Bosnia and Herzegovina; Britain would take over Cyprus. Romania, Serbia, and Montenegro were declared independent from the Ottoman Empire, and Greece, after negotiations, gained Thessaly and a part of Epirus in 1881. The Treaty of Berlin sanctioned the gradual replacement of Turkey in Europe by the new Balkan states; Serbia, Montenegro, Romania, and Greece were enlarged territorially.

Bulgaria elected young Alexander of Battenburg, German by birth, as ruler in 1879. But the influence of Russia upon him was so great that he was considered its agent, despite his efforts to serve the people. In 1885 a revolution took place in East Rumelia, which was united with Bulgaria. This increased the jealousy of other neighboring countries, particularly Serbia (which invaded Bulgaria unsuccessfully) and Greece; as a result, a new doctrine of a Balkan balance of power emerged. In 1887 Prince Ferdinand was crowned ruler of Bulgaria, and a few years later he supported agitation and underground activities in Macedonia—an action that stimulated similar activities and speeded up invasions by Serbia and Greece. Economically, notable progress took place in Bulgaria after liberation. Highways and railroads, connecting the interior with Varna on the Black Sea and Ruse and other ports on the Danube, helped improve internal communications and exports of cattle, wheat, and other agricultural products in exchange for manufactured goods. Similar developments occurred in education and culture.

In the Treaty of Berlin, the European powers designated Crete, Macedonia, and Armenia as objects of their concern. The Turkish sultan Abdul Hamid II, who had been associated with the Bulgarian massacres of 1876, resorted to organized genocide of the Armenians. Utilizing religious passions for political ends, he extended the slaughter of Armenian Christians not only to the mountains of Armenia bordering Russia but also to the streets of Constantinople (1894–96, 1909). By the end of 1898 the sultan, under pressure from the world powers and the rebels, withdrew his troops and administrators from Crete, which voted to join Greece in 1908. By that time disturbances had broken out in Macedonia, which later became an important area of interest in Balkan politics because of its geographical location (including the three Turkish *vilayets* of Kosovo, Monastir, and Salonika) and its variety of races and nationalities (mainly Greeks, Serbs, and Bulgarians). Other people in the area, besides the handful of Turks (landlords, or beys), were the Albanians of western Macedonia, the Kutzo-Vlachs (related to the Romanians) in scattered highland villages, and the less numerous Jewish merchants exiled from Spain (called *Spanioles*), who lived mainly in Salonika. Propaganda and secret groups, used primarily by Bulgarians and other ethnic groups against the Turkish garrisons, later experienced serious animosities among themselves. From 1908 on, military uprisings were carried out by the Young Turks in Macedonia, and later spread to other Turkish areas. For a short period of time, this Young Turks movement, which started with democratic appeals, unified the ethnic groups in Balkania, but it later proved to be as nationalistic as the Ottoman expansionary movement.

Throughout the last years of the nineteenth century and the beginning of the twentieth, the Industrial Revolution in Western Europe brought the need for new markets. Fired by the promise of good returns from investing in backward Balkan countries and other areas, the European powers increased their imperialist desires. Thus, France occupied Algiers and Tunis, England took over Egypt and Cyprus, and German enterprises moved into the Balkans and Asia Minor. The opening of the Suez Canal in 1869 gave new impetus to commercial and industrial development of the eastern Mediterranean. In the early 1890s German companies built railroads in Asia Minor, including the important line from Haidar Pasha, opposite Constantinople, to Angora, the old Seljuk capital of Konya, and as far south as Baghdad. This railway opened up trade between Europe and Asia, carrying passengers and goods from Hamburg to the Middle East. The German economic and military influence in the area alarmed not only England and France but also Russia, because of its possibility of blocking the Black Sea outlet at the Dardanelles.

In the south, as a result of the Turco-Italian war of 1912, Italy occupied Rhodes and the Dodecanese Islands, while almost all other Aegean islands, which had been considered the historic home of the Hellenic race, were evacuated by Turkey and handed over to Greece. In the meantime, an alliance of the four Christian Balkan states (Serbia, Bulgaria, Greece, and Montenegro) was formed against the Ottomans. They defeated the Turkish army and annexed neighboring territories. The Serbs occupied Uskub (Skopje) and moved as far south as Monastir, the Greeks moved northward into Epirus and Macedonia, the Bulgars moved south through the Maritsa River valley to the Aegean, and the Montenegrins moved into northern Albania. (These changes were later incorporated into the Treaty of London on May 30, 1913.) Just a month later, however, war among the Balkan allies led to the defeat of Bulgaria and the signing of the Treaty of Bucharest. Greece acquired Epirus, Serbia acquired Kosovo and eastern Novi Pazar, and western Novi Pazar was given to Montenegro.

During World War I, the Ottoman Empire and Bulgaria took the side of Germany and Austria-Hungary (the Central Powers) against France, Great Britain, and Russia (the Allies). Serbia, and later Greece and Romania, joined the Allies. Germany, Austria, and Bulgaria attacked Serbia and drove its army to the Adriatic coast, from which it was transported to Corfu by the Allies (1915). In the meantime, an Allied attack on the Dardanelles failed, but a new front was created in Salonika. In 1916, Russia attacked Austria and pushed into Bukovina. Romania was badly defeated by Austria, and was driven not only out of Bucharest but also out of the province of Walachia.[23] On the other hand, the British army, helped by the Arabs, pushed the Turks north from the Persian Gulf and Suez, and occupied Baghdad, Jerusalem, and Aleppo, cutting off the Baghdad Railway (1917). In Greece, despite the refusal of King Constantine to enter the war on the side of the Allies (because of his family connection with Germany), the army in Salonika started an attack against Bulgaria in September 1918, and advanced north through the Vardar valley, threatening Sofia. In the meantime, the United States entered the struggle (1917), filling the gap that had been created by the withdrawal of Russia from the Allied ranks after the Bolshevik Revolution. As a result, the balance of power turned in favor of the Allies. President Woodrow Wilson was instrumental in drafting the Treaty of Versailles (1919) and other treaties drawn up by the Allies (including Italy and Japan), all of which gave territorial advantages to the Balkan Allies (Serbia, Greece, and Romania).

By the Treaty of Neuilly, Bulgaria was required to pay heavy reparations to Greece, Romania, and Serbia in the form of money, cattle, and coal. This led to the abdication of King Ferdinand in favor of his son Boris III and to the accession of Stambuliski to the premiership (1919–23). As leader of the Peasants' Party, Alexander Stambuliski introduced compulsory labor and land expropriation laws. Crown and church lands, as well as private lands larger than seventy-five acres, were confiscated, with small compensation. These lands were distributed to the poor peasants.

After the establishment of borders in 1919, territorial grievances cropped up between Bulgaria and Greece, Romania, and (mainly) Serbia. Bulgarian border bands (*komitadjis*) resorted to massacres, kidnappings, and assassinations, especially on the Macedonian frontier. Stambuliski's policy of Balkan cooperation and friendship led to the suppression of the komitadjis and the voluntary exchange of populations. In 1922 large numbers of Bulgarians had to be dispossessed from Macedonia and Thrace to make room for thousands of Greek refugees from Asia Minor. As a result of these difficult economic problems, heavy taxation and hard collective labor remained the lot of the Bulgarian people for decades.

After World War I, Romania was rewarded by the Allies, receiving Transylvania from Hungary, Bukovina from Austria, and Bessarabia from Russia, and the Dobruja boundaries with Bulgaria were reestablished. However, Bessarabia, with a large number of Ukrainians living in the south and the severe russification carried out by the tsars, remained as the sword of Damocles over Romania.

Agricultural reforms similar to those carried out in Bulgaria were enacted in Romania between 1918 and 1921. Lands belonging to the crown, the state, foreigners, and absentee owners, as well as to landlords with large estates (above 100 hectares), were expropriated and distributed among the peasants having small farms. Compensation was granted to the owners in the form of state bonds with fifty-year maturity and 5 percent interest. However, a large number of peasants with small farms still remained. After Julius Mania, the leader of the National Peasant Party, became premier in 1928, export taxes were gradually abolished, rural banks were created to help provide credit to the peasants, state enterprises were improved, tariffs were reduced, and foreign investments were encouraged. Among other foreign commitments, a British firm agreed to build a canal connecting Bucharest with the Danube.

In the postliberation years, the death rate in the Balkan countries, as in the rest of Europe, declined because of medical advances and improved nutrition. However, the birth rate did not drop as much as it did in other European countries, resulting in a sharp increase in population. Immigration was curtailed by the United States and by some areas of the British Empire that either closed or drastically reduced their quotas during the interwar period. At the same time, industrialization in the cities, which could have absorbed some of the underemployed peasants, proceeded at a very slow pace, if at all. Therefore, the pressure of overpopulation upon agricultural areas was obviously great all over Balkania. It was estimated that the rural surplus population in 1930 was 50.3 percent in Greece, 51.4 percent in Romania, 53 percent in Bulgaria, and 61.5 percent in Yugoslavia.[24]

The rapid increase in population and the distribution of large estates that belonged primarily to the Magyars in Transylvania, the Russians in Bessarabia, and the Muslims beys in the other Balkan areas led to the subdivision and redivision of land into small, scattered plots given to the peasantry. This parcelization, which wasted much of the land in the formation of boundaries and paths, reduced the productivity of the land by making it difficult to apply mass-production techniques. Credit availability to the farmers was also limited, and the costs of fertilizers, farm equipment, and agricultural machinery were high enough to make them inaccessible to the peasants. For example, agricultural machinery cost three times as much or more, and fertilizers two-and-a-half times more, in Yugoslavia than in Western Europe. In every Balkan country agricultural production per hectare was far less than that in Western Europe. Likewise, production and income per person in the rural sector were as low as one-fourth or less than in France, Germany, or England. Low income left little surplus for investment, causing a pervasive low productivity and thus perpetuating the vicious circle of poverty in Balkania.

The lucrative concessions given to foreign investors also helped to maintain semicolonial economic conditions. Foreign investment concentrated on low-risk and high-profit ventures concerned with production of raw materials and semifinished products, neglecting formation of long-term capital so badly needed for self-sustained growth. Moreover, large amounts of the extremely high profits from the generous concessions were siphoned off to foreign shareholders, draining the financial resources of the Balkan nations still further. On the other hand, domestic investors concentrated on protected industries in which they could establish monopolies. All these factors were responsible for the misallocation of resources, the low level of industrialization, inadequate absorption of surplus urban population by the cities, and the perpetuation of low land and labor productivity.

During World War II, Albania, Greece, and Yugoslavia waged bloody struggles against the Axis and suffered from internecine fighting between rival groups; Bulgaria and Romania, having allied themselves with the Axis, avoided a similar ordeal. As liberation approached, the Allies, mainly Britain and Russia, increased their influence to the point of shaping postwar trends in the Balkan Peninsula. By November 1943, when the Teheran Conference took place, the British had about eighty separate missions working with the partisans in the region, sometimes supporting and coordinating them, and at other times dividing them. The main goal of the

British, inferred from the statements of Prime Minister Winston Churchill, was to restore (more or less) the prewar status quo with kings and governments sympathetic to Britain. However, the rapid advance of the Allied forces on all fronts and that of the Red Army toward Balkania led to the Moscow Conference in October 1944, at which Churchill proposed, and Stalin accepted, that Russia would "have ninety percent predominance in Rumania, for us (Britain) to have ninety percent of the say in Greece, and go fifty-fifty about Yugoslavia."[25] Russia also would have 75 percent predominance in Bulgaria and 50 percent in Hungary. This arrangement was accepted by Churchill, Franklin Roosevelt, and Josef Stalin at the Yalta Conference in February 1945.

The peace treaties signed at Paris during February 1947 gave Yugoslavia the port of Pola, the Isonzo valley, and Istria, while Trieste was placed under international control. Moreover, Italy surrendered the Dodecanese Islands to Greece and Saseno (Sazan) Island to Albania. Bulgaria restored the Greek and Yugoslav territories and acquired southern Dobruja from Romania, while Romania acquired Transylvania from Hungary and confirmed the cession of Bessarabia and northern Bukovina to Russia. As a result of the Churchill/Stalin division of the area, the northern Balkans were dominated by Communist governments until 1989, while Greece and Turkey remained under Western influence.

Hellas (Greece)

HISTORICAL PERSPECTIVE

Because of the geographical location and composition of Hellas (Greece), the main economic activities of the inhabitants were and still are shipping and trade. From the times of the Minoan (Cretan) and the Homeric civilizations (about 3400–750 B.C.) to the Athenian Golden Age (fifth century B.C.), the inhabitants of the region were distinguished by their maritime and commercial activities along the shores of the Black Sea and the eastern Mediterranean.[1]

The Achaeans and the Dorians, descendants of the same Hellenic race, migrated from the Alps and central Europe at about the beginning of the second millennium B.C. and moved to central Hellas and to the many coastlands of the eastern Mediterranean. A branch of the Achaeans became the architects of the Mycenaean civilization, which was influenced by the Minoans.

Other people, such as the Ionians, the Aeolians, and the Makednoi (or Macedonians) originated in the northern Greek mainland and were driven south and eastward. After the successful siege of Troy in about 1200 B.C. by the Mycenaeans, an amalgam of Achaeans, Ionians, Aeolians, and even the pursuing Dorians settled in the coastlands of Asia Minor, now part of Anatolia, Turkey. Smyrna and Miletus became great cultural and commercial cities after the eleventh and tenth centuries B.C., respectively. Later, these cities, together with others on mainland Greece and the islands, established many colonies along the coasts of Spain and Italy (Syracuse, Taranto, Crotone) and Libya (Apollonia and Cyrene), as well as on the coast of the Adriatic and Black Seas. In these colonies, which remained in close touch with the mother country, commerce, craftsmanship, art, and philosophy were developed.

From the sixth to the third century B.C., Athens had become an important economic and cultural center. As other city-states, such as Sparta, Corinth, Cleitor, Thebes, and, later, Salonika developed, trade and handicrafts greatly expanded. The appearance of silver and iron coins facilitated transactions and improved trade not only among the city-states but also between Greece and other lands.

However, Greek philosophers, including Plato and Aristotle, opposed profit making and interest accruing trade transactions and loans. Interest, named *tokos* or "child" of the "parent" principal in a metaphorical sense, was considered unnatural and immoral. Money cannot literally have a child; two drachmas cannot bear a baby drachma, in a natural sense, as human beings or other creatures can. Despite such philosophical arguments, profit and interest were the prime motives in trade and banking activities, which were enhanced after the invention of coins.[2]

Problems of Public Finance

With the establishment of political democracy and Draegon's laws in Athens came the development of public finance. The constitution of Solon (sixth century B.C.) abolished bondage and gave people a share in the government in a democratic fashion. However, together with the people's right to share in government affairs came their obligation to pay taxes in proportion to their incomes, derived primarily from landed property.

Thus the richest class (*pentacosiomedimni*) with evaluated property (*timema*) of 6,000 drachmas or more and income higher than 500 drachmas per year would pay 24 percent income tax, the second income class (*knights*) with estimated property of 3,000 to 5,000 drachmas and an annual income of 300 to 500 drachmas would pay 20 percent income tax, while the third income class (*zeugites*) with property estimated at 1,800 to 3,000 drachmas and an annual income of 150 to 300 drachmas, would pay 13.3 percent income tax. Finally, poor people (*thetes*) with less than 150 drachmas in annual income were exempted. In wartime, when higher government expenditures were needed, heavier taxes were imposed.[3]

This tax system, which Plato seemed to support in his *Laws*, can be characterized as a form of progressive taxation based on income differentiation. Taxed incomes were estimated primarily on the basis of landed property. Although there were tolls at the gates of the city-states and sales tax at times, income tax, levied according to property, prevailed mainly because of fewer difficulties in assessing the tax base. Regarding tariffs, it was suggested, primarily by Plato, that duties would not be levied on imports or on exports, and that imports of unnecessary luxuries and exports of necessary commodities be prohibited.

As Xenophon pointed out, government revenues were also collected from the silver mines of Lavrion, near Athens. In addition to aliens' duties (*metoikion*) and the rents from public warehouses and other buildings, the inexhaustible mines of silver provided large amounts of revenues.[4] The proprietor of the mines was the state, and those who worked in them were obliged to pay the public a tribute of one–twenty-fourth part of the silver found. The state either operated the mines itself or leased them out to private entrepreneurs, who could also form joint-stock companies. With an efficient administration, national revenue could be improved and, in periods of peace, used to construct public buildings and trading vessels, increase foreign trade, and train youth.

Originally, the citizens of Athens voluntarily contributed to the support of many public works. However, a number of officials became fully occupied in governmental services and many citizens participated, on a rotating part-time basis, in the activities of the city-state assembly (*ecclesia*) for pay. Then public expenditures grew rapidly and reserves suffered, especially during the Peloponnesian War. Under the pressure of raids from Sparta and other hostile city-states, people from the countryside fled into Athens, which provided for their sustenance from public funds (*theoricon* or Theoric Fund). This welfare system increased the proportion of idle persons, reduced production, destroyed the treasury, demoralized the citizens, and accelerated the decline of Athens. Furthermore, deficiencies in the public finance system of Sparta led to the decline of that city-state.[5] The narrow tax base of property, the income of merchants and artisans, and excises on a few commodities could not support the state's needs for defense and other expenditures for long periods. Similar phenomena can be observed today not only in market economies with a growing public sector, such as that of Greece and the other European Union (EU) countries, but also in the United States and other economies with many functions and services performed by the public sector.

Trade Expansion

In addition to the general national wealth of the mines of Lavrion, there was the valuable, splendid marble of Mount Pentelicus used for the construction of the Parthenon and other monuments, as well as for export. Also, honey was produced in Attica, Thebes, and Corinth, while olives, wine, and other agricultural products were produced in the plains and hills of these areas. Some of this produce was sold abroad. Export and import trade thrived primarily through the warm water ports of Piraeus and Salonika and those of the Aegean Islands, which have always facilitated trade between the West and the East and with the Mediterranean lands to the north.

To expand trade, the seafaring Hellenes established a number of colonies along the coast of the Balkan Peninsula and the eastern Mediterranean. Further improvement of commercial activities and crafts took place when Philip II, emperor of Macedonia, and his son Alexander the Great unified the Greek city-states (338 B.C.).

The conquests of Alexander the Great opened new horizons to Greek trade, or emporium, from the eastern Mediterranean coasts to the rich markets of the far-off East. The main commodities exported by the Greek cities at that time were metals, pottery products, textiles, and similar industrial goods. By then trade had assumed an international character following on political evolutions and very often preceding them. The products exported by the Greek cities were mostly industrial because the soil was not rich enough for large quantity production and the export of agricultural products. Trade during the Roman and Byzantine periods was, more or less, a continuation of the ancient Greek trade. Even during the long period of the Turkish occupation, trade was dominated by Greek merchants, both in the vast Ottoman Empire and in a number of cities in Western Europe.

ROMAN CONQUEST AND BYZANTIUM

Under the Roman rule, Greece (then called Achaea) lost importance, but Greek culture influenced the Romans to the extent that the invaders were themselves conquered culturally by the country they conquered physically. Greek architecture had a marked influence on that of Rome, and Romans sent their children to Athens to study. General Sulla and later other Romans shipped home Greek sculpture and kept Athenian workshops busy making replicas (after the sack of Athens in 86 B.C.).[6]

Salonika became an administrative and trade center for the Romans and the Byzantines. Its advantageous location at the crossroads of the Balkans made it an important commercial city. People and products moved from Adriatica to Byzantium and vice versa mainly through Egnatia Street (still used in Salonika).

As mentioned earlier, the Aegean Islands, particularly Delos and Rhodos, were used by the Roman armies and merchants as way stations for the transport of merchandise and slaves from the Middle East.[7] After the separation of the eastern section of the Roman Empire, cultural and commercial activities moved largely to New Rome (Constantinople), which became the capital of East Rome, or Byzantium (A.D. 326).[8]

The emperors of Byzantium introduced a common (Hellenic) language and (Christian) religion and stimulated trade by reducing taxes and making administrative reforms. Silk production, pottery, jewelry, and shipping were the main industries that flourished in Constantinople, which became an international trade center. Constantinople remained, for some ten centuries, the economic and political heart of the Byzantine Empire and the center of the Greek Orthodox religion and intellectual life. However, the spread of Christianity changed the ancient Hellenic culture, caused the closing of ancient Greek temples, and ended the Olympic games after the fourth century.

As mentioned previously, during the ninth century, two missionary brothers from Salonika, Cyril and Methodius, introduced the Cyrillic alphabet, based on the Greek. They were also responsible for the Byzantine (Eastern Orthodox) religious and cultural influence on large segments of the Slavic population. Together with other scholars, they nurtured Byzantine culture throughout the Balkans. To this day, some religious and cultural aspects of Byzantium have been preserved (since the tenth century) by many monasteries, mainly that of Mount Athos near Salonika.[9]

With the increase in imperial expenses, the weight of taxation became greater. The main levies were land taxes and hearth taxes. The latter may have been payable by every head of household while the former seems to have included taxes on arable and pasture land, vineyards, and mountain land. For humanitarian reasons, tax relief was accorded lands that had suffered disasters. Local administrators, at times, resorted to the use of labor services in road construction, shipbuilding, and similar public works, instead of levying provincial taxes.[10]

During the millennium of Byzantium, Athens wasted away, but Salonika kept its commercial importance and became a vital port in the Mediterranean. After the eleventh century, the empire and its capital city began a slow process of decline. However, a number of scholars fled or were summoned to Western Europe, carrying with them Greek philosophy and culture, "the seeds" of which "grew into some of the finest flowers of the Renaissance."[11]

Crete came under the Arabs for over one hundred years around the ninth century, and Candia, now Herakleon, became an important commercial port during that period.

In 1204, the same year that Constantinople fell to the Crusaders, Venice occupied Crete, a rich and lovely island, as Homer called it, strategically located amidst the dark blue sea, almost equidistant from Europe, Asia, and Africa. Crete, which remained for over four centuries under Venetian rule, developed a prosperous commerce, as did other islands and Greek coast-lands, where old Venetian fortresses can be seen today. Also, Franks, anxious to enjoy the sun, climate, and pleasant way of life of Greece, established their feudal system in various parts of the country, particularly in Achàea and Athens, as did the Genoese along the Anatolian coast and on various Aegean islands in the thirteenth century.

Venetian and Genoese merchants competed fiercely with the Greeks for the capture of the lucrative Mediterranean markets. They established a number of commercial outposts in many islands and coastal areas where they were engaged in trade and banking activities. With the Crusaders they occupied Constantinople (1204–61) and drained the financial resources of the Byzantine Empire by collecting tariffs and not paying taxes. Most of the land of Hellas was distributed among Venetian and Genoese barons, and a feudal system was established.

From a sociopolitical point of view, the roots of modern Greece, so the story goes, are sunk in Byzantine soil, and the attitudes of the people stem from that time.[12] The importance of the church (at least with its wealth), the centralized bureaucratic state headed by hereditary rulers, the dominance of personalities in politics, and the primacy of politics over economics in Greek policy discussions are mostly the heritage of the Byzantine and Ottoman mentalities. On the other hand, the system of centralized public administration was largely borrowed from France.

OTTOMAN OCCUPATION

The Ottoman Turks, coming from Mongolia, defeated the Byzantine army and gradually occupied Greece and Balkania. In 1430 they captured Salonika; in 1456, Athens; in 1460, Peloponnesus; in 1453, Constantinople; and in 1566, Chios and many other Aegean islands.

The Turkish newcomers distributed conquered lands to their warriors and collaborators (*spahis*). This practice helped to ensure their permanent settlement and occupation of Greece and other Balkan areas for some four centuries. The forceful recruitment of infant Christian males converted to

Islam (*janissaries*) and the toleration of the Christian religion also helped establish and sustain Ottoman rule in the area for such a long period.[13]

A number of handicraft industries and production cooperatives, including that of Ambelakia, in Thessaly, manufacturing cotton thread, were created. The Ambelakia enterprise was an outstanding example of a handicraft cooperative. It was founded in 1795 in Mount Ossa in Thessaly. Its initial capital, estimated at 100,000 francs, was gradually increased to 20 million francs by 1810. The cooperative had two branches, one agricultural and one manufacturing, which provided raw materials and produced and sold textile products primarily to Central Europe. The cooperative also provided free meals to its poor members and maintained schools and hospitals. Its dyed yarns became famous in European markets, competing effectively with similar British products. However, after the introduction of steam engines, Britain's cotton thread became cheaper than that of Ambelakia, which was spun by manual labor.

Shipping industries also operated along cooperative lines, at that time, with seamen, captains, lumber merchants, and carpenters pooling their resources and sharing the profits. However, a large portion of the ships was destroyed during the revolution against the Turks.[14]

In all of the other areas occupied by the Ottomans, however, heavy taxation, export tariffs, and the bureaucratic centralism of their empire discouraged rapid expansion and modernization of production enterprises. Large fertile areas that had become prosperous during the Byzantine period and the Frankish and Venetian occupations were left idle after the Ottomans captured them.

Toward the end of the eighteenth century, a number of teachers were sent to Western Europe by rich merchants, shipowners, and a few *phanariots* (high clergy and Greek elite) to revive studies of the Greek past.[15] These teachers became interested in bringing the French revolution's principles of liberty and equality to Greece, and one of them, Rhigas Pheraios (Valenstinlis), composed revolutionary battle hymns to encourage the Greek *rayahs* (semislave subjects) to participate in the struggle for liberation from the Turks. For this reason he was captured and executed in 1798.

From an economic and social point of view, the feudalistic system of Western Europe prevailed, to a large extent, in Greece during the Byzantine and the Ottoman periods. Aristocrat landlords and Turkish chiefs (*pashas* and *agas*) lived luxuriously while the masses lived in poverty. Between them was the class consisting of a few well-to-do local people who retained and enlarged their privileges and their large properties, sometimes through collaboration with the foreign masters.

In each village area there was a Christian *kodjabashis* responsible for the collection of taxes, which were delivered to the Turkish masters. *Haratsi* was a heavy tax imposed on Christians as a punishment for not converting to Islam. Another form of taxation was the *decati*, levied every year on produce. The most fertile lands in each area were confiscated by the Turkish chiefs, who transformed them into their own estates (*chifliks*). When the owners and tillers of the land objected, they were summarily executed or tortured by Turkish troops. Under such conditions, many people gave their property to monasteries, which were exempted from property confiscations (*vakoufia*). As a result, large and rich farms and properties, were accumulated by the monasteries (*metohia*). Even today, a number of monasteries in Greece own such farms, which are cultivated by the monks or leased to individuals or agricultural cooperatives.

During Ottoman rule, a number of phanariots served as administrators and even dragomans of the Porte (in Constantinople). They became rich and powerful under the Turks and, as a result, they opposed the rebellion of the rayahs. They remained a group apart, hated by many Greeks struggling for their own freedom. High priests, with some exceptions, were criticized for their exhortation to submit and acquiesce to Ottoman rule and the prevailing authority.[16] This attitude retarded intellectual progress and discouraged efforts at political liberation. However, local priests helped preserve the Greek language and heritage in secret night schools and sparked resistance in the villages. As members of the elected councils, together with the village heads and teachers, they were responsible to the Ottomans for tax collection and other administrative duties. At the same time, though, many of these councils helped unite the Greek people against their oppressor.

Heavy oppression and economic exploitation of the Greek and other Balkan rayahs by the Muslim rulers resulted in the struggle for liberation against their masters, which started in Morea (Aghia Lavra at Kalavryta) on March 21, 1821.[17] Helped by Greek merchants and mariners living abroad, as well as other philhellenic societies and governments in Europe and elsewhere, the Greek *klefts* (revolutionaries) managed to liberate their land and establish a free Greek state that included the Peloponneus (Morea), Sterea Hellas, and Thessaly (by 1828).

GROWTH OF MODERN GREECE

Postliberation Period

After liberation from the Ottoman occupation in the 1820s, Greece began the process of rehabilitation and development under difficult economic and sociopolitical conditions. Over 200,000 people had lost their lives. Houses, olive orchards, and vineyards had been largely destroyed. Most of the land belonged to the Turks, who owned eighteen times as much land per capita as did the Greeks. Even after liberation, land distribution was slow and highly unequal. The primates and other powerful persons helped themselves first, acquiring titles to large and rich Turkish estates. Only one out of six peasants had land of his own. Land appropriations through legal recognition of squatters' rights and title gains (if land was cultivated continuously for a period varying from one to fifteen years) helped land distribution somewhat but gave rise to frequent litigation and violence among the peasants.

The struggle for independence and nationhood distracted the infant nation from economic development. The area of the new nation was small (about one-third of its present size), as was its population (some 753,000 people). It included central Greece, below the Arta-Volos line in Thessaly, the Peloponnesus, and the Cyclades Islands in the Aegean Sea. The rest of what is today Greece was then still in Ottoman hands, except the Ionian Islands, which were controlled by the British.

The new Greek nation began its life under the influence of the great powers. Even the political parties were based on Russian, British, or French interests. Ioannis Capodistrias and Theodore Kolokotrones were connected with the first, Alexander Mavrocordatos with the second, and Ioannis Kolettis with the third. The first republic was established in 1827 as a result of the first constitution, drawn up by the revolutionary founding fathers in the Convention of Troizin. Ioannis Capodistrias, an educated cosmopolitan who had served as Russia's secretary of state, became the president of the republic (1827–31). After his assassination by chieftains of the Mani area (from the Mavrocordatos family), the protecting powers, primarily Britain, selected Prince Otto of Bavaria, a Roman Catholic, to be the king of Greece without consulting the Greeks.

During the thirty years of his reign (1833–63), King Otto, introduced an autocratic system of centralized administration, which, ever since, has resulted in a slow-moving bureaucracy. He also imported his own artisans and a brewer, Fuchs (Fix), whose firm remained active for decades later in Athens.

Due to occupancy and inheritance of land without legal proofs, usurpation and squatting were widespread. Traditional occupants had mostly been sharecroppers on lands that the Turks controlled during the Ottoman period. The Greek-Bavarian regime of King Otto refused to recognize the cultivators as owners and obliged them to pay heavy usufruct taxes as tenants. To end many property disputes between the state and its citizens, important land distribution laws were enacted in 1835, 1855, 1864, and 1871.

Greece, as a weak and poor agricultural nation, resorted to foreign borrowing in order to finance its growing government expenditures. The revolutionary governments of 1824 and 1825 issued bonds that were sold abroad. In 1832, the large Rothschild loan, guaranteed by the three major powers (Britain, France, Russia), was received for servicing prior debts, the indemnity to Turkey, and administrative and military expenses. Such expenses were largely increased after 1833, when Otto recruited paid foreign soldiers and civil servants, mainly Germans. Military expenditures alone absorbed from 40 to 100 percent of annual revenues from 1833 through 1841 and about one-third thereafter. More loans to service the debt and to cover budget deficits continued to flow, and the country faced serious problems of payments.[18]

From a political and economic point of view, directly or indirectly, Greece was controlled by foreign powers. Thus, President Capodistrias had to submit to the allied representatives at the Poros Conference in 1828 statistics concerning frontiers, tribute, and indemnity for lands, including large estates that belonged to the Turks (chifliks). British, Russian, and German rivalry for regional influence played an important role in the formation and development of the new Greek state and its financing.

In 1862 Otto was deposed by a revolt ignited by students and middle-class intellectuals. By that time, the population had doubled, as had the shipping industry, while foreign trade had more than quadrupled.

When the new and small Greek nation was established, all the fertile plains of Thessaly and Macedonia remained in Ottoman control. However, in the hills and plains of Attica and Boeotia and the coastlands of Peloponnesus, the farms produced cereals, olives, grapes, and other fruits as in ancient times. Grapes, combined with resin from the pines of Attica, were and still are used to make retsina, a pungent local wine. Athens, Thebes (where Oedipus lived in ancient times), Patras, and Corinth were the main market towns for such products. After 1833, when the capital of Greece was transferred from Nauplion, Athens gradually increased in wealth and became a magnet city, as it had been in ancient times. Most of the Greek islands, however, remained poor, and a number of their inhabitants immigrated to other countries.[19]

The typical Greek peasant was engaged in subsistence farming. Agricultural techniques were poor. Rudimentary tools and wooden plows were still in use. Crop rotation was little known, and wasteful scattering of seed by hand was widespread. Lack of transportation limited the available markets for agricultural products. Grain was mostly imported from Trieste, Alexandria, and the Black Sea ports. Taxes in the form of tithes on threshing floors were heavy and unjust, and collection was time consuming.[20] Grain had to remain piled up for months awaiting the tax collector's inspection. Fowls, pigeons, and other birds, as well as rats and other creatures, assembled at the threshing floor to get their share of the poor harvest of the peasants. Animal husbandry was neglected, agricultural credit was limited, and interest rates ranged from 20 to 24 percent on mortgage loans and from 36 to 50 percent on personal loans.[21]

To pay for grain imports, Corinth grapes, currants, and later tobacco were exported primarily to Britain, Austria, and Germany. Currant exports steadily increased from 6,000 tons in 1821 to 42,800 in 1861, and 100,700 tons in 1878. Industrial development remained in the embryonic stage. However, shipping kept its traditional importance. Lumber merchants, carpenters, captains, and seamen pooled their resources along cooperative lines to build and operate new ships. A limited number of small, labor-intensive enterprises were developed in the Piraeus-Athens area, Syra, and Patras, especially after 1882 when the Charilaos Trikoupis administration expanded the transportation network. By 1877, there were 136 plants in Greece employing 7,342 workers.[22]

Through fighting and negotiations, the Greek state expanded, slowly and tortuously, to incorporate territories and peoples of Greek background. Such territories included: the Ionian Islands from Britain in 1864; the rest of Thessaly in 1881, Crete (liberated in 1898), Macedonia and Epirus in 1913, the Eastern Aegean Islands in 1914, and Thrace in 1919, all from the Ottomans; and the Dodecanese in 1948 from Italy. The Treaty of Sevres provided that Smyrna and its environs, as well as eastern Thrace, be turned over to Greece, but the Treaty of Lausanne (1923) eliminated this. Cyprus, with a population of 600,000 (about 82 percent Greek and 18 percent Turkish) and rich in copper, achieved its independence from Britain in 1959, after enduring centuries of foreign occupations.

As a result of new acquisitions, Greece's production capacity increased significantly. Production of grain, cotton, and tobacco in Thessaly, Macedonia, and Thrace improved domestic economic conditions and helped increase exports. The city of Kavalla became an important port for tobacco exports. However, much of Epirus, with rugged mountains, eroded lands, and limited means of transportation, remained an economic liability to Greece. This is why many people left it for other areas and industrial centers in search of a better living.

The following is a brief description of the frequent political changes that were responsible for the economic and social instability in the country at that time.

In 1863, Prince William George of the Danish Glucksberg dynasty was enthroned in Greece at Britain's support. King George I of the Hellenes and his descendants were to rule Greece, primarily through obedient conservative governments installed, until 1967, with some interruptions (mainly 1924–35 and 1941–46). On the economic front, the country was plagued by financial difficulties. Large amounts of money were borrowed mainly for military expenditures to police the long new borders and to promote the idea of Greater Greece. A number of economic concessions were given to British-owned public utilities and other foreign companies.

Trading and professional groups were dissatisfied with economic conditions under George I, and popular discontent with the monarchy increased. Then in 1909 young army and navy officers revolted and demanded the removal of Prince Constantine from the army, where he exercised dynastic influence.[23] They summoned Eleutherios Venizelos, a Cretan revolutionary and statesman, who became prime minister of Greece in 1910. On October 1912, Greece, along with other Balkan nations, entered the war against Turkey. King George went to Salonika to celebrate its liberation by the Greek army. He was shot and killed there in March 1913, and his son became King Constantine I of the Hellenes.

King Constantine I, who married the sister of Kaiser Wilhelm II of Germany, and Prime Minister Venizelos, a liberal politician, were in almost constant disagreement over constitutional questions and Greece's alliances, as were the voters (royalists versus Venizelists). The former wanted to join the Central Powers, dominated by Germany; the latter pushed for Greece's entrance into the war on the side of the Allies (Britain, France, and Italy).

GRECO-TURKISH WAR AND ITS AFTERMATH

The assassination of the heir to the Hapsburg (Austrian-Hungarian) throne, Archduke Francis Ferdinand, on June 28, 1914, at Sarajevo, the capital of Bosnia, was used as a reason for the outbreak of World War I. However, other factors such as nationalistic and imperialistic expansions were in the background of the ignition of this bloody war that engulfed Greece and Turkey as well. These two nations had already been enemies in serious fighting during the Balkan Wars, 1912–13.

Turkey joined the Central Powers on November 2, 1914, and German warships entered the straits of the Dardanelles. Winston Churchill, the First

Lord of the British Admiralty, persuaded the cabinet and the Allies to send an expedition to take Constantinople and the straits. On April 25, 1915, Allied forces, mainly British, landed on the Gallipoli beaches but were badly defeated by the Turkish and the Central Powers troops.

On March 18, 1915, the Constantinople Agreement among Britain, France, and Russia promised Russia Constantinople, the Dardanelles, part of eastern Anatolia, and Inbros and Tendedos, among other areas. But the Bolsheviks renounced all claims to Turkish territories in 1917. Greece entered World War I on the side of the Allies in 1917.

In July 1918 Sultan Mehmet V died, and his brother, known as Mehmet VI, succeeded him. His policy was to remain sultan, no matter how much of his territory might be taken by the Allies (British, French, Russians, and later Italians and Greeks). On November 13, 1918, Allied vessels, including the Greek ship *Averoff*, anchored at Istanbul, where French troops were disembarked on February 8, 1919.

For purposes of fighting the Bolsheviks in Russia, Greece sent 45,000 soldiers to join the other Allied forces, but they were defeated and returned home.

On May 6, 1919, Woodrow Wilson, the president of the United States, advanced a proposition to the Council of Four (Britain, France, Italy, and the United States) to unite the Smyrna district and the Dodecanese with Greece. On May 15, Greek forces landed in Smyrna, under the cover of British, French, and U.S. vessels. This was the beginning of the terrible Greco-Turkish drama of 1919–22. With the blessings of Lloyd George, Greek troops fanned out of the Smyrna zone on June 22 and occupied large territories, enclosing Bursa, the Panderma railway, and Ushak.

On August 10, 1920, the Constantinople government signed the Treaty of Sevres, under which Greece was to receive eastern Thrace and the islands of Inbros and Tenedos, while Smyrna and its hinterland were to be administered by Greece for five years. Thereafter, a plebiscite would decide the future status of the region. Also, an autonomous Kurdish state and an independent Armenia were to be created.

Venizelos, who survived an assassination attempt in Paris on August 10, returned to Athens to organize the November 14 national elections. However, people were tired of some ten years of war and put him out of office. His Liberal Party won only 118 of 369 parliamentary seats, and Venizelos himself was not elected, in spite of his political and diplomatic successes.

The Greek royalists, with Constantine I back on the throne, decided to advance further into Anatolia, although they had promised during the election period to bring the soldiers back home. On the other hand, Allied financial support for the Greek forces was withdrawn, and strained relations developed with the departure of Venizelos to Paris. After a new offensive on March 23, 1921, and bloody fighting, especially in June and July, the Greeks captured Kutahya and Eski Shehir. Marching under a broiling sun through the Anatolian Desert they crossed the Sakarya River, some fifty miles from Ankara.

In the meantime, improvements in Turkey's diplomacy achieved striking successes. By October 1921, France and Italy had withdrawn from Anatolia, while the Soviet Union signed a treaty with the Turkish nationalists recognizing them and arranging the borders between Russia and Turkey.

As the Greek army advanced from Smyrna toward Ankara, Turkish resistance was organized, primarily by Yoruk Ali Efe and the efficient leader Kemal Ataturk, who later became president of the republic. Kemal was known as the hero of Gallipoli, where he was victorious against the invasion by the Allies in 1915 for which Winston Churchill, Britain's navy minister, was primarily responsible. The Turks did not react intensely against the loss of the external provinces, but the invasion of the homeland itself aroused fierce resentment, especially by the nationalists under Kemal Ataturk, who rejected the Treaty of Sevres outright. In the meantime, Kemal's forces were armed secretly by France and openly by Russia. Lenin supported the liberation Turkish forces against the imperialistic aims of the Greeks, who were supporting the expedition of the Allies against the Bolsheviks.

On August 26, 1922, the Greek army, with unreliable communications and limited supplies, under heavy artillery fire and a ferocious attack by the Turkish infantry, broke and fled in panic back to Ismir (Smyrna) with heavy losses. On September 9, the victorious Kemal came to Ismir hoping to stop the massacres and terror inflicted by the Turks on the Greek and Armenian populations. For days the streets were hideous with murder and pillage, while half of the city was destroyed by fires whose marks are still visible today. A number of Allied vessels (U.S., British, French, and Italian) anchored off Smyrna refused to allow the terror-stricken people to embark for protection. The Turkish massacre and cruelty continued to the degree that George Horton, the American Consul, stated that a feeling of shame that I belong to the human race prevailed. About 125,000 Greeks and Armenians were killed in Smyrna alone.

On October 11, 1922, an armistice was signed at Mudanya, which represented the Allied surrender to the demands of the nationalist Turks. A week later, Lloyd George, the British prime minister who encouraged the Greek army and the palace to undertake the adventure in Asia Minor, handed in his resignation. On July 24, 1923, the Treaty of Lausanne was signed, under which Greece lost eastern Thrace and the Smyrna zone. About 500,000 Greeks were killed. This was the Greek tragedy of ten years of war and some 4 million refugees (from Russia, Asia Minor, and eastern Thrace). In spite of the severe economic and social suffering, the new blood and talent imported with the refugees contributed to the development of the country thereafter.

This defeat led Colonel (later General) Nicholas Plastiras and a group of officers on the island of Chios to issue an ultimatum in September 1922 demanding the abdication of the king. When Plastiras came to Athens, six leading advisors of the king who were considered responsible for the catastrophe in Asia Minor, were court-martialed and executed. Then George, the eldest son of King Constantine I, became King George II. He, in turn, left the country in 1924 and remained in exile until 1935.

After the Greek expedition in Asia Minor (April 13, 1919) and the disaster thereafter (autumn 1922), a massive population exchange took place. Some 1.5 million Greeks left Asia Minor, where their ancestors had lived for possibly thirty centuries, for Greece, and 400,000 Turks left Greece for Turkey, while another 40,000 Greeks and 40,000 Bulgarians were exchanged between Greece and Bulgaria. Although there were serious housing and employment problems at the beginning, in the long run the progressive and industrious refugees proved to be a great asset to the Greek economy. A rug industry was transplanted from Asia Minor, and new textiles, pottery, copper ware, and shipping were developed by the skilled labor of the refugees.

As a result of the policy of conciliation and friendship pursued by Eleutherios Venizelos and Kemal Ataturk, president of Turkey, as well as other leaders of the Balkan countries, trade and development in the area were stimulated. Genuine efforts to achieve closer economic cooperation among the nations of the Balkan Peninsula were made after 1924, primarily by Alexander Papanastassiou, a premier of Greece and Nicolas Titulescu, foreign minister of Romania. In a number of conferences among the Balkan states, emphasis was given to further collaboration in tariffs, tourism, credit, and protection of agricultural products.[24]

During the period of the second republic of modern Greece (1924–35), economic and political instability led to a brief dictatorship (January-August 1926) by the chief of the army staff, General Theodore Pangalos, who was also the leader of the Republic Officers' League. As in all dictatorships, puritanism was proclaimed. Thus, a law was passed that forbade women's skirts to be more than fourteen inches from the ground.[25] In August 1926 General Kondyles overthrew the dictatorship and held elections, which failed to give the republicans enough votes to govern, and a coalition with royalists was formed. There was no tradition of discipline and obedience in Greece, and disagreements among political leaders persisted. In 1927, the Bank of Greece was established to stabilize the currency and the balance of payment. In 1928, Venizelos returned and became prime minister. At that time, unemployment, inflation, and other economic problems were growing. They were further aggravated in the early 1930s because of the worldwide depression. After attempted military coups by General Nicholas Plastiras in 1933 and 1935 failed because of lack of popular and army support, a plebiscite restored the monarchy, and King George II returned at the end of 1935.

WORLD WAR II AND POSTWAR YEARS

In August 1936 General John Metaxas and King George II imposed a dictatorship and instituted martial law, suspending constitutional liberties. Freedom of the press was abolished, and opponents were jailed or sent to isolated islands (especially Anafe, where some prisoners were forced to take castor oil for ideological cleansing). Also, Greek classical dramas and Pericles' orations were censored. Metaxas, who had been educated in Nazi Germany, turned more and more to Germany for trade while the palace was sympathetic to Britain.[26] Despite the introduction of minimum wages and social insurance, Metaxas' dictatorship was unpopular with the liberty-loving Greek people, as were other dictatorships.

Suddenly Benito Mussolini, the Italian dictator, launched an attack against Greece from Albania on October 28, 1940. The poorly equipped Greek troops managed to push the invading Italians back to Albania, probably because, as Napoleon's dictum goes, in war the proportion of moral to material factors is as three to one. However, Greek troops, fighting on so many fronts, were unable to resist the well-equipped armored units of Adolf Hitler, which on April 6, 1941, penetrated far into the country, while Piraeus, the main port of Greece, was heavily bombed.

Greece, under occupation by Germany, Italy, and Bulgaria (in Macedonia and western Thrace), suffered heavy losses. During the first year of occupation the Germans printed inflationary money and drained the country of needed resources, while imports dropped significantly because of the Allied blockade. Some 450,000 people died of starvation alone, primarily in Athens. Adults and children suffered from malnutrition, malaria, and tuberculosis. Factories were destroyed, transportation and communications throughout the country almost disappeared, and about three-fourths of the country's large commercial fleet was sunk. Civilian massacres were carried out by the Nazis throughout Greece. At Kalavryta alone, a town near Patras, 1,300 unarmed persons were gunned down on December 13, 1943, while all the houses were burned to the ground.[27]

Within five months of the occupation of Greece, the National Liberation Front (EAM), a political resistance organization with people from all walks of life, was created. Later on (April 1942) the National Popular Liberation Army (ELAS), the military arm of EAM, started offensive activities against the Germans. The United All-Greece Youth Organization (EPON) was also formed to train and provide recreation for young boys and girls. The Caretaking Committee for the Partisans (ETA) was responsible for helping feed and equip the partisans. Another resistance group of some importance was the Greek National Democratic League (EDES), organized by Colonel Napoleon Zervas mainly in Epirus. Zervas was preoccupied with promoting his own interests, and his group did not manage to expand as EAM did. Instead, it grew weaker, while EAM-ELAS took the initiative in fighting the Germans and reforming the countryside.[28] Gradually, EAM-ELAS was dominated by the Communist Party, particularly toward the end of German occupation.

During World War II, the strategic position of Greece became apparent. As Winston Churchill said, "the spasms of Greece . . . stood at the nerve center of power, law and freedom in the Western World."[29] The British had more than fifty missions working with the partisans in Greece and Yugoslavia and provided equipment and munitions to the resistance groups, mainly to ELAS and EDES, during the struggle against the Axis. Because of the Nazi occupation and the hardship suffered by the inhabitants during that time, local conflict appeared in many parts of the country. Some people, promoted by selfishness, jealousy, political differences, and previous disputes about property and personal interests, made accusations against others to the occupation authorities or to the partisans of EAM-ELAS. At that time, the British, seeing the growing Communist domination of EAM-ELAS, secretly supported with ammunition and sterling the formation of new organizations composed primarily of former officers and rightwingers (such as the National Organization), which turned against EAM-ELAS. On the other hand, certain heads of the EAM-ELAS resistance groups committed a number of crimes at the suggestion of local political representatives. In many instances, people were killed by both sides not for serious political or ideological reasons and without due process and supportive evidence. Local people did not trust each other and frequently resorted to conflicts, hatred, revenge, and even open group fighting. The dismal situation in which the nation found itself toward the end of the occupation period was the background for the severe civil war that followed (1946–49).[30]

Churchill decided to crush EAM-ELAS, which had been gradually infiltrated and dominated by the Communists, to support the government of George Papandreou (an old-line republican with oratorical and maneuvering skills), and finally to restore King George II. On October 4, 1944, British troops of Operation Manna entered Patras and after ten days reached Athens. On December 3, clashes between ELAS and the police (mostly German collaborators) started in Athens, and clashes between ELAS and the British went on until February 1945. After a rigged plebiscite, royal rule was installed in 1946. Before the people could lift their heads above their starvation and tragedy, mutual hatred between left-wing and right-wing groups flared up into a serious civil war which persisted until 1949.[31] In the meantime, King George II died, and his brother Paul I became king in 1946.

On March 31, 1947, Britain terminated all aid to Greece, and soon thereafter all of its troops were withdrawn. Thus British political and economic tutelage in Greece, which prevailed for more than a century, came to an end. On May 22, 1947, $300 million in aid was initially appropriated by the United States (under the Truman Doctrine), most of which went for the army and the expenditures of largely corrupt public administrations. American experts were assigned to administer the program and to supervise related policies.[32]

During the internal conflict, Yugoslavia provided sanctuary to the Greek Communist battalions until 1948, when Tito broke ties with Stalin. As a result of military support from the United States and the closing of Yugoslav borders, the civil war came to an end, and Greece and Yugoslavia established friendly relations in 1950.

With the promulgation of the Truman Doctrine, American aid, favoring mainly military needs at the neglect of other economic considerations such as inflation and unemployment, began flowing into Greece and Turkey. As Walter Lippmann remarked, these two countries had been selected "not because they are specially in need of relief, not because they are shining examples of democracy . . . but because they are the strategic gateway to the Black Sea and the heart of the Soviet Union."[33] Venal politics, ineptness, nepotism, and corruption were rampant in Greece, which has so often been plagued by social-political turmoil. The country's political and economic life was in a state of bankruptcy. As former Prime Minister George Papandreou observed, there was "a people worthy of their history" but "a leadership unworthy of the people."[34] Greece was perhaps the only country in which enemy collaborators continued to exercise power after World War

II instead of being prosecuted. Mostly, they became right-wing royalists, who used direct and indirect (psychological) terrorism on the part of the dossier-keeping security forces, paramilitary right-wing organizations, such as the X-Group, the National Security Battalions (TEA), and the rural gendarmerie, to coerce the electorate to vote for conservative governments favorable to the royal family. Complaints of fraud and intimidation at the polls were common, while criticism of the high costs of maintaining the royal family was widespread. The annual salary of the king alone was $566,000, or more than three times that of the president of the United States.

Such political and socioeconomic pressures prevented the Greeks from exercising their passion for talk and argument about domestic politics or *politiki* (derived from *polis*, the word for city in ancient times), and turned their discussion instead to international events.

In 1952 Greece and Turkey became members of the North Atlantic Treaty Organization (NATO). U.S. advisors exercised control on weaponry and had great influence on important decisions through the palace and the Greek army command, not only on military but also on political and economic matters. American military and economic aid to Greece amounted to about $100 million per year.[35]

After an official visit by Tito, president of Yugoslavia, to Greece in 1955, better relations were developed with Yugoslavia. Trade agreements were also concluded with other Balkan and Eastern European nations.

Frequent elections, with a great deal of gerrymandering and vote-rigging were the main characteristics of the postwar crowned democracy of Greece. Unstable governments and mounting social and economic problems led to extensive emigration of workers and educated people to Canada, Australia, the United States, and later to West Germany.

In the years following the elections of 1961, which were criticized by the two main opposition parties (the Center Union and the United Democratic Left) as dishonest and fraudulent, the monarchy came under mounting challenges. King Constantine II, who succeeded his father Paul in 1966 at age twenty-four, was greatly influenced by his mother, Queen Frederika, a German by origin. On the other hand, strong individualism and the cult of personality in Greek politics led politicians to spend time beating dead political horses and digging in old records. All this and the absurd actions of the king, who wanted to rule as well as to reign, led to the military coup in April 1967. The end of the monarchy took place in December of the same year, after the king's unsuccessful attempt at a coup against the dictatorship of Colonel George Papadopoulos.

On the economic front, the reforms of 1953 by Spyros Markezinis (the minister of coordination) which included devaluation of the drachma (from 15 to 30 drachmas per U.S. dollar), improvement in public administration, and incentives to attract foreign investments (Greek Public Law 2687/1953) somewhat improved domestic and foreign trade conditions. With political and fiscal stability in the late 1950s, money deposits increased, exports improved, and the wheels of industry began moving more rapidly. Instead of buying gold sovereigns and land or luxury apartments, people put their money in savings accounts for investment financing.

In addition, increasing numbers of tourists from Europe and America came to enjoy the sun-drenched haven and Homer's "wine-dark" sea of Greece. However, unemployment and underemployment remained high, and the gap in per capita income between the city and the countryside increased. Government subsidies on wheat, tobacco, and other crops did not accomplish much. Instead, together with large military expenditures, they increased budgetary deficits. Moreover, the growth of imports over exports had detrimental effects on the balance of payments and the international position of the country.

During the period 1947–66 total U.S. aid to Greece amounted to $3.75 billion, about half of which ($1.85 billion) was military assistance, and half was economic aid. The largest part of the aid ($3.41 billion) consisted of grants, and the rest of loans. Technical assistance was terminated in 1962, and major economic aid was ended in 1964.[36] Only military assistance under the auspices of NATO continued thereafter. Together with aid, U.S. economic and political influence was extensive.

Although a number of investment incentives were offered, entrepreneurs were reluctant to invest in anything other than family enterprises. Under the protection of foreign investment, however, a number of new ventures, such as the Esso-Pappas petrochemical complex in Salonika ($200 million) and the Aluminium de Greece, exploiting the rich mineral deposits of bauxite ($125 million), were completed by 1966. However, large amounts of investment continued to be channeled into housing and urban land specu-lation, particularly in Athens, while the gap in the balance of trade was widening.

STABILIZATION AND DEVELOPMENT

After the collapse of the military junta in July 1974, the New Democracy (ND), under Prime Ministers C. Caramanlis (1974–80) and G. Rhallis (1980–81), Greece came back to democratic stability and became the tenth member of the EU (1981). During the period 1981–89, the Pan-Hellenic Socialist Movement (PASOK), under Prime Minister A. Papandreou, came to power. It was followed again by the New Democracy, under Prime Minister S. Tzanetakis (1989–90) and the Government of National Unity (1990–91), with the agreement of the two large political parties (ND and PASOK), under X. Zolotas (an economics professor and governor of the Bank of Greece for many years). Thereafter, the New Democracy, under Prime Minister C. Mitsotakis, was voted to power (1991–93), followed again by PASOK (1993–present).[37]

In all these years since 1974, and especially in the 1980s, emphasis was given to government expenditures for social programs and employment of personnel that was not needed in the public sector. This policy led to large budget deficits and huge government debts (domestic and foreign). Moreover, the unwise policy of taking over private enterprises by the government made things worse. Although inflation was reduced to around 8 percent, the large budget deficits (approximately 12 percent of the GDP, in contrast to no more than 3 percent required by the Maastricht Agreement of the EU) and the huge total debt (about 120 percent of the GDP, in contrast to no more than 60 percent required by the EU) present serious problems for the country's economy. However, Greece receives significant financial support from the EU for the construction of such projects as the new airport in Spata (a location near Athens), a subway (Metro) in Athens, and a tunnel connecting Rio and Antirio (near Patras).

An important state-owned enterprise under reconstruction is the Olympic Airlines with big annual losses (dr. 135 billion or $597 million in 1994). After the agreement of the Greek government with the European Commission, Olympic's eighteen unions accepted a pay freeze for at least two years and a cut of 1,700 out of 10,600 jobs, partly because of benefits offered for early retirement. In addition, the large debt (dr. 491 billion) write-off by the government benefited the company from not having to pay interest charges. Nevertheless, Olympic would continue to face serious financial problems as long as it remains under the government and the political appointees.

In order to modernize its public utilities and under the pressure of the EU, Greece started to privatize a number of big state-owned firms. Thus, according to a proposed law, the private sector can produce electric power and sell it to the Public Power Corporation (PPC), which has a monopoly in the distribution and production of power. It is expected that production of energy from lignite, oil, coal, and hydroelectric dams, as well as from sun and wind, would increase, and the cost per kilowatt-hour would decline.

In the other eleven countries of the EU, there are more than 1,000 producers of electric energy, compared to only 1 in Greece, and some 38 distributors. In Germany, there are 452 producers of electric energy, in Italy 496, and in Britain 9. In the privatization process of the electricity production unit of Lavrion, foreign electric companies, such as the EDF of France and the ENDESA of Spain, participate.

State subsidies to the "problematic" state firms are not permitted by the EU regulations. Also, the EU demanded the privatization of the Greek shipbuilding enterprises, along with other state firms such as EKO (gasoline distributing firm) and the KSENIA hotels.

A partial privatization of the Organization of Telecommunications of Hellas (OTE), which was announced by the Greek government in 1993, included the sale of 35 percent stake to a "strategic investor," who would be the manager of the firm. The investor would first acquire 25 percent and then sell additional shares worth 10 percent of the value of the firm through the increase of the capital stock. The collected revenue would be used for the modernization of the telecommunication services. The employees and the retirees would control 4 percent, the government would keep control of 51 percent, and the rest of the stock would be sold on the Athens Stock Exchange. The procedure of foreign sales would be arranged by the CS first Boston and the Schroders companies. This process seemed to be attractive for the first stage of privatization of OTE. However, this policy was changed by the new government of PASOK, which came to power in the fall of 1993.

On May 23, 1994, the Greek government announced that it would sell up to 25 percent of OTE on the stock market. An unspecified stake of the firm would be for sale in the United States and Japan. The sale of shares of OTE, with profits of more than $600 million annually, was expected to revitalize the Athens Stock Exchange and attract domestic and foreign capital. However, an offer to foreign investors in London in 1995 was not attractive and was postponed. This made the government cautious and announced that it would float the first 8 percent of the shares of OTE on the Athens Stock Exchange, whereas 1.5 percent of the company's equity would be sold to its employees and pensioners at a discount.[38] Nevertheless, it would seem that the rapid changes in technology, with wireless phones and cellulars, would necessitate the rapid privatization of OTE.

Other firms under privatization are the Piraiki-Patraiki (a cloth industry in Patras, Karpenisi, and Syros), the Greek Auto–Assembly Industry, the NAFSI, and the Athinaiki Hartopiia (Athenian paper industry).

In spite of the opposition of the workers and the people of the regions involved, the state shipyards of Scaramaga, near Athens, and Neorion of

Syros, an island in the Aegean Sea, came under the process of privatization. The memorandum of the Greek government, submitted to the EU Commission stating that these shipyards are of strategic importance for the country, was rejected. Again, the main reason for transferring these and other state firms to the private sector is their deficits which are covered by the governmental budget, the large deficits of which increase total debt, the servicing of which leads to further increases in debt or inflation. As Figure 3.1 shows, velocity of money was constant and money supply increased significantly to cover part of the deficits. This fuels new inflation, which remains relatively high compared to other EU countries.

In the private sector, employee stock ownership plans (ESOPs) are gradually spreading in Greece as well, but at a slower pace than in other countries such as the United States, the European Union, and the Eastern European nations. For example, the Petzetakis A.E., a pipe and related products company, gave 20 percent of its shares to its workers and employees, according to their salaries and the years they served in the company. Such incentive plans proved to be effective from the standpoint of workers' motivation and labor productivity.

Figure 3.1
Money Supply (M1) and Velocity of Money (GDP/M1) for Greece

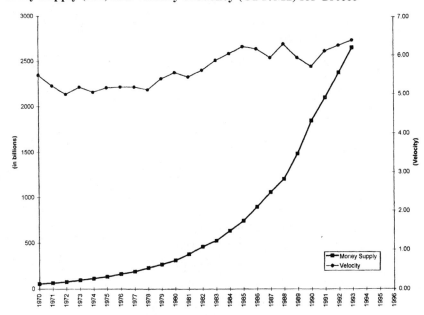

Source: International Monetary Fund, *International Financial Statistics*, various issues.

INTRAREGIONAL GREEK TRADE AND INVESTMENT

Hellenic exports to Albania increased from $12.2 million in 1991 to $221 million in 1994, those to Bulgaria increased from $87.8 million in 1991 to $446 million in 1994, whereas those to Romania remained about the same and around $100 million. Moreover, Hellenic exports to Russia increased from $183 million in 1993 to $240 in 1994 and in Ukraine from $31 million to $80 million, respectively. New Hellenic trade and investment inroads are made in other former Soviet republics, particularly in Armenia, Georgia, and Azerbaijan, with exports to these republics reaching $106 million in 1994.

As ethnic conflicts and regional disturbances in the Balkans are subsided, joint investments among the neighboring countries are rising rapidly. Thus, many mixed investment and trade Hellenic companies are operating in Albania. They include Gatic AE and Prive Ltd., both cloth firms; Pekor AE, a shoe industry; Market Petra, a construction material firm; Buka and Clina, refreshments companies; and Gentos-Krietary, a metal accessories company, all in Argyrocastro. Moreover, the Albpunndimpeks and the Industrial TR, both commercial companies; Varship, a transportation firm; and Terlana, a textile company; operate in Tirana, whereas Union Tekstile operates in Coritsa.

A large number of Hellenic companies are also investing in Bulgaria. They include the Bottling Hellenic Company, which is involved in the production and distribution of juices and refreshments; the Mechaniki AE, a construction company with operations in Albania, Odessa, and other places; and the Thraki AE, a company manufacturing meat and similar products in almost all Balkan countries. Other Hellenic investment companies in Bulgaria are: Delta AE, 3E AE, and Athenaiki Zythopiia AE, as well as Intracom AE, Giotis AE, Nikas AE, Misko AE, Mimikos AE, Pitsos AE, Fidas AE, Agapiou AE, Sato AE, Neoset, Erga AE, Agno, Fourlis AE, and Dromeas AE, primarily in textiles and clothing industries.

An important investment in the area is a pipeline worth $1 billion to connect the Bulgarian Black Sea port of Bugras with the Hellenic port of Alexandroupolis. According to the agreement between Hellas and Russia, oil would be shipped to Bugras from the Russian port of Novorossiyisk, a pipeline terminal from the Caspian Sea. The 174-mile pipeline would have a capacity of 600,000 barrels a day. However, Turkey is favoring its own plan for an 1,190 mile–pipeline to Ceyhan on the Mediterranean, worth $3 billion.

A Hellenic state-owned firm, Egnatia Odos, is under the management of Brown and Root Civil, the British-based companies to oversee the 680 km Egnatia highway construction and operation. The project, worth $3.5 billion, which is the largest in Europe, would partially follow an ancient Roman route connecting the port of Igoumenitsa in northwestern Hellas with Alexandroupolis in Thrace, close to the Turkish border. The construction of the Egnatia highway is expected to take about six years, and it would be financed by the EU of at least $1 billion, loans of up to $1.2 billion from the European Investment Bank, private sector financing of about $700 million, and the rest by the Hellenic state.

Another highway, almost parallel to that of Egnatia, would be constructed through Albania, Scopja, Bulgaria, and Istanbul, linking the Adriatic Sea with the Black Sea. This would be the result of an agreement signed by the presidents of Albania (Sali Berisa), Bulgaria (Zele Zelev), Scopja (Stogian Anotov), and Turkey (Suleyman Demirel) in New York on October 22, 1995, during the meeting of the world leaders for the celebration of the fifty years of the United Nations. This is considered by the EU commissioner Hans Van Der Brooks, who was present in the signing of the agreement, as one step to bringing the Balkans closer to EU membership.

Although Hellenic investment in Romania was not as numerous as in Bulgaria, a number of Hellenic companies were established in Romania. They include: the Commercial Bank and the Bank of Credit, as well ad 3E AE, Delta AE, Sato AE, Thraki AE, Mimikos AE, Giotis AE, Neoset AE, Biosol AE, Seka AE, Star Foods, and Hellenic Heteria of Biskots.

Hellenic Shipyards, which were set up by shipowner Stavros Niarchos in 1956 with $8 million and now controlled by ETVA, a state-owned development bank, is under privatization. Now, it is building three German-designed frigates for the Hellenic Navy and rolling stock for the Hellenic state railway company. The Peraticos Group, a London-based shipping group, offered dr 16.5 billion ($73.7 million) to buy Hellenic Shipyards, the biggest in the eastern Mediterranean, but the deal did not go through mainly because of the expected unemployment problems of the Hellenic's 3,000 strong workers. The firm was nationalized in September 1985 because of the big deficits and the lay-offs after 1981. Peraticos already controls Eleusis Shipyards, acquired from the Commercial Bank of Hellas, a state-owned bank. The European Commission postponed related deadlines for selling or shutting down the shipyard (or paying a $220 million fine) with a turnover, including repairs, of about dr 100 billion ($417 million) a year. Alpha Finance of Hellas and Samuel Montagu of Britain are expected to be the joint financial advisors to finding an international shipbuilder to manage the firm, whereas ETVA plans to sell a 49 percent stake to the workers for $35 million, who agreed to cuts of up to 1,000 jobs.

Noell-KRC of Germany signed a contract with the Public Power Corporation of Hellas worth $92 million to install a desulphurization unit in the ten-year-old power plant in Megalopolis (Peloponnesus). The utility, which burns local lignite with high sulphur, is under pressure from the European Commission to improve environmental standards.

Greece, as a member of the EU, is expected to attract sizable foreign investment in the near future. However, investment in productive and jobs-creating ventures should be encouraged more than investment in casinos and similar services, which are related to social problems and the financial draining of the country rather than its development.

Turkey

INTRODUCTION

Turkey is located in an area where Greek, Roman, and Oriental cultures collided and colluded. At times, Turkey is included in Balkan studies, and at other times, it is excluded as an Asian or Middle Eastern country. It is located at the crossroads of three continents (Europe, Asia, and Africa) and, as a strategic region, has attracted continuous involvement of the great powers throughout history.

Asia Minor, or Anatolia, which was invaded by the Turks in the eleventh century, has a recorded history that dates to the Hittites in the second millennium B.C. The Indo-European Hittites were flanked by the Hurrians who had crossed the Caucasus earlier (third millennium B.C.) and built a kingdom southeast of Anatolia. Related to the Hurrians were the rules of Urartu in the Lake Van region close to the Ararat mountain. After the fall of Urartu, the Armenians arrived (before the sixth century B.C.) and established a kingdom stretching from the Black Sea to the Caspian Sea. Also, the Kurds, descendants of the Medes who migrated from the Eurasian region (second millennium B.C.), settled in eastern Anatolia. In the western part of Anatolia, the Thracians (third millennium B.C.), the Ionian Greeks (twelfth century B.C.), the Phrygians (eighth century B.C), and the Lydians (seventh century B.C.) were in control. Thereafter, and before the coming of the Turks (A.D. eleventh century), the Hellenistic, the Roman, and the Byzantine civilizations flourished in Anatolia.

During the Roman and Byzantine periods, the economy of the area remained primarily agricultural and pastoral. When the Turkish conquerors came from Mongolia in 1071 and later, the Ottoman Empire was established. The sultans ruled the area and all the other Balkan lands from Constantinople, the previous capital of Byzantium, in an autocratic fashion. During the more than 400 years of the Ottoman occupation of the neighboring Balkan countries, economic and cultural stagnation largely prevailed.

Toward the end of the nineteenth and the beginning of the twentieth centuries, the Industrial Revolution in Western Europe brought the need for new resources. Backward Balkan countries, including Turkey, offered opportunities for good investment returns. In the early 1890s, German and other European companies built railways, including the line from Haidar Pasha, opposite to Constantinople, to Angora, and as far south as Baghdad. Turkey exported tobacco, grapes, and other agricultural products, especially to Germany, Britain, and Austria. Industrial development, though, remained in the embryonic stage.

The defeat of Turkey during World War I led not only to its losing vast occupied areas in Arabia, Syria, Mesopotamia, and Balkania, but also to the determination of its present boundaries. The Treaty of Lausanne (1923) restored the boundaries of 1914 and changed the treaty of Sevres (1920), which provided, among other things, for the expulsion of Turkey from Europe (eastern Thrace) and the creation of an independent Armenian state. After the extermination, or dispersion, of the Armenians and the elimination of the Greeks from Anatolia (Asia Minor), Turkey achieved a national homogeneity with the exception of the non-Turk Kurd minority of 12 million people in eastern Anatolia, which from time to time rebels, seeking independence. Occasionally, dispersed Armenian avengers renew the decades-old feud in retaliation for the massacre of over a million Armenians in 1915.

Mustapha Kemal, born at Salonika in 1881, proved to be an effective reformer of modern Turkey. He joined the Young Turks and later organized his own nationalist movement, which finally led him to the presidency of the newly created Republic of Turkey. He rapidly abolished the autocratic sultanate and caliphate, which had prevailed for centuries in the Ottoman Empire. Kemal introduced a policy of secularization and westernization. He appropriated all religious endowments and foundations, abolished the institution of polygamy, replaced the Arabic with the Latin alphabet, and introduced a number of economic reforms aimed at securing higher agricultural productivity and self-sufficiency. Along with the emancipation of women and the abolition of the veil came the replacement of the Oriental fez with the Occidental hat. Protective tariffs were raised, domestic savings were encouraged, and the building of highways, railroads, and other public works was expanded. Intellectual and social progress proceeded vigorously, parallel with industrial progress.

During the years between the two world wars, relations of the other Balkan countries with Turkey remained at very low levels mainly because of the belligerent conditions that prevailed in the area. After the Greco-Turkish war of 1921–22, the influx of some 1.5 million refugees from Asia Minor, in addition to the 5.5 million population of Greece and the other refugee movements in other Balkan nations, created serious housing and employment problems. Rug and textile industries, pottery, and shipping were rapidly developed thereafter.

The policy of conciliation and friendship, which was pursued by the Greek leader Eleutherios Venizelos and Kemal Ataturk (1928–33), as well as other leaders in the Balkan Peninsula, stimulated economic development in the area. Balkan politicians, made genuine efforts toward a closer economic and political cooperation among the Balkan nations in the early 1930s. As a result, a number of conferences were held for further collaboration on tariffs, credit, protection of agricultural products, tourism, and foreign trade. Similar conferences of the Balkan countries, including Turkey, were organized later but with limited results.

After the death of Kemal in 1938, the government of Ismet Inonu (1938–50) emphasized higher agricultural growth instead of rapid industrialization. However, this policy failed to increase productivity substantially.

The weakness of the private sector and the lack of entrepreneurial know-how during the years of "emergence" of the Turkish economy (1923–50), under the governments of the Republican People's Party, may be considered the main reasons of growth of state enterprises. The state economic enterprises (SEEs) started with the creation of the State Railroad Company, and were expanded in the 1930s and later.[1]

Turkey did not suffer great destruction as a result of World War II, and was not compelled to rebuild and modernize its industry, as other Balkan countries, mainly Greece and Yugoslavia, were. Moreover, special interest organizations, which remained and increased over time, inhibited the effective competitive functioning of the economy and led to inflation and balance-of-payments deficits.

In 1950–60 the government of Adnan Menderes pursued a policy of expansion. The growth of the economy may be attributed to the rapid growth of agricultural exports, especially during the Korean War, which resulted in the inflow of foreign investment and the establishment of needed infrastructure. However, the more liberal economic policies of the government aimed at achieving great leaps forward that were unrealistic for the culturally and religiously conservative Turkish society.[2] Furthermore, the opening to the West increased the propensity to import, with no equal rise in exports, and led to trade deficits and the gradual depletion of foreign currency reserves.

On the other hand, the implementation of some form of indicative planning after 1963 was not integrated into the "financial programming" suggested by the International Monetary Fund (IMF), and it proved to be ineffective in solving the problems of inflation and the balance of payments. Such macroeconomic planning, which also was used in Greece after 1958, usually includes optimistic projections for the overall and sectoral growth of the economy with little, if any, practical effect. Only for the projection of public investment may they have some importance. The continuation of the ineptly administered development policies and the overexpansion of the money supply led to even higher inflation.

The inflationary policy of money and credit expansion, which continued during the 1970s, was due primarily to the significant increase in remittances from Turkish workers in Europe. In order to avoid social unrest due to high inflation, the government froze the prices of products of state enterprises. However, because of the lag in tax collection, large deficits appeared in the public sector and were financed by further increases in the money supply, thereby fueling more inflation. Moreover, interest rates were fixed, and as a result the quantity and quality of investments were lowered. These unwise domestic policies, as well as the use of fixed exchange rates in foreign transactions, led to extensive balance-of-payments deficits and further weakening of the Turkish lira.

In order to improve economic conditions, the Turkish government has begun reforms, through privatization, scrapping subsidies and eliminating protectionism that has kept inefficient enterprises in operation. These austerity measures are used to reduce consumption, reduce inflation (which runs at high rates annually), and stimulate the economic growth of the country. Also, economic and military aid provided by the United States and its Western allies is expected to help stabilize the ailing Turkish economy, which has a relatively high unemployment rate. The geographical location of Turkey, between Europe and the Middle East, is a major factor influencing Western policies on foreign aid to the country.

Turkey is very much a country with a split personality. One segment of the population, living mainly in the cities, is in many ways modern and Western; the people in the rural regions form a traditional Middle East society where Islam holds sway. The process of economic development leads to the migration of poor, uneducated peasants into the slums of the cities, which in recent years have been the main areas of the extremism.

A member of the North Atlantic Treaty Organization (NATO) since 1952, Turkey has received large amounts of military and economic aid from the United States under the Truman Doctrine (1947). The 1960s and 1970s have been marked by outbursts of public disorder and frequent changes in government. On September 12, 1980, the country came under a military dictatorship (the third in the postwar years) headed by General Kenan Evren.[3] This dictatorship seemed to be milder than those in 1960 and 1971, and tried to reduce the killings and the skirmishes between the Sunni majority and the Shiite minority of the Muslim population. Turkey, with inflation more than 100 percent (126 percent in 1994), budget deficits of about $6 billion, and trade deficits of more than $1 billion annually, has a population that is 99 percent Muslim. The Islamic Welfare Party of Necmettin Erbakan, which came in first in the 1995 elections, favors pulling Turkey out of NATO and establishing an "Islamic Common Market."

As mentioned earlier, the majority of the Kurdish population, estimated at 12 million (out of a total of 20 million), lives in Turkey. While the Kurdish nationalists are not as well organized as they are in neighboring Iraq and Iran, a number of attempts have been made to awaken nationalism and achieve independence. Another priority of the military rulers in Ankara was and still is to discourage such movements and to calm the unrest that has been growing in the underdeveloped, predominantly Kurdish areas of eastern Turkey.

HISTORICAL TRENDS

Anatolia in Ancient Times

Turkey was known to ancient geographers by the Greek word *Anatolia* (*the rising of the sun*) and in Turkish as *Anadolu*. Around the seventh and sixth millennia B.C., Anatolia was inhabited by prehistoric people known as the Hatti. Their language was known as Hattic. Around 2500 to 2000 B.C., tribes from the north and the east, known as Hittites, coming by way of the Caucasus, settled in Anatolia, northern Syria, and Mesopotamia, and superimposed their Indo-European speech on the indigenous Hattic. They were noted for their working of iron and the use of eight languages found in numerous clay tables in Hattusas (present-day Bagozkoy).

After the second millennium B.C., Anatolia, or Asia Minor, primarily its central and eastern part, was under the Hittites. The city of Hattusas, east of present-day Ankara, was their capital. The Hittites adopted the deities and even their name from the indigenous Hatti people, whom they conquered. After 1200 B.C., the Hittite Empire collapsed when the Phrygians from western Anatolia rebelled and burned Hattusas.[4] Later, Assyrians and the emerging Aegean powers, primarily the Greek Dorians, conquered the area.

On the northwestern section of Anatolia were the lands of Troy (close to the Dardanelles, or Hellespont). From the third millenium B.C., the Thracians controlled the area of Troy and levied tolls on traffic across the Dardanelles. The region was settled about 1900 B.C. by newcomers related to the early Greeks. In about 1300 B.C. an earthquake devastated the city of Troy, while around 1200 B.C. the city was sacked and burned by the expedition force of Mycenae and other Greek city-states under Agamemnon, as Homer's *Iliad* indicates. Later, the site was known as the Greek Ilion and Roman Ilium. From 1200 B.C. onward, the Aegean coast of Anatolia was largely affected by the Minoan-Mycenaean civilization.

In western and southwestern Anatolia, Ionian Greek settlers appeared (1200–900 B.C.). In this region the Phrygians had a strong state between 750 to 300 B.C., with Gordium as their capital and Midas as their fabled king (725–675 B.C.). Later, Lydian kings, such as Croesus (560–546 B.C.), controlled the area. The city-states of Lydia, Lycia, and Caria flourished briefly as part of the Ionian Greek civilization.[5] In Lydia the first coins appeared during the sixth century B.C. In 546 B.C. the Persian king Cyrus defeated the Lydians, and Anatolia became part of the Persian Empire of the Achaemenid dynasty for two centuries.

In the eastern part of Anatolia were the Armenians, stretching from the Black Sea to the Caspian, and the less organized Kurds, who migrated from the Eurasian steppes in the second millennium B.C. to the southeastern part of Anatolia, as described by Xenophon (400 B.C.) and other writers and ethnographers. The Armenians (after 600 B.C.) were settled in the area for good, mainly south of the Caucasus mountains. They had come earlier from the east and had merged with the Hittites of the region. They preserved a distinct Indo-European language and were to endure in the region as a separate ethnic group.

In 334 B.C., Alexander the Great crossed the Hellespont, defeated the Persians at the nearby Granicus River, and, cutting the Gordian knot, advanced into Asia and incorporated Anatolia into his empire. After his death (323 B.C.), Anatolia was divided among a number of small kingdoms. During the third century B.C., Gallic peoples from Europe settled in central Anatolia, an area known as Gallatia during the Roman times.

Roman and Byzantine Periods

During the second century B.C., the Romans, coming from the Adriatic coast, conquered the Balkans and then Asia Minor. Their main contributions were the construction of an efficient transportation network and the security of life and property. Under these conditions, a number of trade centers and local industries developed.[6]

Ephesus, a masterpiece of urban planning and Hellenistic architecture, was annexed to the Roman Empire in 133 B.C. It became the capital of the rich Roman province of Asia. An extraordinary cosmopolitan city with its monumental Temple of Artemis, it was a major port and commercial center both before and after the Romans came. Situated on the southwest coast of Turkey, near Smyrna, it was known for its outstanding theater, where Mark Antony greeted Cleopatra, and the famous Library of Celsus. (As I observed during my research trip to Ephesus, this library and other surroundings were under renovation by a Danish group.)

The Byzantine Empire existed for some 1,100 years and extended over parts of Europe, Asia, and northern Africa. From that point of view, knowledge of Byzantine economic history requires extensive research and volumes of publications. Here, an attempt is made to present a short review of the main features of Byzantine economics, with emphasis on agriculture and public administration (see also chapter 2 of this book).

The geographical position of the Balkan Peninsula, with its mountainous area and the protection given by the Danube to the north, enhanced the prospects for the survival of Byzantium. As a result, the reputation of Constantinople (the capital of Byzantium) as a commercial and industrial center was furthered. Likewise, Smyrna and other cities in Anatolia were developed through more trade and investment.

Fiscal and monetary policies of the Byzantine Empire were used not so much in support of trade but primarily to supply the state's needs for revenue, to pay the army and administrative personnel mainly in the capital city, as well as to pay bribes for keeping enemy powers in check. Such policies proved to be effective in providing stability and serving the empire well across so many centuries.

Economic mismanagement, high taxes, currency debasement, and the luxurious living of the Byzantine rulers led the empire to the point of bankruptcy. Moreover, internal strife and external invasions, mainly by Mongols from the east, brought about the final collapse and the occupation of the empire by the Seljuk Turks. Conquest by the Latins from the west and the Turks from the east made the Byzantine Empire look like a slender and miserable body upon which rested an enormous head.

OTTOMAN EXPANSION

The Ottoman Turks gradually advanced from the Central Asian steppes to the Anatolian plateau. Toward the close of the thirteenth Christian century, flying before the face of the Mongols, the nomadic stock-breeding invaders passed from the basin of the Oxus and Jaxartes, on the northeastern marshes of Islam, to their new settlements.

The Islamic Ottoman Empire grew up very alien and hostile to the contemporary Christian communities that had sprung from the soil of the West during the Greco-Roman civilization. To extract a livelihood, these nomadic herdsmen kept constantly on the move in search of pasture at different seasons with their cattle and other animals (dogs, camels, horses) that assisted them.[7]

In 1345, John Cantacugenus, a Byzantine official, invited the Ottomans to support his bid for the throne. In 1349, the Ottomans were invited again to help save Salonika from the Serbs (under Stephen Dushan). Thus the Ottomans, further strengthened by additional troops, began to settle down in eastern Thrace (Gallipoli). From 1354 onward they began pushing westward to the rich lands of Thrace, Macedonia, Thessaly, and the rest of Greece and the Balkans. Eventually they captured Adrianople (1360), Salonika (1430), Constantinople (May 29, 1453), and almost all the Balkans by 1460. From time to time Venetian fleets gained control of coastal areas and many islands, including the Ionian Islands (1386–1797) and the Peloponnesus (1687–1718).[8]

For purposes of maintaining the gulf between the Eastern (Orthodox) and Western (Catholic) churches and precluding any combined Christian resistance to Ottoman rule, the Turks practiced religious tolerance and permitted exemptions from taxation and expropriation of church properties, like the Byzantines before them. This helped preserve and promote the rapid growth of monasteries, which acquired large estates, even outside individual Balkan countries (*metochia*), from the donations of the heavily taxed peasants. The transfer of the accumulated properties of the monasteries to the tillers or the government presented, and still presents, serious problems in the Balkans' agricultural economics.

Following their usual practice, the Turkish invaders distributed conquered lands to their warriors and collaborators, while the other Balkan peoples (the *rayahs*) were subjected to heavy taxation and economic exploitation. Rich lands were confiscated by the Turkish chiefs, who transformed them into their own estates (*chifliks*) and used them in a feudalistic manner.[9]

From an economic and social point of view, the feudal system of Western Europe prevailed, to a large extent, in the Balkan areas during the Ottoman period. Turkish chiefs (*pashas* and *agas*) lived luxuriously while the masses lived in poverty. Between them was the class consisting of a few well-to-do local people who retained and enlarged their privileges and their large properties, mainly through collaboration with the Turkish rulers.

During the Ottoman years, a limited number of new manufacturing units were created primarily with European capital and know-how. To pay for imports from Europe, exports of cotton and thread from areas under the Ottomans increased while export tariffs declined from 5 to around 1 percent of the value of exports. European markets dictated, to a large extent, the pattern of production for cotton, silk, and other raw materials.

In order to promote the economy, the sultans renewed the privileges that Venice enjoyed under Byzantium and even wanted to repopulate occupied areas with mainly merchants and seafaring Greeks. A number of cultural and commercial centers, such as those of Salonika, Athens, Smyrna, and Ioannina, developed, and the Greek language gradually spread throughout the Balkan areas, especially in the ports of the Black Sea. Handicraft industries and production cooperatives were also created.[10] In addition to the Ambelakia enterprise in Thessaly (1795), which manufactured textile products, Bursa in Asia Minor also became an important center of silk and textile industries in the Near East. It used to compete with other nations, mainly Persia, in local and European markets. Salonika was a center for production and export of primarily wooden products.

However, the tax form of stamp duties on cloth and price fluctuations in European markets led, in many instances, to instability and stagnation of the textile industries. Moreover, the use of hand-operated looms and other primitive Ottoman technology, compared to more efficient steam-powered machines in Europe, increased production cost and squeezed profits in these industries. Bursa and other cloth centers, though, continued to specialize in producing the raw materials demanded by the hungry industries of Europe, mainly those of France, England, and Holland.

The capitation tax was the major personal tax (*harach* in Turkish), which each adult Christian male was required to pay. It was computed for the whole village, regardless if the number of taxpayers was reduced as people fled to the mountain areas to escape oppression and heavy taxation. In mountain communities, such as Arcadia, Roumely, and Kosovo, where people found asylum from Ottoman oppression, one could meet precipices where a few men with stones might destroy armies.

Another major land tax was the tithe (*dhekati* in Greek, *usr* in Turkish), varying from one-tenth to one-half of the produce. Also, a tax paid by the Christian subjects was that in lieu of military service, as well as an irregular impost (*avariz*) which varied in purpose and amount. There were cases, as in Epirus, for example, in 1867, in which taxes and all kinds of charges under the Turkish rule amounted to 67 percent of the farm proceeds.[11] Such large payments and other charges were very difficult to meet; even the mythological giant Cyclops would be distressed.

Although the establishment of a common Ottoman system put an end to internal strife in the occupied areas and perhaps brought some economic development, this was accomplished with the sacrifice of the liberty of the people and their cultural improvement. For four centuries, the Balkan peoples were subjected to ruthless exploitation. But, "far worse than the material injuries were the spiritual wounds, the traces of which it will require generations of educational effort and moral reconstruction to obliterate."[12] Under the laws of Islam, polygamy was permitted and harems (where women were treated as inferior beings) were common. The sultan and his family ruled the empire for the benefit of Muslims, who monopolized the professions and exploited their Christian subjects in the occupied principalities.

THE ESTABLISHMENT OF MODERN TURKEY

During the Balkan wars and World War I, the Ottoman Empire slipped to its doom. The heterogeneous population that inhabited its farflung and unwieldy area, the differences between Muslims and Christians, and the economic, social, and military disturbances at home and pressures from abroad were among the main causes of decline.

The disintegration of the Ottoman Empire was associated with territorial claims and occupations by the victorious Allies. So, "the sick man of Europe," as Tsar Nicholas I of Russia described (1833) the Ottoman Empire, was dismembered, as Britain, France, and Italy took over Arab and other provinces.

Another element of crisis in the empire came from the Young Turks. After the suppression of their movement in 1876, they started an underground movement that flourished, especially in Salonika. Advocating racial and religious equality and the end of autocracy, the movement, represented by the Committee of Union and Progress, was supported by some young army officers, including Enver Bey and Mustafa Kemal. Although the Young Turks managed to introduce some reforms, especially in 1909 and 1910, they faced serious problems of inflexibility on the part of the Muslim judicial institutions that dominated the Ottoman society. Moreover, the formation of the Balkan League in 1912 by Greece, Serbia, and Bulgaria and their concerted attack on Turkey in the autumn of that year liberated almost all the European sections of the Ottoman Empire. On the other hand, the alliance of Russia with Britain, France, and Italy made some Young Turks favor alliance with Germany and war against the Allies, who wanted the partition of Turkey. Thereafter the Young Turks became, to a large extent, nationalistic and abandoned their movement for reforms for equality and progress. However, they were able to record some progress. With French advisors, they reformed the tax system toward eliminating the curse of the old regime of tax-farming, while with British supervisors they reformed the customs duties. In any case, their movement subsequently helped the westernization and modernization of Turkey.

After the Greco-Turkish war and the rise of Kemal Ataturk, the borders of today's Turkey were determined (Treaty of Lausanne, July 24, 1923) and economic reforms were introduced. Ataturk (meaning "father of Turkey") wanted the de-Islamization and westernization of Turkey. This transformation, although slow and painful, reached partial fulfillment, at least in economic development terms.

Among the major reforms introduced by Kemalist nationalists were: abolishment of the sultanate and caliphate, the fez was outlawed and the veiling of women discouraged, new civil penal and commercial codes based on European models and a new constitution were adopted, a new alphabet based on Latin was introduced, women could vote and hold office, and a state capitalist control of the public sector (etatism) was introduced with the new constitution.

The Young Turks, influenced by the Russian Revolution and the English Fabian ideas, were enthusiastic about state control over the economy of the Ataturk regime, according to which if the private sector did not perform well, then the state would interfere and even take over productive operations. At that time and especially during the 1930s, protective tariffs were raised, transport rates were reduced, and lands for industrial sites were granted, particularly for sugar and textile factories.[13]

The five-year plan, which was announced by Ataturk in 1935, incorporated a number of reforms for the modernization and development of the Turkish economy. Investment in plants and equipment, not only by the private but also by the public sector, was emphasized. Public sector investment was to be financed through taxation. Direct taxes, which were about 30 percent of total taxes, included income taxes that were graduated from 15 to 45 percent. Indirect taxes, about 60 percent of total taxation, provided the largest part of government revenue.[14]

During the prewar and early post–World War II periods, the economy of Turkey was primarily based on agricultural production, mainly tobacco and grain. Mining, textiles, leather, and food processing were also important. After the economic reforms of Kemal Ataturk, protective tariffs were raised, domestic savings were encouraged, and highways, railroads, and other public works were built. Agricultural productivity and self-sufficiency were emphasized. Industrial progress was also pursued but less intensively. The government of Ismet Inonu (1938–50) continued to emphasize the agricultural sector at the neglect of the industrial sector. During the years of "emergence" of the Turkish economy (1923–50), the lack of entrepreneurship and the weakness of the private sector were largely responsible for the rapid growth of state economic enterprises (SEEs). However, the policy of self-sufficiency pursued by the Turkish policymakers during that period did not permit much trade expansion with neighboring and other countries.

Gradually, and particularly in the 1930s, Germany penetrated and established a firm position in Turkey. The Germans trained the Turkish army, projected and assisted the construction of the Berlin-Baghdad Railway, and invested in a number of industries.[15] During World War II, the Turks managed to preserve neutrality and stay out of the ordeal and the destruction of war faced by other Balkan countries.

Due primarily to World War II conditions, economic growth in the 1940s was impressive. High growth rates of the Gross National Product (GNP) continued in the 1950s as well, due mainly to an increase in the nonagricultural labor force rather than to productivity growth.

However, the gap in per capita income between the urban industrial workers and the rural workers was and still is large. Moreover, the opening of the economy to the West increased the propensity to import without a substantial increase in exports. Then the government's optimistic policies, projecting great leaps forward, proved largely ineffective because of the difficulties of changing a culturally and religiously conservative society in a short period. This is a familiar phenomenon in developing nations such as Turkey. There it could be observed as early as the intensive developmental efforts of Kemal Ataturk years ago.

THE ARMENIAN TRAGEDY

After the victory of Russia over the Turks in 1877–78, the Treaty of Berlin was concluded in June 1878. It permitted Britain to take Cyprus, and sanctioned the gradual replacement of Turkey in Europe by the Balkan states, while Armenia, Crete, and Macedonia were designated as objects of the Great Powers. The Turkish sultan Abdul Hamid II, "The Great Assassin," who had been associated with the Bulgarian massacres of 1876, utilized religious passions for political ends and resorted to organized genocide of the Armenian Christians, extending not only to the mountains of Armenia bordering Russia, but also to the streets of Constantinople (1894–96, 1909).

Article 61 of the Treaty of Berlin, designating Armenia as an area of concern for the Allies, served as a pretext for inflaming the Turks' hatred of the Christian element and became the cause of its ruin. This led to the formation and execution of a diabolical scheme of extermination of the Armenians in Istanbul and in Armenia proper by Turkish soldiers and wild Kurdish horsemen. Among other crimes, women were sold as slaves after being bestially violated. In the words of the historian Arnold Toynbee, "The intermittent sufferings of the Armenian race have culminated in an organized, cold-blooded attempt on the part of the Turkish rulers to exterminate it once and for all by methods of inconceivable barbarism and wickedness."[16]

A systematic slaughter of some 1.5 million Armenians, including women and children, took place on April 24, 1915, close to the Russian borders. Those who survived the massacre were ordered to make a long disastrous walk, "a death march," toward the Syrian borders. Most of them perished from hunger, hardship, and torture or were hanged along the way, especially in the desert of Des-Es-Zor.

The premeditated, systematic annihilation of the Armenian people in 1915–23 has been recognized. However, scholars trusted by the Turks, such as Ezel Kural Shaw and Bernard Lewis, do not agree as to the number of people killed. While Armenians claim that as many as 2 million were massacred, writers sympathetic to the Turkish arguments base their calculations on the Ottoman census of 1914 and argue that the Armenian population was only 1.3 million. They contend that 400,000 Armenian people were actually transported in 1915–16, some 700,000 fled to the Caucasus, Western Europe, and the United States, and 100,000 remained in Turkey. Therefore, they estimate that about 100,000 were slaughtered.

Regardless of whether there were 300,000 or 2 million or, more probably, 1.5 million people who perished, the truth is that these horrible atrocities by the Turks between 1915 and 1923 aimed at the extermination of the Armenians. In addition to those slaughtered in their homes, many died during their transfer, or "death march." Clemenceau had to admit that "the history of mankind has never presented such an example of organized horror." Mothers saw their children die of starvation in their arms. A little girl told her mother that when she died she did not want to give her body to the others to eat because they did not give her meat from the others' bodies while she starved. This was an organized Hitler-like genocide of worldwide importance.[17]

In 1987, the European Assembly recognized the Armenian genocide in the sense of genocide as defined by the General Assembly of the United Nations. However, it also recognized that the Turkey of today must not be held responsible for the tragedy of the Armenians belonging to the Ottoman Empire.

During the period of the Armenian genocide by the Turks, many Armenians fled to the Armenian Soviet Socialist Republic. There they erected a monument in memory of the massacre, which is still open to visitors and tourists. The author visited this monument during a research trip to Eastern Europe. An eternal flame, under a high metallic arch, and a historical account of the Armenian ordeal in the background are the sad characteristics of this place.

Another ordeal of the Armenians occurred in Smyrna in 1922. When the Greek troops retreated from the disastrous expedition into Asia Minor, Smyrna was burned and pillaged, raped and wrecked by the Turks. "The Armenians, with nowhere to go, were slaughtered although they played no part in the Greek recklessness."[18] As Ernest Hemingway reported, the retreating Greeks, on the other hand, smashed the legs of their loyal mules so that they might never carry Turkish masters.

To avoid being caught and persecuted by a recalcitrant Turkey, the Armenian people, with one of the most ancient civilizations in the world, are still fleeing their homeland to other countries and scrambling for a safe position elsewhere. It is estimated that only about 60,000 Armenians remain in Turkey now, primarily in Istanbul, and about 6 million are spread all over the world, mainly in the Soviet Union and the United States. This is the tragedy of the Armenian people who continue to struggle for going back to their homeland in Turkey under difficult conditions.

United States congressional joint resolutions are presented from time to time to designate April 24 as a day of remembrance honoring Armenian victims of the genocidal massacre and dispersion in 1915. However, the American government discourages the approval of such a resolution on the grounds that it would harm relations with Turkey, which is regarded as an important ally. To remember the ordeal of their ancestors, Armenians parade in New York on April 24 every year. As George Deukmejian, a former governor of California, said, the idea is that mature societies admit their past mistakes to avoid repetitions similar to that of Hitler who decided he could get away with the extermination of the Jews because, as he put it, Who still talks nowadays about the extermination of the Armenians? In revenge, underground Armenian groups, such as the Justice Commandos Against Armenian Genocide and others, have resorted to bombing Turkish airline and tourist offices and to assassinating Turkish diplomats in different countries and cities, such as Paris, Lisbon, Geneva, Athens, and Los Angeles.[19]

On September 21, 1991, the Republic of Armenia (with a population of 3.4 million), which was under the former Soviet Union, voted for its independence from the USSR (which it joined in 1922). After the collapse of the USSR in 1989, Armenia and other neighboring Black Sea countries formed the common market of the Euxene; then in 1991, it joined the Commonwealth of Independent States (CIS) with ten other former Soviet republics.

THE KURDISH STRUGGLE FOR INDEPENDENCE

The Kurds, a fairly homogeneous Muslim tribal society of some 20 million people, are of Indo-European origin. They live in an area extending from western Iran (Kermansach) to northern Iraq and Syria, but they are mostly located in the eastern provinces of Turkey, especially in the regions of Kars and Arntachan. Primarily, they belong to the Sunni branch of Islam, opposing the Shiite Muslims, sharing no common characteristics with the Turks, the Persians, or the Arabs. The region in which they live has been divided mainly among three countries (Turkey, Iran, and Iraq), and this makes it difficult for their union in one independent Kurdish nation. Moreover, each of these countries at times uses its Kurdish minority against the other neighboring countries for its own benefit, or makes alliances to coordinate policies toward annihilation of the autonomy-seeking Kurds.

These stubborn Kurdish people opposed the Seljuk Turks and later the Ottoman oppressors for a long time, but being under the antagonism of powerful Turkey and Persia, they could not achieve independence.[20] Kurdish nationalism expanded during the nineteenth century and especially at the beginning of the twentieth century. The Treaty of Sevres in 1920 gave to the victorious powers (mainly Britain, France, and Italy) the possibility to grant autonomy to the Kurds. However, with the Treaty to Lausanne in 1923, the Treaty of Sevres was void, and the Allies did not keep their promise. Since then, the Kurds have been continuing their struggle for independence.

After Turkey became a republic in 1924, the Kurds rose, from time to time, against Turkish oppression. Thus, in the uprising of 1924, some 15,200 Kurds were killed and 206 villages were destroyed. Also, similar revolts broke out in 1925 and 1930, as well as in 1937 and 1938. In the serious battle of Tunceli (Dersim) in 1938, the Kurds were defeated by the Turks. As a result, the Tunceli province was placed under martial law until 1946. The Soviet Union occupied northwestern Iran in 1945–46 and allowed the creation of the state of Kurdistan (Mahaband). After the Soviets left, the Iranians reoccupied the new state and executed its president, Zaki Mohamant.

After World War II, the oppression of the Kurds in Turkey began to relax in some ways, and some religious and nationalistic activities were tolerated. However, after May 27, 1960, the military dictatorship in Turkey again started prosecuting Kurdish separatists and sentenced some of them to death.[21]

Major Kurdish rebel attacks occurred mainly in Iraq after 1960. The Kurdish struggle for independence in Iraq forced the Baath Party of Saddam Hussein to recognize some form of autonomy and to include some of their leaders in the General Assembly. Also, limited but temporary autonomy was offered by Iran after the disturbances of March 1979, in which more than one hundred people were killed.

Similar improvements in the status of the Kurds occurred in Turkey in the 1960s and the late 1970s, when liberalism was flourishing. The Kurds were attracted to liberal and leftist parties like the Turkish Workers Party that was sympathetic to Kurdish aspirations. However, when the party was dissolved by the military regime in 1971, some Kurds began to form their own clandestine organizations. Others, like Serafettin Elci, joined the Republican People's Party, a social democratic group. Elci served as minister of public works when this party was in power under Prime Minister Bulent Ecevit in 1978 and 1979, and supported the economic development of the backward eastern region where the Kurds lived.

After the armed forces came to power on September 12, 1980, the junta once again began to arrest and prosecute Kurdish nationalists, including Elci, who argued that the eastern region has been left to poverty and misery and that "it is natural that there should be reactions in an underdeveloped society that is oppressed."[22] Massive trials of Kurds have taken place since the military coup of 1980 for "illegal" activities inside Turkey and abroad (mainly in Sweden) aiming at introducing a language other than Turkish and "attempting to divide the Turkish nation into ethnic groups."[23]

At present, the largest Kurdish segment lives in Turkey, where unemployment is high and people feel neglected. The economic backwardness of the area and the Kurdish independence movement are responsible for disturbances and violence from time to time. Some 12 million Kurds are believed to live in Turkey. They are among the poorest people of the country. Diyarbakir, the capital of what Kurdish clandestine nationalists call Kurdistan, Van, and other cities around the river Tigris are known for poor housing, unpaved streets, and economic backwardness. Turkish security and armed forces are busy in their drive against Kurdish nationalist organizations, said to number about ten. A principal clandestine Kurdish organization is Apo, a name derived from that of its leader, Abdurrahman Ocal. These organizations that demand independence put slogans on walls and elsewhere in Turkish and in Kurdish and call for "Freedom for Kurdistan." Frequently visitors can hear a student, a clerk, or a writer declare: "I am Kurdish, not Turk." The separatists are centered mainly in high schools and universities.

However, there have been no serious revolutions since the insurrections in the 1920s and 1930s. In the 1980s, it was estimated that about 80 people of Kurdish origin were sitting in the 635-member Turkish Parliament. Although Turkish authorities try to understate the Kurdish movement for self-determination and independence, the problem remains and at times becomes serious as disturbances and massive trials occur.

Kurdish separatist fighters have been conducting hit-and-run raids, especially in recent years. Sometimes, Kurds in Turkey receive help from Kurdish people in neighboring countries. Under a 1984 agreement between Turkey and Iraq, Turkey was permitted to carry out operations against these camps on Iraq territory. Turkey has conducted a number of raids with aircraft and ground forces. However, Iran objects to such operations, saying they help Iraq. In May 1983, the Turkish infantry crossed the Iraqi borders, hunting and killing Kurdish separatists.[24] In August 1986, Turkish planes entered Iraq and bombarded Kurdish camps. In a similar air attack on March 4, 1987, it was estimated that one hundred people were killed. Some thirty planes from the Batman and Diyarbakir airfields were used for raids against three locations in Iraq.[25] In the previous attack 242 partisans, fighting for self-determination, and 211 civilians were killed.

In November 1994, some 220,000 soldiers, nearly half of the Turkish army, were sent to southeastern Turkey against about 20,000 Kurdish separatists in a campaign to depopulate Kurdish regions through forced evacuation and burning of some 1,500 villages. At least 13,000 people, including thousands of civilians, have been killed in a decade, according to the Turkish military. Moreover, because of the jailing of elected Kurdish legislators and the war on Kurds, the United States restricted military aid to Turkey, whereas the European Union (EU) warned President Suleiman Demirel and Prime Minister Tansu Ciller about the effects of human rights violations by Turkey.

In March 1995, at least 35,000 Turkish troops crossed the border into Iraq against Kurdish separatists. This region, with some 3.5 million Kurds, is protected by the United States and its allies from the genocidal fury of Saddam Hussein, the leader of Iraq, since the end of the Gulf War over Kuwait in 1991.[26] The result of that campaign, severely condemned by the fifteen EU members, were new destructions and killings of the much-suffering Kurds. For this, the thirty-four members of the Council of Europe voted to suspend Turkey and demanded political reforms.

It seems that for decades now Turkey has been under either a concealed or open military dictatorship. Political leaders are largely following the directives of the military leaders, who have a racist mentality similar to that of the Nazis, and dream of the revival of the Ottoman Empire. The use of such racist slogans as "The Turkish race is superior to every other" and "Happy is he who calls himself a Turk," are behind the recent murders of over 1,700 people, some 2,000 Kurdish villages burned, and 2.5 million people exiled.[27] As it appears, Turkey does not tolerate other minorities and ethnicities.

For the self-determination of the Kurdish population, Kurds in Europe created an exiled Kurdish parliament in The Hague in April 1995, aiming at the recognition of a new state, Kurdistan.

HUMAN RIGHTS AND THE EUROPEAN UNION

Alawites, a sect of about 20 million Muslims who believe in a more liberal laissez-faire brand of Islam, feel the threat of fundamentalism, toward which Turkey is drifting rapidly. In a land that is 98 percent Muslim, the Alawites, which include ethnic Turks and Kurds, are discriminated against and persecuted by the Sunni majority, mainly because they do not observe the strict rules of Islam and do not attend mosques run by Imams. Moreover, their children are taught a Sunni brand of Islam in required religious classes at schools built with state money in their neighborhoods. After the 1980 military coup, Sunni Islam began to gain the upper hand. In Istanbul (March 1994) the Sunni fundamentalists in the Welfare Party won municipal elections, as they did in Ankara as well. As a result, municipal workers are under pressure to join in prayers and observe the Muslim fast of Ramadan, and women must wear head scarves. Alawite protests in Istanbul in March 1995 resulted in clashes with the police and thirty-four deaths.[28]

With the lifting of the veto by Greece, it is expected that Turkey would join the EU customs union. However, the European parliament warned that ratification would depend on political reforms and respect for human rights by Turkey. Moreover, Turkey should stabilize its economy and reduce inflation, resulting primarily from increases in money supply, as Figure 4.1 shows. (More on Turkish relations with the EU in chapter 7.)

Some groups oppose accession of Turkey to the EU on religious (Islamic fundamentalist) and ideological or political grounds. "The more you make yourself a European the more you become a stranger in your own land," a Turkish editor said.[29]

Figure 4.1
Money Supply (M1) and Velocity of Money (GDP/M1) for Turkey

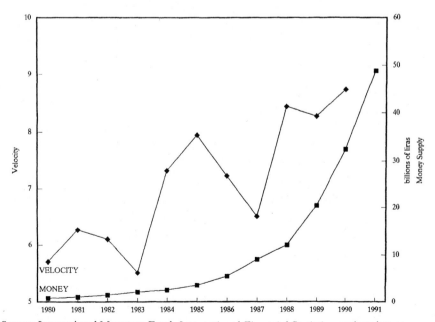

Source: International Monetary Fund, *International Financial Statistics*, various issues.

Turkey wants to be a member of the EU not only for economic reasons but for sociopolitical reasons as well. Turkey's "Europeanization" seems to have an appeal for the Turkish people and their leaders, even from the time of Kemal Ataturk. However, EU member nations have reservations, not only because of the great economic gap regarding the level of development between Turkey vis-à-vis the EU, but on political grounds as well. Reports from Amnesty International charge that torture is still widespread, and some "Eurocrats" feel that for Turkey to be a full member of the EU full restoration of western-type pluralistic democracy with respect to human rights, particularly of the Kurdish people, is needed, not a system of "democracy under military supervision." Moreover, Greece, an EU member, argues that Turkey cannot belong to the same politico-economic group and at the same time threaten another member, to wit Greece, in the Aegean with anachronistic designs of expansionism. However, after Greece lifted its objections, the EU Parliament voted on December 13, 1995, to accept Turkey into the EU customs union.

EFFECTS OF THE CONFLICTS OVER CYPRUS

The strategic position of Cyprus attracted the involvement of the Great Powers in its affairs for the promotion of their own interests. From ancient times, through the Roman and Byzantine periods, on to the Ottoman and British occupations, and primarily during its recent postliberation years, the island has had a turbulent history that perhaps no other region can match. It survived many invasions, occupations, and intrusions by a number of superpowers.

In about 1200 B.C., Greek warriors returning from the Trojan expedition with their fleet were misdirected by strong winds and sailed to Cyprus. They were mainly Arcadians, under General Agapenor, and they settled in the area of Paphos where they built the sanctuary of the goddess Aphrodite.

In July 1570, Cyprus fell to the Ottomans, in spite of the heroic defense by a mixed force of Greeks and Italians under the command of Bradadin, an experienced Venetian general. With the Treaty of Berlin, concluded in June 1878, the island passed from Ottoman Turkish hands to Britain, which annexed it outright in 1914. At the end of World War II, the population of the island (600,000) was and still is approximately 80 percent Greek and 18 percent Turkish.

After World War II, the Cypriot Greek majority wanted an end to the British occupation, and in the 1950s started guerrilla fighting for liberation. On August 29, 1955, the British, following their usual practice of divide and rule, organized a conference in London, in which Turkey was invited to participate as a third member in the arrangements for Cyprus's independence. This three-member conference became and still is the source for serious conflicts between Greece and Turkey over Cyprus.

On September 6–7, 1955, some three to four days after a pro-Cyprus demonstration in London, new serious disturbances broke out in Istanbul, and to a lesser extent in Smyrna, because of bomb explosions in the house where Kemal Ataturk was born, and in the Turkish consulate, both in Salonika. Although the damage was not severe, the media (especially newspapers in extra editions), the Turkish foreign minister, and other government officials exaggerated the events. Then a mob of youngsters demonstrated and proceeded to burn stores and houses owned by Greek people in Istanbul (Constantinople). The police and the responsible authorities of the Menderes government did not offer protection.[30] In Smyrna, though, violence was not as serious as in Istanbul and destruction was less severe. However, attacks in Smyrna against Greek officers, working in the NATO offices, and their wives had serious emotional effects in Greece. In Ankara, though, the chief of prefecture (*nomarchis*) offered enough protection and avoided serious disturbances.

As a result, a new wave of refugees left Istanbul for Greece to avoid atrocities. Of 180,000 Greeks living there, only a few thousand remained. The explanation of the Menderes government, which neglected to provide needed police and army protection, was that the disturbances were instigated by "red agents."

In the late 1950s, Greece and Turkey tried to improve their political and economic relations through high-level political contacts. Constantine Caramanlis, prime minister of Greece, visited Ankara in 1959 and had friendly discussions with Menderes, the prime minister of Turkey, and other government officials. Celal Bayar, the president of Turkey, also visited Athens.

In 1960, Cyprus secured its independence from British control, with Archbishop Makarios III as president.[31] The issue of the Greek majority rule versus the Turkish minority rights remained after Cyprus became an independent republic. Internal stress and conflicts caused major crises in 1964 and 1967, during which Greece and Turkey verged on war. In 1964, President Lyndon Johnson warned against Turkish intervention in Cyprus, threatening that the United States would not defend Turkey against a possible Soviet attack.

In 1964, a Turkish discriminatory decree (No. 6/3801/11.2.64) was imposed against Greek citizens that deprived them of their rights to carry out legal dealings with regard to the transfer of property. This measure was in contradiction to the association agreement between Turkey and the EU, and Greece (a member of the EU since 1981) was using it to refuse entry of Turkey into the EU.

In July 1974, the right-wing military junta in Athens, which had governed Greece since 1967, conducted a coup against the government of Cyprus under Archbishop Makarios III.[32] Some 650 Greek army officers assigned to Cyprus's National Guard, according to the 1960 independence agreement guaranteed by Greece, Turkey, and Britain, were used to install Nicos Sampson as president, after overthrowing the legitimate president, Archbishop Makarios. They aimed mainly at *enosis*, union of Greece and Cyprus.

On July 20, some 6,000 Turkish troops, reinforced over the next few days by more than 25,000 additional troops with U.S. equipment, invaded and occupied some 40 percent of Cyprus, in spite of UN Secretary Council resolutions and the objections of Britain, the United States, and the EU. Some 200,000 Greek Cypriot refugees (out of a total population of 600,000) fled to the south, and about 10,000 Turkish Cypriot refugees were flown to northern Cyprus. At that time and later, the Turks sent in settlers from Anatolia to colonize areas and properties that belonged to Greek Cypriots. Some 1,619 Cypriot refugees (including 5 Americans) were taken prisoner by Turkish troops. Their whereabouts are not known as yet, although more than twenty years have passed since their capture.

In protest over the continued occupation of Cyprus by Turkish forces, the U.S. Congress imposed an embargo on military assistance to Turkey. The embargo seemed not to have had much practical results and was lifted in 1978. In 1983, Decktash, the leader of the Turkish Cypriots, declared the creation of a separate Turkish Cypriot republic, which was not recognized by any nation but Turkey. After so many years and despite the repetitive resolutions of the UN for the withdrawal of the Turkish troops and settlement of the Cyprus conflict through negotiations between the Greek and the Turkish communities, the problem still remains unsolved and irritates the relations of Greece and Turkey, as well as the EU and Turkey.

Thus, Cyprus, Aphrodite's isle, which has always been a pawn on the Mediterranean chessboard, is still a source of contention between Greece and Turkey, as Turkish troops have occupied about 40 percent of the island since 1974. In addition, Turkey continues its provocations against Greece over the Aegean islands, including the Imia rocky islets (January 1996). Three Greek Navy officers lost their lives when their helicopter fell down while flying over Greek territorial waters.[33]

5

The Former Yugoslavia

The history of Yugoslavia is related to the territorial complexity of the area, the expansionary trends of different neighboring powers, and the related resistance of the native peoples, as well as their efforts to absorb and unite with each other. The valleys of the Danube, the Sava, and the Morava have served as the main gateways of migrating people and invading armies for centuries, while the Dinaric Alps and the other Balkan mountains served as a bastion against these movements.

Although little is known of the inhabitants of Yugoslavia before the coming of the Slavs, many archeological remains attest that the area was peopled even at the early times of the Iron Age (Hollstat Period). However, about the fifth century B.C., the Greeks were the first to mention that the Illyrians had occupied the area west of the Vardar and north of Epirus, driving the Thracians to the central and eastern regions of the Balkan Peninsula. During the seventh, sixth, and fifth centuries B.C., a number of Greek trading colonies were established in such locations on the coast of the Adriatic Sea as Vis (Issa), Korcula (Korkyra nigra), Hvar (Pharos), Trogir (Tragurion), and Split (Salona). However, the interior had been affected little, if at all, by the spread of such trading colonies. Moreover the infiltration of "Celtic" peoples from the north at the beginning of the fourth century B.C. had little and only temporary influence on the Illyrians.[1]

Trade interruptions by the pirates from the Illyrian coasts and the expansionary policies of the Roman Empire led to repeated Roman expeditions from the year 229 B.C. until A.D. 9, when Tiberius annexed the area named Illyricum, which at times incorporated areas from Vienna to Athens. The transportation network and the effective Roman administration stimulated commerce and mining operations, particularly in gold, silver, and copper, in the area.[2] The eastern part of the Roman Empire from near Lake Scutari to the river Sava was separated administratively by Diocletian (A.D. 285). After A.D. 395, this eastern part became the Byzantine Empire, with its own Greek-speaking Orthodox world, contrasted to the Latin-speaking Catholic world of the western part of the Roman Empire.

With the collapse of the Roman Empire, Visigoths, Huns, Ostrogoths, and some other groups captured the whole coastal area of Dalmatia. This was reconquered by Justinian, the Byzantine emperor, by A.D. 535 but then was captured and devastated by the Avars coming from the Danube plain during the second half of the sixth century. At the same time, and into the seventh century, the Slavs dispersed by the Avar menace in eastern Europe moved southward as far as the Peloponnesus. By A.D. 650 they occupied Illyria and settled there permanently. It was mainly the Slovenes, the Croats (who came under Roman Catholic influence), and the Serbs in the south who were influenced by the Orthodox church of Constantinople. Although the Croats used the Latin, and the Serbs the Cyrillic alphabet, they both continued to speak the same (Serbo-Croat) language, while the Slovenes continued to use a different language. At the beginning of the tenth century, the Magyars, a Finno-Ugrian race, established itself in what is now Hungary and separated the southern Slavs from the others in the north. The remnants of the Roman provincials, primarily Vlachs, were scattered in different mountainous areas and were gradually slavicized.

During the period of the Byzantine and Ottoman empires, Dalmatia's city-states came repeatedly under Venice or Hungary, but they managed to preserve a high degree of autonomy. As a result, the development of industries, fisheries, and seaborne commerce, primarily with neighboring Italian cities, brought real prosperity to the area. However, the interior economy remained primarily agricultural and pastoral. Gradually, though, and as a result of the economic awakening in Europe especially during the thirteenth and fourteenth centuries, production of cereals, hemp, flax, wine, oil, and other agricultural products greatly increased in the fertile basins of the Ibar, the Vardar, the Drim, and the Morava rivers, supplementing the cattle, pigs, wool, and skins that always kept a prominent position in domestic and foreign markets. Furthermore, with the help of immigrants from Italy and Germans from Hungary (named Saxons), the mining of silver, gold, copper, and tin, particularly in the north, proved to be important for the economic development and the hiring of workers by the rulers of the region.

The Serbs, under Stephen Dushan (1331–55), achieved a high level of prosperity, along with the expansion of their country from the Danube and Drima rivers to Dalmatia, Albania, and parts of Greece (up to the Gulf of Corinth). The transportation network that the Romans had established, particularly the east-west roads, proved to be beneficial for agricultural and mining products and the expansion of domestic and foreign trade during that time.

When the Ottomans first came into the Balkan Peninsula, they established military and administrative officials in strategic regions. In 1389, the Ottoman Turks defeated the Serbian forces of Prince Lazar in Kosovo. Turkish chiefs (*beys*) received large tracts of land (*chifliks*), while Turkish peasants were transported from Asia Minor, mainly Konia, and were implanted in different areas.

The Turkish conquerors did not press heavily on the Christian subjects (*rayahs*) during the early years of occupation, and taxation was not excessive. Large regions (*pashaliks*) were subdivided into provinces (*nahies*). Each province had an elected native chief (*obor-knez*) and each village a headman (*knez*), both of whom were responsible for tax assessment. The *obor-knez* represented the natives to the Turkish *kadi*, who presided in each *nahie*, and was responsible to the pasha, the governor of pashaliks. Nevertheless, some nobles managed to keep their lands and their independence, as long as they paid the taxes, being responsible directly to the pashas. This administrative system proved to be successful at the beginning.

The Turkish authorities stood above local conflicts and let the knezes do the dirty work of collecting taxes and policing their own people. However, when the central authority gradually lost control and the kadis and the pashas became corrupt, heavy oppression was exercised upon the Slavs and other Balkan rayahs.

During the period 1797–1814, the economic conditions of the western provinces of the Balkans from Carniola to Dalmatia and Ragusa, under Napoleon's rule, were greatly improved.[3] The administrative system of these Illyrian Provinces, with Ljubljana as capital, was reorganized. Roads were built, trade was revitalized, and intellectual life, influenced by the liberal ideas of the French Revolution, was stimulated. From 1815 to 1849 the area came under the Austrian Empire.

Directly or indirectly, the neighboring big powers opposed cooperation among the Balkan countries so that they could continue to exercise their influence in the area. Thus in 1906, Austria objected to tariff negotiations between Serbia and Bulgaria and imposed high duties on livestock passing through Austria-Hungary (the Pig War). Since nine-tenths of Serbian exports were involved, such restrictions would have led to the economic collapse of the country if new markets had not been opened in western Europe and exports facilitated via Salonika.

Macedonia, which extends roughly from Lake Ohrid in the west to the river Nestos (Mesta) in the east, and between the mountain Kara Dagh and Sar Plainina in the north and the Aegean Sea in the south, remained a troubled area for a long time. Because of its strategic location, its great port of Salonika, and its fertile plains, it was always coveted by the neighboring countries, mainly Bulgaria, Greece, and Yugoslavia. Before liberation from Turkish occupation, rival educational activities, nationalistic propaganda, and even revolutionary secret societies, such as the Internal Organization (VMRO, 1893), the Greek Ethniki Hetairia (1894), and the Bulgarian Supreme Macedo-Adrianopolitan Committee (1895), quarreled in their efforts to gain the support of the people of Macedonia, which at that time included the three Turkish *vilayets* of Salonika, Monastir (Bitolj), and Kosovo. The passion for education was so strong that parents were often induced by scholarship to enroll their children in schools belonging to rival races. Thus, sometimes a "Greek" father would have "Bulgarian," "Serbian," or "Romanian" children.[4] Moreover, armed groups, such as the Bulgarian *komitadjis* in the east, the Greek bands (mainly Cretans) in the south, the Serbs in the north, and Albanians in the west, renewed their activities against each other and against local people opposing their aims.

As a result of the long Turkish occupation and the frequent raids by the revolutionary and nationalistic bands, the development of the land and mineral resources of the country was neglected. The Ottoman landlords (beys) were interested in the short-run returns of the occupied lands and neglected their long-term development. River banks were allowed to erode, irrigation projects were neglected, many people were homeless, and agricultural and mining methods remained backward. However, the fertile plains of the countryside and the unexploited rich mineral wealth provided high potential for the production of cereals, fruits, cotton, tobacco, and wine as well as silver, iron, lead, bauxite, and manganese. Slovenia, Croatia, and Vojvodina (Hapsburg provinces) were more advanced in agriculture and industry than Serbia, Montenegro, and Macedonia (former Turkish territories).

With the departure of the Turks, the area remained underdeveloped. About 80 percent of the population was engaged in agriculture and less than 10 percent in industry. While in other regions a great number of latifundia remained, in Serbia and other Yugoslav regions land was split among the peasants. The Serbs did not have the same opportunity to emigrate and this, coupled with the rapid increase in population, led to extensive fragmentation of peasant property.[5] Under such conditions, even the *zadruga* (village cooperative) gave way to the individual farm unit. The pressure of the population increase forced the peasants to grow mostly corn, barley, and wheat and reduce the land for pasture.

Under tariff protection, a number of industrial units were established at the beginning of the twentieth century. They included milling, sugar refining (established mainly by German concerns), meat packing, brewing, textiles, mining, and other industries for the processing of raw materials. Also, more roads and shipping facilities were created. Railroads were built from Austria and Hungary to Trieste and Fiume through Slovenia and Croatia (1846), and from Vienna through Yugoslavia to Salonika (the Orient Express) and Constantinople.

The last railroad was built by a French firm in 1888 and was expanded by the Serbian government in 1912. However, the financing of economic development required rapid growth of money and credit, which in turn led to high government spending and indebtedness. Thus government expenditures in Serbia increased from 12.5 million francs in 1869 to 120.1 million in 1911, while public debt rose from 2.3 million in 1867 to 903.8 million in 1914.[6] The debt primarily owed to Austria, Germany, and France, was guaranteed and paid by the revenues from taxes on tobacco, salt, liquor, and petroleum, over which the government, together with foreign bond-holders, had control.

The need for money to pay taxes and buy agricultural tools and other industrial products forced the peasants to borrow primarily from village usurers and pay high interest rates reaching, at times, 120 percent.

THE ESTABLISHMENT OF THE YUGOSLAV STATE

Interwar Years

The Yugoslav state was born out of the collapse of the Central powers in World War I. Its formation was the result of the Declaration of Corfu on July 20, 1917, signed by Nichola Pashich, Serbian premier, and Ante Trumbich, president of the Yugoslav committee in exile. This agreement, which was supported by Russia and the United States, provided for a constitutional and parliamentary monarchy under the Karageorgevich dynasty, and the union of all Serbs, Croats, and Slovenes was proclaimed in Belgrade. The main defects of the new state, South Slav Kingdom, seemed to lie with the domination of the other ethnic groups by Serbia, a fact that condemned it to domestic disturbances and even danger of full-scale civil war.

In spite of internal political strife, weak federalism, and foreign pressures, the kingdom managed to achieve a satisfactory degree of economic progress in the interwar years 1919–40. Transportation and communications were improved, tourism increased, especially on the Dalmatian coasts, and agricultural production rose significantly, allowing exports to exceed imports. As a result, the war debts to the United States and Great Britain were repaid, the dinar was stabilized, and foreign investments were attracted. The textile industry, using machinery from Germany in payment of reparations, advanced rapidly, and the growth of domestic and foreign investment increased the material wealth of the country. Public administration was also reorganized.

Two parties have been dominant in the political life of Yugoslavia: the Radical Party, under Nichola Pashich (1881–1926), and the Croatian Peasant Party under Stefan Radich (1905–28). Both parties remained active until the German invasion of 1941. In 1919, land reforms were enacted. Feudal and quasi-feudal institutions were abolished, and land was distributed among some 500,000 peasant families, despite strong opposition from (mainly Muslim) landlords. The Constitution of 1921, influenced by the unionists of Pashich, created a centralized monarchy that led to the dictatorship of King Alexander in 1929. The name of the country was then changed from the Kingdom of the Serbs, Croats, and the Slovenes to Yugoslavia. Alexander was assassinated in 1934, and the regency continued until 1941.

Like the rest of the Balkan countries, Yugoslavia was devastated during World War I. The loss of livestock was extensive, especially of pigs and sheep (47 and 55 percent, respectively). Credit was limited, interest charged by individual lenders reached 200 percent or more, and taxation was heavy (40 to 50 percent of the peasant's cash income). Agricultural productivity was low, which discouraged new capital investment. A labor surplus of more than 60 percent was estimated in the rural sector (disguised unemployment), and illiteracy was more than 50 percent in the interwar period.

It was realized that to carry out a rapid economic development, industry had to be stimulated through protective tariffs and other subsidies. As a result of the industrialization policy, foreign investment increased, transportation and communications were improved, and large lumber and steel mills and many manufacturing and mining units were established. However, domestic and intra-Balkan markets were poor, and Yugoslavia became largely dependent on German markets for economic survival.

As a result of the worldwide depression after 1929 and of domestic sociopolitical unrest, the Yugoslav economy deteriorated in the 1930s. Exports fell dramatically, German reparation payments stopped (in 1931), and the deficits in the balance of trade increased. The dramatic decrease in prices of agricultural products forced the government to buy up imported products in exchange for more of its own products. Limited storage facilities and the lack of bank credit worsened economic conditions. Increases in taxes and decreases in administrative salaries and pensions intensified social unrest without improving the economy.

Cattle exports decreased as slaughtering increased and peasants, unable to pay debt, became embittered at usurers and the urban gentry (*gospoda*). Bankrupt cities were widespread, currency controls were intensified, and foreign credit was not available. To pacify the poor peasants, the government suspended debt payments for more than a year. The whole economic picture was dismal, especially in 1932–34. Then, the economic influence of Nazi Germany penetrated the country further with the Commercial Treaty of 1934 and the new preferential treatment of Yugoslav exports in pigs, cattle, wheat, and other raw materials. By 1938, Yugoslav exports to Germany accounted for 38 percent of total exports, while imports from Germany were close to 33 percent of total imports.[7]

World War II Period

Despite the efforts of the Balkan Entente (Greece, Romania, Turkey, and Yugoslavia) to preserve peace in the area, economic pressures and aggressive acts by Germany and Italy divided the Balkan nations again. With Italy's attack upon Greece on October 28, 1940, and the Bulgarian alliance with Germany and Italy, the situation was further complicated. Encouraged by the Greek success in the battles in Albania against Italy, the Yugoslavs refused to allow Italian troops to cross Yugoslavia to outflank the fighting Greeks. Instead, they expressed interest to help Greece defend Salonika, where they had an outlet for their foreign trade (the Free Trade Zone). Furthermore, Turkey warned Bulgaria that she would support Greece in case of a Bulgarian attack.

On April 6, 1941, Hitler's troops in Bulgaria entered Yugoslavia and Greece simultaneously. In a few days and after intensive air attacks on Belgrade, Yugoslavia was in the hands of the Axis, as was Greece. The Italians conquered Dalmatia, the Hungarians reached Osijek and Novi Sad, and the Bulgarians occupied southern Yugoslavia. The Germans occupied northern Slovenia, while Croatia (except Dalmatia) and Montenegro were nominally designated independent.[8] Albania took southwestern Yugoslavia and Kosovo. The puppet state of Croatia was left to the control of Ustashi fascists under Ante Pavelic, who, in alliance with Muslims, turned against the Orthodox population of Bosnia and Serbia as well as against the Jews.

During the years of German occupation, a nationalistic group operated in Serbia (the Chetniks) under Draza Mihajlovich, a former officer who wanted to restore the exiled government of King Peter II. Both Ustashis and Chetniks turned against the partisans of the National Liberation Movement under Tito and gradually collaborated with the occupation forces of Germany and Italy.

Tito, the Croat metalworker Josip Broz who joined the Austrian army and later the Bolsheviks in Russia, managed to mobilize and unite large segments of the Yugoslav population against the occupation forces of Germany and Italy. Although he headed the Communist Party in Yugoslavia since 1938, as chief of the wartime partisans he declared that all the peoples of Yugoslavia, regardless of party or religion, must join hands against the fascist occupation forces. In his efforts he was helped by efficient colleagues such as Alexander Rankovich, Edvard Kurdelj (from Slovenia), and Miholovan Djilas (from Montenegro).

The partisan bands, using hit-and-run tactics, achieved many victories. The savage reprisals of the Germans, such as the massacre of 7,300 people (including schoolchildren) in the industrial town of Kragujevac, helped further the recruiting and resistance of the partisans. Moreover, Tito's strategy in organizing a national rather than a Communist resistance, coupled with the austere discipline of the partisans—no drinking, no looting, no sex—increased fighting spirit and aided in unifying the resistance movement. The local, popularly elected National Liberation Committees, like the Russian soviets in 1905, provided the resistance with the needed supplies and new members. Using the slogan of self-determination and federalism Svetozar Vukmanovich, a Montenegrin and trusted lieutenant of Tito, organized effective resistance in the south and established liaison with the partisans in Albania, Greece, and Bulgaria. On November 29, 1943, the Anti-Fascist Council for the National Liberation of Yugoslavia, known as AVNOY, established a presidium with Dr. Ivan Ribar as president and Tito as the head of the thirteen acting ministers, and forbade the return of the king and his government in exile.

On the battlefield as well as in diplomacy, Tito (the Lion of Belgrade, as he was called later) proved to be effective enough to unite the long-embittered ethnic groups of Yugoslavia and to be president of the country for thirty-six years (from 1944 until his death in May 1980 at the age of eighty-eight). He was also able to combine the Orthodox Christian Serbs and Montenegrins with Roman Catholic Croats and Slovenes and to make room for Muslims, Hungarians, Albanians, and other minorities.

In the Moscow Conference of October 1944, Churchill proposed (on a napkin), and Stalin accepted, that Russia would have 90 percent predominance in Romania, Britain would have 90 percent of the say in Greece, and go fifty-fifty about Yugoslavia. Russia also would have 75 percent predominance in Bulgaria and 50 percent in Hungary. This arrangement was accepted at the Yalta Conference in February 1945, in which President Roosevelt participated. As a result, the northern Balkans were dominated by Communist governments, while Greece remained under Western influence.

POSTWAR YEARS

In 1944, and officially in the 1946 Constitution, Tito established a federal state with six republics (Bosnia-Herzegovina, Croatia, Macedonia, Montenegro, Serbia, and Slovenia) and two provinces (Kosovo and Vojvodina). To make the Serbs weak, he split them up among surrounding republics and provinces. Tito named the southern part of Yugoslavia (the Vardar area) as Macedonia for expansionary reasons into the Greek region of Macedonia and the Aegean Sea. In 1948, Tito broke with Stalin and the Cominform and gradually replaced the Soviet planning system with a self-management system.

The name of the south Serbian region, which Tito baptized "Socialist Republic of Macedonia," was "Vardanska Banovina."

In 1946, Athens protested Tito's carving a piece out of Serbia to call it "Macedonia." However, later the United States and the West forced Greece to not bother Tito because he broke with Stalin (1948) and received sizable assistance from the West so that Yugoslavia would stay out of the Soviet bloc. Nevertheless, in 1952, under U.S. pressure, the government of Greece recognized the Republic of Macedonia as one of the six republics of Yugoslavia.

In his efforts to reform the economy of the country, Tito was supported by the poor peasants, who were exploited by the landlords and neglected by the Yugoslav governments during the interwar years. Among the fundamental reforms introduced immediately after the war were: the replacement of the prewar currencies by a new dinar in a ten-to-one ratio; the confiscation of the property of Nazi collaborators; strict rent controls; limitation of land ownership to those who cultivated it (35 hectares for individuals and 10 hectares, or 100,000 square meters, for institutions); and nationalization of about 80 percent of the country's industry, including mining.[9] Also, banking and insurance activities, wholesale and foreign trade, and foreign-held property were placed under direct state control.

The main problems Yugoslavia faced immediately after the war were the rehabilitation of the economy, which was devastated as a result of fighting with the Nazis; the pressure from the Soviet Union for the extension of the Russian perimeter of defense, particularly after the growing U.S. influence over Greece and Turkey that resulted from the Truman Doctrine and the Marshall Plan; and the need for national and ideological consolidation.

The Soviets were interested mainly in exploiting agricultural and mineral resources in the Balkans and in other Eastern European countries in order to repair their own wartorn economy. After the war they bought raw materials at low prices in exchange for expensive industrial goods and equipment of poor quality, a policy similar to that practiced by the Western powers with their colonies. However, Yugoslavia was in no better position than Russia after the war. One quarter of the population remained homeless, more than half of the industrial capacity was destroyed, and about 10 percent of the population (1.7 million people) had died in the fighting. Furthermore, investment in joint ventures with Russia did not prove to be very effective, except in air and shipping transportation.

In order to keep up production incentives and to avoid apathy on the part of the peasants, the first Five-Year Plan of 1947–51 did not abolish private ownership. However, investment emphasis on industry, to the neglect of agriculture, led to low wages, high prices, and shortages in the consumer sector. Many of the goals of the plan did not materialize because they were based on unrealistic premises and overenthusiasm. This first plan, as well as the 1946 Constitution, provided for a closer connection between the various ethnic territories and the establishment of a federal state with six constituent republics—Bosnia-Herzegovina, Croatia, Macedonia, Montenegro, Serbia, and Slovenia—and two provinces—Kosovo and Vojvodina.

Tito tried to establish closer relations with neighboring Albania and Bulgaria. The Bulgarians, subject to more control by Russia, proposed instead a looser and broader association among the Balkan countries. Stalin was suspicious of Tito's movement, which could establish a new Balkan power deviating from the directives of Moscow. He summoned the Yugoslavs and Bulgarians to Moscow in February 1948, but Tito did not go.

Charges of Trotskyism, Menshivism, and revisionism were directed against him. Russian advisors were withdrawn from Yugoslavia, and economic sanctions were imposed. Tito was recognized as a national leader, and started following a policy independent of Moscow. He also stopped his support of the Communist side in the Greek civil war, in order to avoid involving his country in a conflict in which the Americans were involved with war materials and military advisors. Yugoslavia then accepted some $98 million worth of aid from the Export-Import Bank, the Economic Cooperation Administration, and other Western relief organizations, and even received aid from military programs. Tito, the first Communist to break away from Soviet ideology and control, developed a personality cult. He also proved that there are different socialist paths, a concept that was later accepted by Soviet Premier Nikita Khrushchev in his reconciliation agreement with Yugoslavia.

Tito's policy of purchasing food and other agricultural products at fixed low prices and putting heavy taxes on profits turned many peasants against the regime. Strong opposition also came from religious groups, particularly the Catholics, who accounted for 32 percent of the population in 1953, compared to 41 percent Orthodox and 12 percent Muslim.[10]

The first Five-Year Plan for economic development was introduced in 1947 with the aim of restoring the economy after the war's devastation (1.7 million people dead and close to $50 billion in material losses) and increasing production through high rates of investment. It was an ambitious plan emphasizing heavy industry and based upon promised Soviet technical assistance and loans of over $300 million. However, after the dispute with the Soviet Union and the other Cominform countries in June 1948, implementation of the plan was gradually abandoned. Also, collectivization of the land, into which some two million peasants were coerced in 1949–51, was abandoned by 1953 because low incentives for production resulted in food shortages.

After the break with the Cominform, Yugoslavia turned to the West for trade and aid. By 1958 about $2.5 billion in aid was given primarily by the United States, Britain, and France. Despite the reconciliation efforts by Nikita Khrushchev in 1955 and the mutual suspicion of Western and Yugoslav leaders, relations with the Western countries continued to improve. Industrial production and Yugoslav manufacturing exports to the West increased significantly.

Although peasants could withdraw their land and livestock from cooperatives after 1953, some 216,000 hectares of land remained under 507 working cooperatives by 1958. The new policy was to encourage the formation and strength of general cooperatives in which the peasants would cultivate their own land but participate in joint efforts for buying agricultural tools, seeds, fertilizers, and breeding stock, and which promoted the marketing of their products.[11] This policy was reinforced by abolishing the system of forcing the peasants to sell their products at fixed prices and fixing taxes in advance on an agreed estimate yield. Further support was provided by the government through improvements in transportation, irrigation, marketing, and refrigeration facilities. However, migration of peasants to the cities necessitated purchase of their land by the government, which then organized it into state farms.

Extensive economic and political decentralization was introduced with the establishment of the workers' councils on June 26, 1950. This institution was incorporated in the constitution of 1953. With these new measures, the powers of the six federal republics were increased and more authority was delegated to the communes. The workers' councils, elected biannually in enterprises as well as universities, hospitals, and similar economic units, would decide on production, marketing, income distribution, and work conditions. However, their freedom was somewhat reduced in matters of tax payments, except for investments, salaries, and price determination, especially after 1954. Tourism was encouraged, Yugoslavs were permitted to travel abroad, work incentives were offered, and productivity was improved. Although some limitations were reintroduced by the 1957–61 and 1961–65 Five-Year Plans, the overall process of decentralization continued. Nevertheless, in the political field decentralization was less effective than in the economic field.[12] Further decentralization in 1963 expanded the principle of workers' management and gave more economic and sociopolitical independence to the assemblies of the republics and the communes.

Tito's longevity in power helped him to carry his innovative economic programs of labor-managed enterprises, explained in more detail later. For the formation and implementation of this economic program, which may be considered the first in the world in its application, Edvard Kardelj, Tito's colleague as partisan and economic advisor until his death (1979), played a significant role.

In the international field, Tito was among the first leaders, together with India's Nehru, Indonesia's Sukarno, and Egypt's Nasser, to create and promote the Third World nonalignment group of nations in the late 1950s. In consequence to that policy, he introduced and maintained throughout his presidency Yugoslavia's nonaligned relations. He gave the country a global prominence that could be maintained only with great difficulty by his main successors, Lazar Kolisevski, Stevan Doronjski, and Stane Dolanc. Under

Tito, Yugoslavia built up good political and trade relations with the two main superpowers. These relations, together with a domestic arms industry that supplied 80 percent of the army's needs, bore strongly on the security and safety of the country. Good relations were also created with Yugoslavia's seven neighbors. With Italy, the perennial Trieste issue was settled, as was that with Austria involving the Slovene minority in Carinthia. Moreover, there were elements of genuine friendship with Hungary and all the other Balkan neighbors, particularly Romania. However, from time to time, there were disturbances with Bulgaria and Albania regarding minorities, mainly in Kosovo. But such disturbances did not seem to be instigated by the official governments of the neighboring countries. They might have been the result of ethnic groups inside or outside the country, which continued to implement related policies initiated by the big powers, as frequently happened in the past.

ROTATION IN GOVERNMENT

Despite speculations that the Yugoslav federation might be in trouble after Tito's death, the country remained largely calm for a decade. Only in Pristina, the capital of Kosovo, were there disturbances in which Albanian nationalist riots left nine people dead and scores injured in 1981. Some 300 people were sentenced to jail terms of up to fifteen years, and sixty students and five professors were dismissed from the University of Pristina. Kosovo is the poorest province of Yugoslavia, populated mainly by people of Albanian descent. As a result of the riots, mistrust between majority Albanians and minority Serbs and Montenegrins increased.

More serious problems for the successors of Tito (1980–91) were the debilitating effects of inflation, which ran around 30 percent, and the pressures of the various republics and economic sectors to increase or at least keep their share of an insufficient investment pie. The main dilemma for Tito's successors, who did not enjoy his charismatic authority, was how to keep and promote the twin legacies—unity and self-management socialism. On matters of income distribution, 10 percent of the population received 45 percent of total national income, and the motto "jobs for the party boys" prevailed while more than 90,000 workers were unemployed.

A difficult problem for the post-Tito system of rotation in government was the continuation of the status quo and the lack of reforms because of the short-run (one year) authority of the rotating presidency among the six republics and the two provinces.

Economic and diplomatic relations with other countries were improved, and Yugoslavia gained many friends among Third World nations as a result of the nonaligned movement, an important conference of which took place in Belgrade in 1961. Trade with both Communist and Western economies was expanded, especially with the EU, cooperation with which did not require political alignment. Although economic growth in the 1960s slowed down and inflation and external debts increased, the country was rapidly industrialized, and the standard of living of the poor Yugoslav peasants and workers was greatly improved.

Greece and Yugoslavia are perhaps the only Balkan countries that have not had a war or any military conflict between them. On the contrary, they were allies during the two world wars. A number of abortive discussions on a Balkan federation have been held since 1945. Nevertheless, closer cooperation has been advanced not only between Greece and Yugoslavia, but between them and other neighboring countries. Thus in 1953, the Balkan Pact was signed by Greece, Yugoslavia, and Turkey. This has been superseded by bilateral summitry of greater importance, particularly in the 1970s and early 1980s.

From a geopolitical point of view, Yugoslavia, as well as the whole Balkan region, attracts the big powers' influence and competition. Thus, from time to time, U.S. representatives have visited the country to negotiate the future of U.S. military bases and related matters. Soviet prime ministers have visited Yugoslavia to urge more independence from the West and the creation of a nuclear-free zone in the Balkan Peninsula,[13] along with more trade and investment between the Soviet Union and Yugoslavia. Also, Chinese representatives (among them party leader Hu Yaobang) have visited Yugoslavia and Romania to urge policies independent from both the Western and Eastern blocs.

SELF-MANAGEMENT SYSTEM

Worker participation in enterprise revenue and decision making could play a significant role in promoting workplace democracy and social change. Also, it could stabilize and improve political democracy, especially in the Balkan nations.

Employee and worker control may be exercised by approving or disapproving basic ideas, leaving day-to-day operations to an executive committee or to the managers elected by the employees. This is largely practiced in the former Yugoslav republics, where self-management, practiced for more than forty years, leads to the autonomy of each enterprise from the unending deliberations and bureaucracies of state controls.[14]

In addition, self-managed enterprises may become multinational, as happened with Slovenjales, a Yugoslavian furniture firm which has branches in the United States (Atlanta, Houston, Chicago, and Clifton, New Jersey) as well as in Austria, France, Germany, and Australia.

Since the reforms of 1965 and the 1970s, Yugoslavia has moved further toward the self-management system with the Basic Organization of Associated Labor (BOAL) in each enterprise and self-supporting communes or local communities. Taxes were collected primarily by the republics and the communes but also by special funds, such as "public roads," "waterworks," and "joint ventures." Trade agreements were signed with the EU, particularly in the 1970s and 1980s.

Although the former Yugoslav republics became independent, the worker self-management system, which prevailed for four decades, seemed to remain largely in operation. However, as a reaction to the influence and the controls of the one party (the former Communist, renamed Socialist, Party) and the undemocratic process of decision making, the pressures for changes and abolishment of the system increased. This was so particularly for the advanced republics of Croatia and Slovenia, which began to adjust their economic systems to that of the EU, particularly that of Germany, as they expect an association status and eventually, full membership to the EU.

Nevertheless, the European Union itself has adopted measures of worker participation in enterprise decision making and, to some extent, employee ownership. Moreover, Germany has the system of codetermination, or comanagement, of capital and labor (*Mitbestimmung*).

In any case, Serbia (the largest republic) and Montenegro, as well as the provinces of Vojvodina and Kosovo and to some extent Bosnia and Herzegovina, maintain the system of self-management.

PRESENT YUGOSLAVIA

The growing resentment against the Communist system in the former Yugoslavia added an ideological divide to the historical, cultural, and religious differences of the most prosperous republics of Croatia and Slovenia with Serbia. Out of the six republics (Serbia, Bosnia and Herzegovina, Croatia, Slovenia, Macedonia, and Montenegro) and two provinces (Vojvodina and Kosovo), Serbia was the most populous (with 9.3 million people) and exercised political and economic controls upon others. The Catholic Croatians (4.8 million) and Slovenians (2 million), who were under Austria until 1918, did not want the hegemony of the Christian Orthodox Serbs, who threw off Turkish rule in the nineteenth century.

With the split of the former Yugoslavia into independent republics, ultranationalistic and religious differences, which were suppressed under the Communist regime of Tito, came to the surface. With the hasty recognition of Slovenia, Croatia, and Bosnia and Herzegovina by Germany and other Western countries, the principle of self-determination was difficult to be reconciled with that of territorial determination. Thus, sizable minorities of Serbians were included under these republics without their consent. The internal boundaries of the former Yugoslav republics, as well as their names, were arbitrarily determined by Marshall Tito (a Croat) in 1946, mainly to weaken the Serbs by leaving about one-third of them outside Serbia. Such borders were never negotiated or ratified by free elections. This became obvious with the independence vote of Bosnia and Herzegovina on February 29, 1992, in which the Serbs, about one-third of the population in this republic, objected, and a severe civil war among Serbs, Croats, and Muslims broke out.[15]

The geographic regions of Macedonia, liberated from the Turks, was divided in 1912–14: 51 percent retained by Greece, 38 percent parceled to Yugoslavia, and 10 percent to Bulgaria. For long-term expansionary reasons, Tito carved out southern Yugoslavia as one of the six republics during World War II, and named it "Macedonia." In 1991 the new republic named itself "Macedonia."

Greece objected to the use of the name by Skopja on historical and geopolitical grounds. Together with other nations, it has denied recognition of this republic until its name is changed, because Macedonia, the country of Aristotle and Alexander the Great, is the region where Greeks have been living for centuries.

Serbia

Out of the six republics and two autonomous provinces of former Yugoslavia, Serbia was the largest, with a population of 9.3 million out of a total 23.5 million for the whole of Yugoslavia. It produced about 38 percent of the total output of former Yugoslavia.

Originally, the Serbs immigrated to Serbia from Galicia, close to the Dniester River of Russia, about A.D. 637, when they were dispersed by the Avars. They were invited by the then–Byzantine emperor to defend the region (Illyria) against incursions of enemy tribes. Although they enjoyed political autonomy, they were considered as vassals by the Byzantine emperors.

In the ninth century the Serbs were converted to Greek Orthodox Christianity and used the Cyrillic alphabet, while the Slovenes and Croats were under the Roman Catholic influence and used the Latin alphabet. During the fourteenth century, under Stephen Dushan, Serbia became an important power in the Balkan area, but after 1459 and for more than four centuries, it was under Turkish domination, as were other Balkan regions as well. After World War I and the end of the Austro-Hungarian influence, the Kingdom of the Serbs, Croats, and the Slovenes (South Slav Kingdom) was established on December 1, 1918 (Versailles Conference); the name was officially changed to Yugoslavia in 1929. Bosnia's Muslims were not recognized as a distinct group. In 1934, the king of Serbia, who tried to dominate the country, was assassinated in Paris by Croatian extremists. Serbia, which dominated other ethnic groups, became part of the federated republic of Yugoslavia, with Belgrade as its capital.

On December 9, 1990, Serbia, as well as Montenegro, had its first multiparty election since 1938. The leader of the Serbian Socialist Party (formerly the Communist Party), Slobodan Milosevic (son of an Eastern Orthodox priest) was elected president for five years. Although he promised Western-style economic reforms, he followed, more or less, the same self-management system. Mainly because of the conflicts with Croatia and Bosnia and Herzegovina, no significant changes were introduced. To expand Serbian frontiers, he incorporated Kosovo and Vojvodina into the Serbian republic, keeping the name Yugoslavia, which now includes Serbia, Montenegro, Kosovo, and Vojvodina.

Montenegro

Montenegro ("black mountain") was part of Zeta Province of the Serbian Kingdom during the Middle Ages. It retained its independence by fighting the Turks from the mountains. In 1516 a Greek Catholic Bishop (Vladika) attained civil authority, which was transferred to other prince-bishops until Nicholas I gave the first constitution of 1868. In 1916, Austria occupied Montenegro, which joined the Kingdom of the Serbs, Croats, and the Slovenes in 1918. During the Axis invasion of the Balkans in 1941, it was declared independent, as a protectorate of Italy, and in 1945 it became a republic of Yugoslavia.

The population of the republic is 584,000. Titograd is its capital. It is rich in arable land, and the raising of livestock is the main occupation. Cereal grains, vegetables, olives, and fruits are the main agricultural products. Moreover, electrical engineering and tourism are two major services of Montenegro.

Kosovo

Kosovo, with a population of 1.6 million, a large segment of which is of Albanian origin, is an autonomous province of Yugoslavia, as is Vojvodina. Historically, both provinces faced problems similar to those of the neighboring areas. Kosovo was under the Turks from 1389 to 1878. During World War II, Albania, which was under Italy, took Kosovo and western Macedonia. From time to time, disturbances occur in Kosovo by Albanian nationalists who demand union with Albania. In 1981, for example, nine people were killed and scores injured, while 300 people, including students and professors, were sentenced to jail terms of up to fifteen years. Similar disturbances continued thereafter, particularly in Pristina, the capital of Kosovo. In April 1996, five persons were killed.

Mining of lead, zinc, and nickel, as well as livestock and agriculture, are the main economic activities of the province, which is the poorest territory of the area.

Vojvodina

Vojvodina, the other autonomous province of Yugoslavia, has a population of 2.1 million, the large majority of which are Serbs. Its capital is Novi Sad. In addition to agriculture, oil, and gas, building materials and chemicals are the main products of the province.

Both provinces, Kosovo and Vojvodina, were severed from Serbia by Tito, who arbitrarily drew the internal borders of former Yugoslavia. Tito (part Croat and part Slovene himself) did that, probably, to diminish the importance of the Serbs within the Yugoslav federation by leaving three million Serbs outside of the Republic of Serbia. The same thing can be said about Bosnia and Herzegovina, and the Republic of Macedonia, the misleading name given by Tito for reasons of expansion to Greek Macedonia and the Aegean Sea. Currently, Kosovo, Serbia, Montenegro, and Vojvodina are all included in the state of Yugoslavia.

CROATIA

Little is known about the inhabitants of Croatia and the neighboring regions before the coming of the Slavs (seventh century A.D.). About the fifth century B.C., the Greeks were the first to mention that the Illyrians had occupied the area, driving the Thracians to the central and eastern regions of the Balkan Peninsula. Under Roman rule (A.D. 9 to A.D. 395), Croatia formed part of the Pannonia province. After 395, it became part of the Byzantine Empire. By 650, Illyria was occupied by the Slavs, who moved southward and settled there permanently.

In 1102, Croatia and Slovenia formed an autonomous state under Hungarian rule, which survived for eight centuries, although the Croats were involved in wars with the Venetians and Turks who conquered parts of Croatia at various times. In 1797–1814, Dalmatia came under Napoleon's rule.

In 1815 (after the Congress of Vienna), Croatia and Slovenia became an Austrian crownland, and after the defeat of the Central Powers, they became a province of the new Kingdom of the Serbs, Croats, and the Slovenes in 1918, which was renamed Yugoslavia in 1929. During World War II, the province was the scene of a bitter struggle among the partisans of Marshall Tito (Josip Broz, a Croat), the Serbian Chetniks, and the Ustashi fascists, who were installed by the Nazis in control of the puppet state of Croatia. In 1945, Croatia became part of the federated Yugoslavia. Its capital is Zagrem.

A large part of the coastal and mountainous area of Dalmatia, with the Drava and the Sava rivers, Croatia is rich in timber, cattle, sheep, pigs, fruits, wine, and cereal grains, as well as in deposits of iron, coal, copper, marble, and sulfur. Moreover, shipbuilding and tourism are two major industries of the republic. Its population was 4.8 million and the per capita GDP was $7,232 in 1991. The main language is Serbo-Croat. In May 1994, Croatia introduced the kuna as its new monetary unit.

The democratically elected, non-Communist government of Croatia (in 1990) came openly in conflict with Serbia, especially after the declaration of its independence on June 25, 1991. National aspirations and antagonisms, long suppressed by the Communist governments of Belgrade, dominated by Serbs, came into the open. Serious conflicts, with more than 10,000 deaths, occurred in 1991 and later. Other republics, such as Slovenia where a democratic government also was elected, followed the same movement of independence, and more conflicts with Serbia led to more fighting and killings.

Although a peace was arranged by former U.S. Secretary of State Cyrus Vance, with the use of UN peacekeepers (as in Bosnia, as well) until a political settlement could be reached, Croatia's president, Franjo Tudjman, ordered his army to cross UN lines to capture a narrow territory in a key highway in Slavonia (May 1995). In response, Serbian forces launched rockets on central Zagrem, killing six people and injuring hundreds.[16] Such actions show that further "Balkanization" of the Balkans could continue until the EU and the United States take vigorous steps to arrange EU association or full membership of these troubled countries and steam out ethnic and religious conflicts.

The State Organization of Privatization of Croatia sold shares of six state enterprises worth DM 5.6 billion, or about $4 billion. It sold 10,724 shares, or 34 percent, of the Gradevno d.d., a construction company, and 6,200 shares, or 30 percent, of the Carbon d.d., a hardware and painting company. Also, it sold lesser amounts of the Vela Luka d.d., a merchandise company, and Podravka d.d., a food manufacturing company, as well as two hotel chains, and other firms, some of them at a discount.

SLOVENIA

Slovenia, a northern republic of former Yugoslavia, has about 2 million South Slavic people. Its capital is Ljubljana. The history of this republic is mostly related to that of Croatia. Slovenia's free elections in 1990 gave it a non-Communist, anticentralist government, and in June 1991, it declared its independence. The chief products of the republic are electrical equipment, chemicals, and other advanced industrial products. Agriculture is also more advanced than in Serbia and the other southern republics. Its per capita GDP was $6,540 in 1991.

In addition to political differences among the republics and provinces, there were economic differences as well, which intensified the movement of disintegration. Thus, average monthly net wages per worker in 1990 varied from $167 for Kosovo, $299 for Serbia, and $413 for Slovenia. The more prosperous, Westernized Croatia, which earned 90 percent of former Yugoslavia's tourist income, and Slovenia, which produced more than 30 percent of the country's exports to the West, complained that they shared proportionally more for government programs in support of the poor regions of the south.

The parliament of the republic of Slovenia overwhelmingly passed the declaration of independence on June 25, 1991, which led to full secession from Belgrade, after ethnic fighting.

BOSNIA AND HERZEGOVINA

The population of the republic of Bosnia and Herzegovina, situated in the central part of former Yugoslavia, was 4.1 million in 1990 and consisted mainly of Muslims (39 percent), Serbs (32 percent), and Croats (18 percent). Other national groups included Greeks and Gypsies. Mostly, the Serbo-Croatian language and the Greek Orthodox religion are observed. The main minority religions are Mohammedan and Roman Catholic. Sarajevo is the capital of the republic. Per capita GDP in 1991 was $4,639.

In antiquity, Bosnia, and Herzegovina were parts of Illyria. During the Roman period, they were parts of the Roman province of Illyricum. After the collapse of the Roman Empire the area was overrun by Goths, and in the sixth century A.D., it was occupied by Slavs. Later, various parts of the territory came under the domination of Hungary. In 1463, the Turks conquered Bosnia and, in 1483, Herzegovina, which was an independent duchy. Both areas remained under the Turks up to the end of the Russo-Turkish war of 1877–78, when they came under the administration of the Austria-Hungary monarchy. Bosnia and Herzegovina were merged and became part of the Kingdom of the Serbs, Croats, and the Slovenes (December 1, 1918). On November 29, 1945, Tito carved the region as one of the six republics of Yugoslavia, which was included in the constitution of 1946.

As a result of the long Turkish occupation, many Christians and others were converted to Islam. In 1990, large segments of the population in Albania (more than 50 percent), Bosnia and Herzegovina (39 percent), Bulgaria, and other Balkan regions (up to 10 percent) were Muslims.

In the elections of Bosnia and Herzegovina in March 1992, Alija Izetbegovic, a Muslim, was elected president. Izetbegovic, a lawyer, was convicted in the late 1940s, and again in 1983 with 12 others, and imprisoned until November 1988 for his activities to create a pure Muslim state. Turkey, Iran, and Saudi Arabia are the main backers of the Bosnian government under Izetbegovic.[17] The Serbs (about 33 percent) of this former Yugoslav republic abstained from the elections and objected to being subordinate to a Muslim president, whom they considered as a new ayatollah of the Balkans. This led to an ethnic and religious civil war with thousands of deaths, as the Christian Orthodox Serbs considered the Muslims as a flesh and blood remnant of the Ottoman tyranny, and they do not like being under their rule again. (More on the conflicts in the area and the involvement of the international community in chapter 7.)

On November 21, 1995, the leaders of Serbia, Croatia, and Bosnia initialed the U.S. brokered peace at Dayton, Ohio, officially signed in Paris on December 14, 1995, which ended the forty-three months of ethnic conflict that had left about 250,000 people dead and 2 million refugees from the worst war in Europe since World War II. Some sticking points of this Balkan accord include the slicing of Bosnia-Herzegovina into two main pieces, about half to the Bosnia-Croat Federation and half to the Bosnian Serbs. Sarajevo, including the mostly Serb suburbs, Gorazde, with a wide corridor connecting it with Sarajevo and a corridor in Brcko linking Serb territories in northwestern Bosnia with eastern Bosnia and Serbia proper, are the most difficult regions to arrange in practice. Also, eastern Slavonia would be ceded to Croatia after a transition period of about a year. On April 3, 1996, a U.S. plane crashed in Croatia killing thirty-three Americans, including Commerce Secretary Ronald Brown and two Croatians, who were in the Bosnian area seeking new business investment opportunities.

Ethnic Croats (some 350,000) control about 20 percent of Bosnia's territory, Muslims 30 percent and the rest—50 percent—is controlled by Serbs. In a draft Bosnian constitution, prepared by the United States, a nine-member Bosnian presidency or thirty-six–member parliament was proposed in November 1995. Six members of the presidency would be appointed by the Bosnian Serbs. Also, the draft calls for a rotating chairmanship of the collective presidency, similar to the unsuccessful one established after the death of Tito in 1980. The chairman would be elected by the four-year term presidency and serve five and a half months. Although the Bosnian Serb leaders accepted the peace plan in general, the Serbs of Sarajevo's suburbs, more than 60,000, declared that they are willing to fight again instead of being governed by the Muslims. However, a large number of them left their homes, as the Dayton agreement determined.

According to the peace agreement, some 60,000 NATO troops, 20,000 of them American, were sent to Bosnia. The most difficult function of these troops is to sort out refugee housing and to stop the involvement of other nations, notably Iran, which supplied arms to Bosnia via Croatia, secretly approved by the U.S. government, in violation of the U.N. embargo.

FORMER YUGOSLAV REPUBLIC OF MACEDONIA (FYROM)

As the Greek writers mentioned, in ancient times the area west of the Vardar and north of the Epirus was occupied by the Illyrians. About 1100 B.C., Dorian Greeks entered the area of Macedonia and named it "Makednoi." In the seventh century B.C. Macedonia, or Macedon, was known as the kingdom of Greece which entered a period of growth under King Philip II (Philip of Macedon) and later under his son Alexander the Great, who united all the Greek city-states and expanded his dominion to all the areas below the Danube River, the Middle East, and Asia.

In A.D. 9, Tiberius, the Roman ruler, annexed the area. After A.D. 395, it became part of the Byzantine Empire. Beginning in the sixth century, part of Macedonia was settled by people of Slavic origin. From 1453 onward, it came under the Ottoman Empire.

The population of the republic is about 1.9 million, or 8.8 percent of the total population of former Yugoslavia (Slavs, Albanians, Greeks, and Bulgarians). It produces primarily agricultural goods, such as tobacco, cotton, cereal grains, and fruits. Moreover, sheep and goats are raised, and iron, steel and chromium are the chief mineral resources. Skopje is the capital of the republic. Per capita GDP in 1990 was $3,330.

Elections in 1990 gave a non-Communist government. After a referendum in September 1991, it declared independence from Yugoslavia, using the name "Macedonia," which Tito introduced in 1945, mainly for reasons of expansion into the northern Greek region of Macedonia, Salonika, and the Aegean Sea.[18]

While other names given by Communist regimes changed (e.g., Volgograd from Stalingrad, St. Petersburg from Leningrad), that of "Macedonia" remained, although it was used for the expansion of communism to other neighboring regions. (For more information on the conflict of Greece with FYROM, regarding the name "Macedonia," see chapter 7.)

In May 1993, the former Yugoslav Republic of Macedonia introduced legislation for privatization of state enterprises. Firms with fewer than fifty employees or revenue less than a certain amount were to be sold to the highest bidder, with preference given to the basic buyer who should obtain 29 percent of the capital at the first stage. For big firms, 10 percent of the capital value is sufficient, provided that this first buyer will eventually obtain the rest of the shares or at least 51 percent of the total. From the rest of the shares, 20 percent are offered to associated persons or companies, 15 percent are free to the pension fund of the firm, and the rest is offered to the general public.

Bulgaria recognized FYROM's independence but has not recognized its people as a separate ethnic group, asserting that they are really Bulgarians.

On October 3, 1995, the then-president of FYROM, Kiro Gligorov, seventy-eight, was seriously injured in a car-bomb attack. The Speaker of Parliament, Stojan Andov, became the second president of FYROM.

6

Other Balkan Countries: Albania, Bulgaria, and Romania

ALBANIA

A Brief Historical Review

For Albania, the independence movement started primarily abroad. This was due mainly to the degree of autonomy Albanians enjoyed under the Ottoman rule. However, in 1881 they organized the Albanian League to unite the isolated regions of the country and to counter the interests of neighboring countries in territorial claims or domination, mainly because of its strategic position on the Adriatic Sea. For this reason, Albanians have, at times, supported the Turks, and even joined the Young Turks movement.

The Treaty of London, signed by the six great European powers in 1913, created the Albanian state. However, Greek troops entered southern Albania, including Koritsa and Argyrokastron (1914–16). Montenegrins entered Scutari in the north, Serbians occupied Elbasan and Tirana (1915), and Italians occupied Valona, (later) Argyrokastron, and even Ioannina in Greece (1916). The French, who commanded the Salonika front, extended their position and occupied Koritsa. In 1920, Albania, supported by the British and by President Woodrow Wilson, became a member of the League of Nations; in 1921, its boundaries were confirmed by the great powers, in spite of protests from Yugoslavia and Greece. By 1926, Yugoslavia, Britain, France, and Italy had signed the final agreement determining the present frontiers of Albania. In 1922, Ahmed Zogu became premier, and after a brief

(1924–25) term as premier by Fan Noli (a bishop from Egypt who had been educated in Greek schools and at Harvard, and was the head of the Albanian Autocephalous Orthodox Church in the United States), he regained power and remained premier until 1939.

Premier Zogu, following the example of the other Balkan countries, introduced land reforms and expropriated large estates from Muslims *beys* and the church, and distributed them to the poor peasants. Except for some small handicrafts made from local materials, the country's economy was based primarily on agriculture, in which more than 80 percent of the population was engaged. Albania, with 85 percent of the population illiterate before World War II, was regarded as the most backward state of Balkania and the whole of Europe.

After 1925, Italy penetrated Albania and concluded a number of military and economic agreements with Premier Zogu, who in 1928 became King Zog. Through the Company for Economic Development of Albania, Italian engineers and financiers built roads, ports, agricultural projects, and other public works. They also drilled for oil and discovered two fields, one near Berat and one near Valona. Italian engineers later helped Albania increase oil production from 7,000 barrels in 1926 to 1,659,000 barrels in 1940.[1] The crude oil and asphalt produced, together with other raw materials (hides, wool, livestock, olive oil, wine, spirits [raki], and lumber), were exported mainly to Italy. The Italian protectorate and the established controls continued until 1939, when King Zog was compelled to flee to Greece before the Italian invasion.

After the occupation of Albania in April 1939, Italy attacked Greece on October 28, 1940, using Albania as an army base for a projected gradual expansion into other Balkan areas. However, the Greeks resisted the invasion, pushing the Italians back to the Albanian mountains and ultimately occupying the major cities of Koritsa and Argyrokastron and the naval base of Santi Quaranta. However, Hitler's attack against Greece on April 6, 1941, helped the Italians to recapture the Albanian areas and to occupy Greece, together with the Germans and Bulgarians.

Resistance against the Italian, and later the German, forces of occupation began in 1942, primarily through the efforts of the National Liberation Front (NLF). The NLF was headed by Enver Hoxha (Hoja), a teacher by profession and later the president of the country. Landless peasants, ready to revolt against their Muslim landlords, and intellectual idealists joined forces with the front for the cause of liberation and social reforms. Despite the efforts of British and American agents to unite the NLF with another group of Albanian nationalists, the Ballists, the stronger NLF Communist group prevailed. Most of the Ballists collaborated with the Nazis. This practice, which was followed in Yugoslavia and even more so in Greece, was intensified after Italy's collapse in September 1943 and the consequent control of the country by the Germans. Following the example of Tito, the Albanian NLF assembled a national congress. The congress forbade Zog from returning to Albania, and formed a provisional government by December 1944, when the Nazis were driven out of Albania.

During World War II, some 28,000 Albanians were killed and 800,000 cattle were destroyed by the Nazis; 100,000 buildings were leveled to the ground. Albania claimed, and continued to claim, $4.5 billion for these damages. Another $20 million was claimed from Britain for gold seized at the end of the war. Britain claimed about $2 million in compensation for two British destroyers sunk by Albania in the Corfu Channel in 1946.[2]

After the war, small Albania, under President Hoxha, followed the Soviet economic model. In 1961, however, the leadership changed its mind, and until 1975 came under the ideological influence of the People's Republic of China.[3] Thereafter, the country followed an independent policy that retained many characteristics of Stalin's economic system, which involved strict central planning and detailed controls.

Under the previous occupations and pressures, a large number of Albanians had emigrated to other countries, mainly Greece and Italy, where they advanced culturally and economically. Some 200,000 Albanians settled in Italy at the beginning of the twentieth century.[4] Francesco Crispi, twice premier of Italy, was a descendant of Albanian immigrants, as is Mother Teresa, the nun who won the 1979 Nobel Prize for peace as a result of the valuable social services that the order she founded offers to the very poorest people of India. At present, northern Albania is inhabited mostly by the rough and individualistic Ghegs, among whom the law of the vendetta prevails, while in the south, below the Shkumbi River, live the milder Tosks.

Albania was perhaps the only country in Eastern Europe that did not deviate from the initial course of strict state control over the economy until 1985. The Albanian Labor Party (ALP), in control of the country since World War II, preached that rapid progress could be achieved through a centralist system that would supervise all economic and social activities. As a "true believer" in the Marxist-Leninist-Stalinist dogma, Albania considered the Soviet Union and its faithful ally, Bulgaria, "revisionists." The same thing could be said for Yugoslavia and Romania, which were further removed from the Stalinist system, while Greece and Turkey were considered as capitalist agents in Balkania. From that point of view, Albanian leaders (primarily President Hoxha and Prime Minister Mehmed

Shahu), fearing that their country might fall victim to its neighbors—Yugoslavia and Greece—used extreme caution in dealing with other Balkan countries. However, under pressure from the people for better economic conditions, they did conclude treaties for trade and cultural exchanges, predominantly on a bilateral basis.

Thus, for the first time since World War II, during which Albanian and Yugoslav partisans fought together against fascism, diplomatic and economic relations have begun to warm up between Albania and Yugoslavia, particularly in the 1980s. Being isolated from the outside world, Albania has felt the need for closer trade relations with its neighbors, particularly with Yugoslavia. As a result, the first railway and air connections between the two countries have materialized, and their foreign trade increased, especially after 1978.

The winds of reform that blew throughout Eastern Europe affected Albania, although to a lesser extent.[5] More investment emphasis is now given to the less industrialized regions of Gramsh, Kukes, Librazhd, Mat, Permet, and Tepelene, with less emphasis on the industrial areas of Karja, Shkoder, Tirana, Berat, and Durres. Western enterprises with oil-drilling equipment are invited to increase oil production. Albania is self-sufficient in oil, producing an estimated 20 million barrels a year, small quantities of which are exported to Greece and Italy. It is also the world's third largest producer of chrome, behind South Africa and Russia, and is second in the export of this strategically important product (more than 350,000 tons a year). Other major exports are olives, oranges, and dried fruits, primarily to Italy.[6]

Seeing the tide of European changes, Ramiz Alia, the Albanian leader after Hoxha, introduced limited reforms. They included price changes to reduce the gap between supply and demand, bonuses for key workers, and decentralization in decision making. Albania remains the poorest country in Europe, and many people want to immigrate to other countries, particularly to Italy and Greece (more than 100,000 have already emigrated, mostly illegally).

In the free elections of March 22, 1992, the Democratic Party won 92 of the parliament's 140 seats. The Communists, renamed Socialists, who controlled the 3 million poor Albanians for almost half a century, won 38 seats. President Sali Berisha, a heart surgeon, and Prime Minister Alexander Meksi started moving rapidly toward privatization and free market reforms.

With the extension of nondiscriminatory treatment (most-favored nation status) to Albania by the United States in August 1992, more foreign trade and investments are expected to flow into the country in the coming years.

This would help Albania to implement free market democratic reforms and stabilize this volatile Balkan region. Although limited, foreign investments do flow in. In May 1996 Berisha won the elections, which were criticized as fraudulent.

Privatization

Albania, a tiny country of 3.3 million people, producing mainly agricultural and mining products, such as oil (about 20 million barrels a year) and chrome (the world's third largest producer, with 37 million tons in reserves), started privatizing state enterprises and forming joint ventures with foreigners. Joint ventures in Albania include the Albkrom state enterprise, producing chrome (a metal resistant to corrosion), with the American Mecalloy Corporation and six British companies (including GEC-Alsthom and Compair Holman). Albkrom rejected a previous agreement with the Buero fur Sozial and Entwickle Ungsmanagement (BSE), a German state firm, because of delays. Also, Chevron, one of the big U.S. petroleum companies, agreed with DPNG, an Albanian petroleum firm, to search out and produce coal and petroleum products in an area of 1,800 square kilometers, close to Tirana, the capital of Albania. Moreover, in May 1994, the Coca-Cola Company began operations in the country, opening a $10 million bottling plant, whereas some seventy Greek-Albanian joint ventures already operate in Albania.

Currently, drug smuggling occurs through Turkey, Bulgaria, FYROM, and Albania to Western Europe and the United States. Production of opium and its deadly derivative, heroin, is growing in Iran, Afghanistan, and Pakistan, and the troubled Balkan countries provide fertile ground for lucrative drug smuggling. From Istanbul to Kosovo and the Adriatic Sea, particularly to the Albanian port of Durres, the drug trade provides profit, much of which is used to buy weapons for the ethnic and religious war in Bosnia and possibly other areas. "The main market for the 'Albanian Connection' is Switzerland. Drug smugglers use compatriots living there and in Germany as couriers. . . . In Germany, Albanians share business with Turks."[7]

BULGARIA

A Brief Retrospective

Because Bulgaria was close to Constantinople, the center of the Ottoman Empire, it was the first Balkan country to be occupied by, and the last to be liberated from, the Turks. There were some uprisings, such as that conducted by Michael the Brave in 1598, but they had limited or no success. Only after the establishment of the autocephalous exarchate church in 1870 were serious efforts made to organize the Bulgarian people to seek independence. In addition to the Turkish oppression, the Bulgarians suffered looting by armed bandits (*kirjalis*) and exploitation by *chiflik* (large estate) owners and tax collectors (*chorbajis*, similar to Greek *kodjabashis*). That is why a number of people fled the country, going mainly to Odessa and Bucharest, where they made fortunes.

A number of revolutionaries, outstanding among whom were George Rakovski, Lyuben Karavelov, Khristo Botev, and George Benkovski, were educated primarily in Moscow. They set out from Bucharest, together with the *haiduk* outlaws (the equivalents of the Greek *klefts*), to attempt a number of unsuccessful revolts, the last occurring in 1876, when the *bashi-bazouk* irregulars and the Turkish regulars massacred thousands of people. This helped contribute to intervention by the world powers, especially Russia, which resulted in the liberation of Bulgaria in 1878.

During the postliberation period, the country's economy remained for the most part agrarian, with a gradual transformation toward market-oriented agricultural and industrial development. From a political point of view, the Russian influence was great, despite the fact that Prince Alexander Dondukov-Korsakov (1879–86) tried hard to maintain an independent position. By 1885, East Rumelia was incorporated into Bulgaria. Under the rule of Premier Stefan Stambulov (1887–94) and King Ferdinand (1887–1918), the country experienced considerable stability. Ferdinand, however, secretly permitted the *komitadjis* to raid Macedonia, and committed his dynasty to two disastrous wars (1913 and 1915), while his policy of approaching the Russians was not very fruitful.

Representatives of the Ottoman authority (the *pashas*, the *agas*, and the *bashi-bazouks*), along with the local money lenders and tax collectors, kept the rural status quo, and the agrarian structure of the economy remained the same for a long period of time after liberation. By 1911 agricultural and livestock production still accounted for about 65 percent of national income. However, the tax on grain amounted to about 10 to 15 percent, and the revenues from tariffs were no longer being sent to Constantinople. Instead, they were used by the government for the development of the economy. Thus, the transportation network and the educational level of the country were improved. Foreign competition increased, however, and overwhelmed domestic producers of industrial and handicraft products, particularly after tariffs were reduced to less than 8 percent by the Berlin Treaty. Because of the heavy indebtedness of the country at that time, controls were imposed by foreign creditors over the revenue derived from tobacco taxes. Moreover, the division and subdivision of land into tiny plots and the low productivity of wheat forced changes in agriculture oriented toward the production of poultry, eggs, attar of roses, and tobacco, large quantities of which were exported.

During the interwar period, Bulgaria went through stormy and violent years. The Internal Macedonian Revolutionary Organization (IMRO), which became an instrument of the Bulgarian government, continued its raids and assassinations, not only within Greek and Serbian Macedonia but also inside Bulgaria, where it liquidated leaders and people opposed to or not supportive of its cause. Alexander Stambuliski, the Agrarian Party leader, managed to implement extensive social reforms and to pursue a policy of cooperation with neighboring Balkan countries. He distributed large estates to the peasantry, and introduced compulsory labor service in place of military training, which proved to be beneficial for the infrastructural development of the country.

As premier, Stambuliski signed the Treaty of Neuilly in 1919, revised the tax system to benefit the peasants, and conducted elections (1920) in which the Agrarians received 39.1 percent, the Communists 20.5 percent, and the Democrats 11.0 percent; the rest of the votes were distributed among six other parties. His main goals were to mobilize support from other countries, to unite the peasants, and to establish a Green International in contrast with the White International of the royalists and landlords, and the Red International of the Bolsheviks. In 1923, however, the military seized control in a coup that was recognized later by King Boris.[8] Thereafter, the country experienced disorders arising mainly from the activities of the IMRO, a group split between the Federalists, who supported an autonomous Macedonia, and the Centralists, who wanted its annexation by Bulgaria. From 1934 until 1943, when Boris died, the country was under military and royal dictatorship.

Before World War II, scarcity of natural resources, lack of capital, and unskilled labor and management were the causes of the backwardness in industry and low productivity in other sectors. About half of the total capital in industry and transportation had been invested by foreigners. Agricultural exports, mainly fruits, tobacco, and animal products, accounted for more than 90 percent of total exports, two-thirds of which went to Germany to pay for imported machinery, chemical products, textiles, and other industrial commodities. However, the peasant families remained mostly self-sufficient, the educational level remained low, and even the limited number of university graduates had a difficult time finding jobs, except in crowded government offices where corruption and open nepotism prevailed.

As mentioned earlier, during World War II Bulgaria became an ally of the Axis Powers, as did Romania, while Greece and Yugoslavia joined the Allies, and Turkey remained neutral. When Germany occupied Greece and Yugoslavia, the Bulgarian army was permitted to enter southern Yugoslavia as well as Greek western Thrace and eastern Macedonia. With respect to troop allocation to other fronts, Bulgaria, under King Boris, managed to stay aloof, mainly because of the traditionally large Russophile sentiment in the country.

In the occupied lands of Yugoslavia, the Bulgarian forces tried to win over the inhabitants with the opening of schools, libraries, and theaters, especially in Skopje. But in Greece their policy was more ruthless, for they sought either to convert or to eliminate the Greeks and replace them with Bulgarian colonists.

In mid-1942 the Fatherland Front was organized by Georgi Dimitrov, a Communist leader well known for his defiance against the Nazis during the Reichstag fire trial. The front included Social Democrats, the left-wing Agrarian Party, and the Zveno group, which had connections in the army. The resistance against the Axis, however, was not as significant as in other occupied Balkan countries because the partisans had to concentrate against the Bulgarian army and the gendarmerie, rather than the Germans. Further aiding this decision was the fact that the peasants became more prosperous during the war, because of high prices received for agricultural products. As the Red Army approached Balkania, partisan bands, aided by Allied air raids and the delivery of British arms (dropped by parachute in Serbia), became more effective and finally took power.

As a result of the continuous advance of the Red Army, especially after the declaration of war against Bulgaria by the Soviets on September 5, 1944, the Bulgarian army turned against the Nazis and fought alongside the Yugoslavs and Russians in Yugoslavia and Hungary, where some 30,000 Bulgarian soldiers were killed. At the end of the war, Bulgaria evacuated the occupied Greek and Yugoslav territories.

During the postwar years, Bulgaria has closely followed the Soviet economic model of central planning and strict government controls. However, in order to obtain a better performance from the economy, the government introduced some market-oriented reforms in the early 1960s.[9] But these reforms did not accomplish much, mostly because of inflexibility in the centralized economy. It was difficult for the Communist Party to permit any loss of its authority because of an abstract and mechanical process that requires the use of precise information in order to obtain reliable results.

Capital formation, as a percentage of national product, was higher in Bulgaria than in other Eastern European countries, but there was less independence in production enterprises (subsidiaries and subdivisions).[10] The gap between the growth rate of net national product and net economic welfare was greater than in Western market economies. Todor Zhivkov, the president of the planners responsible for policy making, tried to eliminate consumer frustration by keeping prices low, but inflation would have to rise if consumer lines were to be eliminated.

In the postwar years, Bulgaria has experienced an unprecedented period of peace and progress, mainly because it has not had to confront any external threat and, unlike Romania, did not lose territory to its neighbors. Moreover, it does not suffer from internal disunity, as does Yugoslavia, or the political instability and the internal turmoil of Turkey.

Because of the common culture and the linguistic and ethnic background with the Soviets, a high degree of cooperation has been developed between Bulgaria and Russia. The glorification of the Russian army, which liberated the country from Turkey in 1878 and helped it establish political stability in the postwar years, cannot escape the visitor to present-day Bulgaria. On the other hand, because of Bulgaria's strategic location (close to the Dardanelles and the Aegean coast), Russia has always kept a watchful eye upon the country, especially since 1979, when the Chinese attempted to sow anti-Russian seeds in the Balkan Peninsula.

It has been said that Russia can use its most faithful ally to stir up conflicts in the murky and sometimes conspiratorial world of Balkan affairs. This was especially so with Macedonia, where Yugoslavia fueled the issue, from time to time, to create an external threat and to unify its diverse republics. However, the Bulgarians have declared publicly that they consider the borders with Yugoslavia and Greece as permanent. On the other hand, although they decry U.S. military assistance to Turkey as meddling in the Balkans to exploit political instability in the region, they wait for more concrete results, an attitude that reflects the old Bulgarian saying, "We count the chickens in the autumn."

Economic Reforms

As in the other Eastern Bloc countries, the Bulgarian Communist dictatorship of more than forty years was overthrown, together with the long-tenured President Todor Zhivkov, on November 10, 1989. Thereafter, anti-Communist demonstrators dismantled reminders of Communist rule, including the mausoleum of Georgi Dimitrov (father of Bulgarian communism), burned the Communist Party headquarters, and eliminated other Communist sacred symbols. Free elections on June 10, 1990, though, gave a reformed Communist (now called Socialist) Party 57 percent of parliamentary democracy. However, Bulgaria faces serious economic problems from reduced supplies of cheap Russian oil and gas, food shortages, and a heavy foreign debt of about $12 billion. Also, severe problems appear in the process of privatization of the economy, especially in land ownership.[11] The drastic reforms and the austerity measures introduced recently will suppress the living standard of the 8.5 million Bulgarians for some time to come.

Bulgaria has six Russian-built reactors, four of which are old and the most dangerous in the world. They need repairs to avoid accidents similar to that of Chernobyl, in the Ukraine, in April 1986.

The nuclear power plant at Kozloduy, Bulgaria, a 440-megawatt Soviet-made reactor on the river of Danube, which supplies 40 percent of the country's energy needs, is considered not safe. The Group of Seven leading industrial countries and local and international environmental groups, including Friends of the Earth, Greenpeace, and the World Wildlife Fund, together with a pan-European group of environmental ministers, gathered in Sofia in October 1995 to demand the Bulgarian government shut the reactor down. Western countries fear that it may trigger a meltdown disaster. However, the government of Bulgaria did not agree to shut down the number one reactor of the six operating in the country because of expected severe power cuts. Moreover, the government argues that Energia, a local insurance company, has re-insured the nuclear plant with the American International Group and Lloyds of London. Also, it argues that France put most of the pressure on diverting attention away from debates in the European Commission on the French nuclear tests in Mururoa and to making Bulgaria dependent on energy imports. On the other hand, Electricité de France wants to construct another nuclear plant in Bulgaria. It seems that economic assistance from the West and debt-for-environment swap agreements, similar to that of Sofia with Switzerland (worth $17.3 million), would solve the problem and enhance nuclear safety.

Although significant reforms were introduced, foreign investment remains limited, but further expectations are high. The Coca-Cola Export Corporation, a subsidiary of the Coca-Cola Company, together with Bulgaria's Central Cooperative Union and the Leventis Group subsidiary Clarina Holding SA, created the Coca-Cola Bottlers Sofia Ltd. This is the fifth joint venture of the Coca-Cola Company, making it the biggest foreign investor in Bulgaria. Also, there are some 500 Greek-Bulgarian joint ventures.

Privatization

The Bulgarian government plans to privatize about 340 state enterprises, in addition to 17 sold at the end of 1994 and the other 63 sold previously, by the Bulgarian Organization of Privatization. Among the state companies which are under privatization are the Eltos Company, which produces machines and tools worth about $25 million a year mostly in exports; the Elcabel Company, which produces wires and similar products worth more than $28 million; the Plastchin Company, which produces plastic products worth more than $20 million a year; and the Panoyot Volvo Company, which produces plastics. Most of these firms are expected to be transferred to the private sector through a system of investment ownership titles. Each book of titles, with a certain nominal value, would be sold for a small fraction of this nominal value. The buyers of the investment titles can exchange them with shares at auction.

Among the main investment ventures into Bulgaria is that of Global Finance of Greece in association with Baring of Britain. Some 50 percent of the capital fund of $30 million is contributed by the International Finance Corporation and the European Bank for Reconstruction and Development (BERD). The Euromerchant Bank, controlled by the Latsis shipping group, sponsors the fund, and other Greek and international investors provide the rest of the fund. Since 1990, Bulgaria has absorbed about $100 million in foreign investment, $40 million of which came from Greece. Usually, the Euromerchant Balkan Funds takes minority stakes in Bulgarian and other Balkan companies, mainly focusing on food processing and retailing.[12]

In implementing its privatization or denationalization program, Bulgaria had only sixty-three state firms, worth $43 million (1.2 billion lev), privatized up to 1994. Ten of these firms were sold in auctions with installment payments. About half (thirty-one) of them belong to the service sector, seven to construction, six to the food industry, and two each to the cloth, engineering, and shoe industries, respectively. Only a small number of the privatized firms came under the ownership of foreign investors, whereas the rest were bought by Bulgarian entrepreneurs. Total assets of firms under privatization are 100 billion lev. Some 10 percent of the ownership titles would be distributed to the employees who work in these firms.[13]

Bulgaria, with the largest part of its economy still in the hands of inefficient state firms (compared to less than half of the Polish economy) is slow in the process of privatization. This is so primarily because of the disagreements in the National Assembly by the two main parties, the Bulgarian Socialist Party (the successor to the Communist Party) and the Union of Democratic Forces (a coalition of smaller parties which includes neo-Fascists and monarchists). Moreover, trade unions want privatization, but they like a share in ownership and decision making. Nevertheless, privatization and joint ventures are under consideration for a large state trucking company, the Balkan Airways, and tourist firms.

The BNP, a French banking firm, plans to establish a banking company in Bulgaria, in cooperation with the Dresdner Bank of Germany and the European Bank for Reconstruction and Development. The BNP has sixty-two subsidiaries in nineteen countries, including Greece (with six branches in Athens and Piraeus), Romania, Hungary, and other east European countries.

Bulgaria plans the construction of a tunnel, worth $90 million, for the highway connecting the port of Rus, on the Danube, with the city of Haskovo, close to the borders of Turkey. Some fifteen construction companies have made their financial bids. They include the Greek Mechanical Company AE; the Compenon Bernard SGE and the GTM International Companies, of France; and Dogus Holding, of Turkey.

In September 1994, Greece and Bulgaria signed an agreement for the construction of a pipeline carrying Russian oil to Greece by tankers from the Black Sea to the Bulgarian port of Burgas and, by pipeline, to the Greek port of Alexandroupolis.

Future Expectations

Bulgaria faces a problem of identity, as it is torn between the West and the East. The pro–Western United Democratic Front and President Zhelyu Zhelev, as well as the Atlantic Club of Bulgaria (an active lobby formed by prominent Bulgarians), push toward closer relations with the European Union and NATO. However, the Bulgarian Socialist Party, which returned to power after the election in December 1994, favors a pro-Russian policy. Many Bulgarians, influenced by the gratitude to Russians for freeing them from the Ottoman yoke, and their common Slavic roots, support closer cooperation with Russia. At the same time, they realize that outside the EU they would be isolated and deprived from modernization and rapid economic development.[14]

Expectations are that foreign, mainly European, investment in Bulgaria would grow rapidly. Already, the number of investments at the end of 1994 was 3,087, the largest (573) from Greece, followed by Turkey (304), Russia (191), Germany (152), and the United States (85). In dollar terms, out of a total of $467 million, Germany has invested $178 million; the Netherlands, $57 million; Switzerland, $51 million; Belgium, $36 million; Greece, $33 million; and the United States, $25 million. Through the EU PHARE and TACIS programs, Greek and EU firms increased their investment activities in Bulgaria and other Balkan and Euxene countries. Thus, Vakakis International and Doxiades Enterprises invested in the agricultural sector of Bulgaria and Armenia, whereas Energo Group, Kantor, and L.D.K., invested in the energy sector of Armenia, Azerbaijan, and Uzbekistan.[15]

ROMANIA

A Historical Review

Historically, Romania has perhaps been the nation in Balkania most affected by foreign cultures. During the Byzantine era the Slavonic language and tradition were prevalent, while during the Ottoman period Greek culture was spread by the Phanariots and the monastic schools. Toward the end of the Ottoman occupation, revolutionaries and writers from Bucharest and Jassy spread the ideals of the French Revolution and introduced the French language into the schools of Walachia and Moldavia. However, in reaction to the Greek revolution of 1821, the Turkish authorities replaced the Phanariot *hospodars* with Romanian *boyars*. On the other hand, a number of Romanian students, educated in Jesuit schools in Rome, started a systematic movement to replace the mainly Slavonic language with Latin, which was the tongue of their Dacian and Roman ancestors. During the postliberation years, the influence of France and the rest of Western Europe was predominant.

As mentioned earlier, the long tenure in office of Carol I (1866–1914) helped the economic development of the country. Some 2,000 miles of railroads were constructed. A large bridge at Cernavoda, on the Danube, connected Dobruja with the rest of Romania, and the Iron Gate was blasted to open the Danube to large ships. Moreover, the ever-increasing oil production around Ploesti (from 50,000 tons in 1890 to 1,885,000 tons in 1913) helped improve the financial and borrowing position of the country until 1917, when British engineers blew up the wells to avoid their falling into the hands of the Central Powers. By 1921 oil production was restored to prewar levels and, together with grain and lumber exports, provided enough foreign currency to pay for industrial imports.[16]

Romania, like the other Balkan countries, went through a turbulent period during the interwar years. Under pressure from the poor peasant masses and in order to stop the Bolshevik revolutionary spirit from crossing the Dniester River, King Ferdinand enacted a drastic land reform program between 1918 and 1921. Of 6 million hectares of land expropriated from absentee proprietors, foreigners, the crown, and large landowners, about two-thirds were distributed to some 1.4 million peasants; the rest was held for public use (forests, grazing, model farms, and roads). Although these reforms had political importance, mainly for the Liberal and the National Peasant parties, economically they were insufficient to increase farm productivity. Moreover, under the pressure of the depression of the 1930s, many poor peasants sold their plots and became part of the growing rural proletariat class.

The death of King Ferdinand in 1927 and the succession of his son Carol II, a shrewd maneuverer, led Romania to further turbulence and instability. Although he had Professor Nicholae Iorga, an internationally known historian, as a tutor, his unwise policies and his favoritism stimulated the Fascist movement of the Iron Guards, and led to the dictatorship of 1938–40. Surrounded by a sea of Slavs, old nationalistic feelings and endemic anti-Semitism were growing among the Romanians. Apathy and lack of cohesiveness, similar to that prevailing in Yugoslavia, brought on a national crisis in 1940 that resulted in the cession of Bessarabia and northern Bukovina to Russia, of northern Transylvania to Hungary, and of southern Dobruja to Bulgaria. Carol and his mistress, Magda Lupescu, fled the country to avoid prosecution by avenging nationalists.

Despite the efforts of the government and the political parties to carry out rapid industrialization, the Romanian economy remained largely agrarian. Close to 80 percent of the population lived in the rural sector by 1941, while only about 40 percent of the existing labor in this sector was needed. Ownership of small plots was prevalent. About 58 percent of the plots were less than 3 hectares. Increase in land productivity and employment of surplus rural labor, rather than land distribution, seemed to be the most pressing problems. Land productivity (9.5 quintals per acre) was very low, less than one-third that of Denmark (29.4 quintals per acre). This average output was the lowest in Balkania, except for Greece. Lack of equipment, limited use of fertilizers, the practice of strip farming, and primitive methods of cultivation were the main reasons. In addition, the decline in agricultural prices by half, during the depression of the 1930s, intensified the dismal economic conditions of the population.[17]

Heavy indirect taxes on consumption and high tariffs on agricultural exports (up to 50 percent of their value) made things worse for the starving peasantry. On the other hand, high import duties and quotas to protect domestic industry did not greatly help to stimulate industrial growth. Other restrictive measures on foreign investment (not permitting more than 40 percent foreign ownership and less than three-fourths native personnel) hampered technological development. However, the rich mining and lumber resources of the country helped to establish a few raw material–processing and metallurgical industries. Shortly before World War II, petroleum was providing 46 percent, and lumber 12 percent, of the export total. By that time, Germany had imposed a semicolonial treaty on the country that called for specialization in the production of minerals and agricultural raw materials.

Great inequality in incomes, class stratification, a low level of education (nearly half of the population was illiterate), and poor health conditions (the highest infant mortality rate in Europe, next to Yugoslavia) also intensified misery and poverty in Romania. Average per capita income remained very low ($60 to $70 per year in 1937). As in all Balkan countries, education was limited and misdirected. Classical education was preferred to technical or agricultural training. Students prepared themselves for white-collar, bureaucratic positions and gathered in the towns to swell the mass of applicants for the already overcrowded government offices. Nepotism, favoritism, and corruption were widespread.

Toward the end of the 1930s, the pressures from Italy and Germany were mounting. Italy tried to organize Yugoslavia, Romania, and Hungary in order to avoid Russian penetration across the Danube. At the same time, Turkey, Greece, Bulgaria, and Romania tried to form an alliance supported mainly by Britain. Both efforts were unsuccessful, and by 1940 the Balkan Entente had become ineffective.

Romania then faced serious problems of dismemberment. (It has already been noted that Russia demanded and got Bessarabia and northern Bukovina, Hungary partitioned Transylvania, and Bulgaria took over southern Dobruja.) To avoid further partitions, and pressured by its people, Romania joined the Axis. In the meantime, Hitler had decided to invade Russia, and he needed a secure Balkan Peninsula. German troops were sent to Romania in October 1940, while Mussolini launched his invasion of Greece.

Under the dictatorship of General Ion Antonescu, Romania, provided Germany with oil, munitions, and grain, as well as some thirty army divisions for the Russian front. During the war, the country suffered severe losses in Russia, especially during the winter of 1942–43 and in the battle for Stalingrad. When the Soviet army crossed the Prut River and entered Romania in April 1944, the Russian dominance in the area became obvious. Moreover, after the Teheran Conference, Romania was assigned to the Soviet Union, and Anglo-American nonintervention was assured. On August 25, 1944, King Michael, who was sympathetic to the Allies during the war, broke away from the Axis and declared war. The Romanian army then turned against Germany, fighting alongside the Russians in Transylvania, Hungary, Czechoslovakia, and even Germany. Casualties suffered in this fighting totaled some 170,000.

In contrast with the primarily Communist-led resistance movement against the Nazis in Yugoslavia, Greece, and Albania, no significant resistance movement developed in Romania, mainly because of the territorial disputes with Russia over Bessarabia and Bukovina. At the end of World War II, Romania gave up Bessarabia and northern Bukovina, which had been ceded to Russia in 1940, and regained Transylvania from Hungary.

After 1945, and under the Petru Groza regime, Romania was bound to the Soviet bloc, and its interests were interwoven with those of Comecon. However, after the death of Stalin in 1953 and under Gheorghe Gheorghiu-Dej, initiatives were taken toward some degree of independence and restoration of cultural relations with the West.[18] Despite the Soviet interventions in Hungary (1956), Czechoslovakia (1965), and Afghanistan (1980), Romanian leadership (under President Nicolae Ceausescu from 1965 to 1989) managed to maintain a precarious position while attempting to develop its own identity. Still classifying itself as a Communist country, it pronounced, from time to time, its opposition to both NATO and the Warsaw Pact, and wished to retain its national independence.[19] Although an ally of the Soviet Union, Romania was not as close an ally as Bulgaria, first because its population is primarily non-Slav, and second because of the existing problem of Bessarabia. Moreover, Romanians felt that the Soviet Union and Comecon exploited their country's natural resources during the postwar years.

On December 22, 1989, Nicolae Ceausescu, the Communist dictator since 1965, resigned and was executed, together with his wife, Elena, on December 25, 1989, by the army, which had revolted. This was the result of demonstrations and the massacre in Timisoara and Arad (Transylvania) of rioting people, mostly from the Hungarian minority and other anti-Communist revolutions in other cities and in other Eastern European countries. The Front for National Salvation, with Ion Iliescu as president, which took power on December 26, 1989, won the elections of May 20, 1990 (the first free elections since 1937), with 66 percent of the popular vote.

Romania, in its efforts to turn the state-owned economy into a free market economy, faces severe problems, although it has a small foreign debt when compared to other Eastern European countries. The process of selling state assets to the private sector, including foreign investors who can have full ownership of companies, continues with priorities in housing construction, food processing, tourism, and trade services. Also, free changes in prices are gradually introduced for almost all commodities and services, and economic hardship remains a serious problem for the 23 million Romanians.

Monetary and Investment Policies

The monetary policy of Romania was relatively stable up to the drastic economic and political changes at the end of 1989. After 1991, the money supply increased significantly, as did the velocity of money in 1991, as Figure 6.1 shows.

Although there is currently relative stability in the country, the flow of foreign investment is limited. However, future expectations are promising, particularly from the EU countries and the United States.

The Amoco Corporation and Rompetrol SA of Romania agreed to conduct exploration works for oil in the Carpathian Mountains. The new Amoco Romania Petroleum Company would spend $20 million initially for drilling operations on a 185,000-acre area.

Greek entrepreneurs have undertaken considerable investment initiatives in Romania. There are already 646 joint Greek-Romanian ventures in such sectors as aluminum, cigarette manufacturing, clothing, tourism, medicines, and pesticides. Moreover, a large part of the Romanian merchant fleet has been acquired by Greek shipowners. However, Germany holds the first place, with 2,646 businesses, and Turkey the fourth place, with 1,950.

Privatization

Romania plans to privatize some 3,000 state enterprises, through coupons of temporary titles of ownership, which can be exchanged for shares worth $517 (875,000 lei). About 60 percent of the stock would be sold, and 40 percent would belong to the Organization of Government Property, which would be sold later. Already, some 15.5 million coupons have been distributed during the first stage of privatization starting in 1992. However,

Figure 6.1
Money Supply (M1) and Velocity of Money (GDP/M1) for Romania

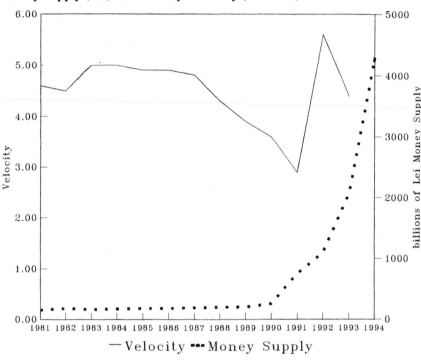

Source: International Monetary Fund, *International Financial Statistics*, various issues.

there are statements from the Romanian government that a good number of these titles have been bought by illegal or mafia-style groups on the black market.

Although the pace of privatization is slow, there are about half-a-million small, private enterprises sold, and their number is growing. Foreign investment is not encouraged, but a number of foreign firms enter Romania and form joint ventures.

The previously unproductive centrally planned economy of Romania, with its guarantee of permanent employment but many surplus workers in state firms and low standard of living for everyone, is generally exposed to efficient but often brutal capitalism. As the joke in Eastern Europe used to go, "They pretend to pay us, and we pretend to work." However, some state enterprises, which have been reorganized to be efficient, face serious problems. Thus, the Magura Colea furniture factory, which was privatized in 1992 through a management buy-out, lost export markets and is about to be foreclosed by IKEA, the Swedish furniture firm, the Ion Tiriac Bank, and other creditors because of a $9 million debt.

Foreign investments in Romania include the BNP French bank, in alliance with the Dresdner Bank of Germany, which created a subsidiary in Bucharest in order to provide credit for investment in the country, as it did in other Eastern European countries. Moreover, some 30 Pizza Hut restaurants, worth $10 million, are expected to be established all over Romania.

In a joint venture with Automobile Dacia (a state-owned carmaker of Romania), PSA Peugeot Citroën, of France, plans to assemble up to 10,000 small family cars per year. Dacia, the largest carmaker in Romania, shares about 32 percent of the total market and exports mainly to China (about 65 percent of its exports). It has thirty-two privately owned dealer shops, which count for half of its domestic sales, and expects to replace the Iatsa chain for state-owned sales and service outlets for the rest. However, Dacia faces severe competition from Daewoo, a South Korean car company, which agreed to rescue Oltcit, a smaller Romanian car company.[20]

Following the direction of the International Monetary Fund and the World Bank, as a condition for loans, Romania passed legislation for bankruptcy and further privatization. President Ion Iliescu and his administration have sold off about 900 state companies under the 1991 plan. Mostly, employee groups and management purchased these companies.[21]

Also in February 1996, 40 percent of the equity of 20 state enterprises were sold in auction for 287 billion lei ($101 million). These enterprises were involved mainly in the tourism, construction, wood, and food industries.

Foreign firms participate in the privatization process or establish their own companies, especially through the EU programs PHARE and TACIS. They include Planet, a Greek information firm with investment in Romania, Moldavia, and other Euxine countries, as well as Triton and Ellconsult, Greek firms with investments concerning expansion of the Black Sea ports.

Moreover, New Holland, a subsidiary of Fiat of Italy, acquired 60 percent of Semanatoarea, a Romanian state-owned group, for $50 million, to make tractors for Eastern Europe.

Economic Growth, Foreign Trade, and International Relations

DEVELOPMENTAL TRENDS

The main economic goal of each society is prosperity and happiness for all its members. Material and spiritual happiness—"the good life," as Socrates called it— includes higher levels of production, security, equal opportunity, dignity, and freedom of expression. Is convergence—that is, a system in which diverse economies adopt similar institutional structures and move closer to each other—expected to lead to such prosperity and happiness? The question is important for the Balkan countries, where a mosaic of ethnic groups and economic systems can be observed.

The effective use of fiscal and monetary policy and the successful management of demand have contributed to continued progress under capitalism. Income policies, tax cuts, investment incentives, and various subsidies have been introduced by the Balkan economies to achieve high growth rates and full employment.

Up to the collapse of communism in 1989, the Balkan countries incorporated a sample of different economic systems. Greece and Turkey followed the market, or Western, economic model, while the others followed the centrally planned or Eastern, economic model, with some varieties. Bulgaria and Romania followed, generally, the Soviet model; tiny Albania tended to imitate the Chinese; while Yugoslavia followed a peculiar model of a mixed market and planned economic system. Later, all moved toward the free market Western system. From this point of view, economic and sociopolitical trends in this peninsula were and still are of considerable interest.

The main problems of the Balkan economies are those that plague any other market economy: inflation and unemployment. Policy measures intended to stimulate employment frequently lead to inflationary spirals. Anti-inflationary policies, in turn, slow down the economy and increase unemployment. This dilemma of trading-off inflation with unemployment is perhaps the most serious economic problem of the market economies, including those of the Balkan countries. As these economies waver between the Scylla of unemployment and the Charybdis of inflation, policy makers in these countries may turn away from relying on the market mechanism and adopt control measures in order to correct undesirable economic trends.

As to the difference of the private versus the public sector, in large scale industries, individual incentives in private enterprises are not much different from those under state enterprises. The greater proportion of laborers and managers work for somebody else rather than their own establishment. However, the question of incentives and productivity in middle-size industries, which constitute a large part of the enterprises in the Balkan countries, remains a field that needs further research and exploration. The establishment of middle level corporations, the encouragement of private farm markets and vertical and regional decentralization of decision making, practiced to a large extent by Balkan economies, are measures which seem to support the trend toward convergence of these economies.

The "middle of the road" process of development may be less painful and more instrumental in bringing these countries together by seeking out rapid growth with the least possible sacrifice of political and economic freedoms. Changes need not be made through revolution but perhaps through gradual evolution. Economic development brings more material satisfaction, and people who have their stomachs full may turn to more individual enjoyments of life rather than to revolutionary insurrections and other conflicts.

Almost all the Balkan countries are at a stage of middle development, perhaps between the take-off, or self-sustained, stage and that of the drive-to-maturity. Through the transfer of technology and capital from advanced countries, these economies can continue to achieve high rates of growth. All the Balkan countries can continue to have high percentages of investment by withdrawing resources from consumers and placing these resources in the capital-producing sectors. However, their economies may then end up with fewer consumer goods. On a per capita basis, all Balkan countries are expected to perform well because of high overall economic growth rates and a low rate of growth in population, except perhaps Turkey, with high growth rates in population.

From a sectorial point of view, agriculture, considered the poor Cinderella in the former planned economies, is expected to turn in a good performance in northern Balkan countries, mainly because there is renewed emphasis on this sector. Also, comparatively speaking, the sector of services, which was not contributing as much as the industrial sector in the developmental effort previously, is expected to thrive in the future.

ECONOMIC GROWTH

Trade among the Balkan countries, which is gradually growing may speed up economic growth and create a favorable environment for further regional cooperation. Such cooperation, in turn, will create a big market, enlarge production units and stimulate development through specialization and economies of scale. As a result of such developments, relative differences in regional endowments of natural resources, capital, and labor may be reduced and eventually eliminated. Such an equilibrating process may hopefully lead to a gradual movement of scarce resources into the more promising sectors and regions so that relative differences in productivity and factor renumeration can be reduced.[1]

Large enterprises, growing in number and size year after year, and subsidiaries of multinational companies that have established themselves gradually in almost all of these countries require autonomy from controls and more corporate authority. This may be considered another trend supportive of the economic convergence thesis and more regional and international cooperation. Such convergence may take place not through a conflict of opposite (thesis-antithesis), but through a peaceful synthesis of these economies. Furthermore, mechanization and computerization of production and distribution, introduced by large enterprises, may reduce the need for individual and entrepreneurial incentives, and prepare the ground for an easier and more permanent convergence. Also, the growing use of mathematical models of the input-output variety may help policy makers more effectively, thereby making controls less necessary.

Economic cooperation among the Balkan countries may prepare the way for closer relations with other countries. The outcome of such efforts may be used as a model or paradigm for other countries to follow, especially Third World countries, which may try to combine the best elements of economic development.

During the postwar years, all the Balkan countries performed well in terms of growth in total production (more than 5 percent per year on the average). From a sectorial point of view, agriculture performed poorly in all countries considered. The northern Balkan economies did better, on the average, in industrial growth, compared to the economies of Greece and Turkey, but they did not do so well in the area of services. In construction, Greece had the highest rate of annual growth, followed by Romania and Bulgaria; while in transportation there was not much difference among all these countries.

Comparatively speaking, per capita income conceals greater inequalities in Greece and Turkey than in the other Balkan countries. However, there is a trend toward wage and price determination (income policies), aiming at a better income distribution. Moreover, the gradual acquisition of corporate shares or company partnerships and the spread of insurance, retirement and similar mutual funds to large segments of the population, although not extensive, palliates the problem of inequality and tends to support the spread of what may be called democratic capitalism, which may be considered as another path toward convergence.

Almost all the Balkan countries have high rates of investment, measured as percentages of gross domestic product (GDP). All these countries exhibit a declining percentage of investment in agriculture as contrasted with a constant or rising percentage in industry (in which manufacturing, mining, and electricity are included), transportation, housing, trade, and other services. However, Greece has relatively high investment rates in housing and transportation. Such high investment rates in housing, while investment rates are low in manufacturing, present serious problems for the economy of Greece from the point of view of industrialization, urban concentration (especially around Athens and Salonika), and environmental protection. In recent years, development policies have been introduced with corrective measures, but limited results have been obtained with their implementation.

The proportions of particular sectors toward output of production (GDP) follow the same proportional pattern as in sectoral investment. The agricultural share declined throughout the postwar years (from around 30 to 15 percent) for almost all Balkan countries. As expected, the share of industry is far higher in Romania, Bulgaria, and former Yugoslavia (around 50 percent) than in Greece (about 30 percent), but that of services was lower. Both sectors, industry and services, seem to present rising shares in recent years. This means that all Balkan countries followed, more or less, the general or universal trend toward a gradual transformation from agriculture to industry and services, although at a slower pace compared to middle or highly developed countries.

On the average, former Yugoslavia and Greece used more capital per unit of output than the other Balkan countries. During the last three decades the ratio of investment to additional output was close to 5 for Yugoslavia, 4 for Greece, 3.7 for Romania, and around 3 for Albania and Bulgaria. All Balkan countries provide free public education at all levels with minor exceptions in Greece and Turkey. Almost all countries have less than a 10 percent illiterate population. However, Greece has the lowest level of annual educational expenditures as a percentage of GDP while Romania has the highest.

Although Balkan countries produce mostly competitive products, such as metal ores, tobacco, vegetables, textiles, machinery, and chemical products, there is a rapid increase in trade among them except for former Yugoslavia. Exports among these countries are expected to increase in the near future. This is particularly so for Greece and Bulgaria.

There is a recent trend toward more cooperation among the Balkan countries. The dilemma of unemployment and inflation, as well as the problem of a better distribution of income and wealth, tend to force a greater degree of cooperation. Low production incentives (especially in agriculture and small scale industries), inadequate consumer satisfaction, and the problem of more efficient resource allocation in the economies of the northern Balkan countries tend to force greater decentralization and a movement toward free markets. Such concurrent trends seem to justify some of the conclusions of the convergence theory among the Balkan countries.

It is difficult to expect, in the near future, what the supporters of convergence suggest; that is, an optimum role for government and an optimum combination of the public and private sectors in the Balkan countries. However, it is equally or more difficult to accept the arguments that "convergence" is impractical. On the contrary, there are indications of economic cooperation and trade coordination which may submerge, in the long run, national differences between these countries, which have many conflicts, and gradually prepare the ground for common policies of development.

Tables 7.1 and 7.2 show the main indicators of the Balkan economies. Greece has the highest per capita gross national product (GNP), followed by former Yugoslavia, Bulgaria, and Romania. Albania, with a population of 3.3 million has a low per capita GNP (about $1,200). Greece and Turkey have high contributions of services to the GDP, whereas Bulgaria, Romania, and former Yugoslavia have high contributions of industry to GDP. They

Table 7.1

Economic Indicators of the Balkan Countries, 1994

Country	Population (millions)	Per Capita GNP (U.S. $)	Average Annual Inflation 1980–92	Current Account Balance ($.bill)
Albania	3.3	1,290	n.a.	n.a.
Bulgaria	8.5	1,330	11.7	0.5
Greece	10.3	7,290	17.7	2.1
Romania	22.7	1,130	13.1	-1.5
Turkey	58.5	1,980	46.3	-0.9
Yugoslavia (former)	23.9	3,060	123.0	-1.2

Sources: World Bank, *World Development Report* (Washington, D.C.: Oxford University Press, for the World Bank); International Monetary Fund, *International Financial Statistics* (Washington, D.C.: International Monetary Fund); and United Nations, *Yearbook of National Account Statistics* (New York: United Nations), all various issues.

Note: In some cases, earlier years' data were available.

Table 7.2

Sectoral Distribution of GDP, Growth, Inflation, Investment, and Government Budgets for Balkan Countries, 1994

Indicators	Bulgaria	Greece	Romania	Turkey	Yugoslavia
Distribution of GDP (%)					
Agriculture	14.0	17.0	19.0	15.0	12.0
Industry	45.0	27.0	49.0	30.0	48.0
Service	41.0	56.0	32.0	55.0	40.0
Economic Growth (1980–92)	1.8	1.7	-1.0	4.9	0.8
Inflation (1980–92, %)	11.7	17.7	13.1	46.3	123.0
Investment (% of GDP)	22.0	18.0	31.0	23.0	21.0
Gov't Expend. (% of GDP)	42.5	66.2	37.0	29.4	5.2
Budget deficits (% of GDP)	-5.1	-29.0	-1.2	-6.2	0.3

Sources: World Bank, *World Development Report* (Washington, D.C.: Oxford University Press, for the World Bank); International Monetary Fund, *International Financial Statistics* (Washington, D.C.: International Monetary Fund); and United Nations, *Yearbook of National Account Statistics* (New York: United Nations); and OECD, *Economic Surveys: Greece* (Paris: OECD), all various issues.

Note: In some cases, earlier years' data were available.

all have relatively high rates of investment and high rates of inflation. Greece has high amounts of government expenditures and budgetary deficits, compared to the other Balkan countries.

SALONIKA: THE GATEWAY OF THE BALKANS

Historically, Thessaloniki (Salonika) has been an important crossroad for East-West commercial and cultural activities. From the days of its creation in 315 B.C. by the king of Macedonia, Kassandros, who named the city after his wife, the daughter of Philip II and step-sister of Alexander the Great, Salonika has had periodic ups and downs. During the Hellenistic period (315 B.C. to 168 B.C.) and the Roman period (168 B.C. to A.D. 325) the city was used as a transportation and commercial center. Ignatia Street was the main route from which the Roman armies, as well as weapons and merchandise, were moving eastward. Merchants from Egypt, Phoenicia, Rhodos, and Rome used the port to transport such valuable commodities as diamonds, gold, silver, perfume, papyrus, jute, cloth, animals, and metals. After the conquering of Macedonia by the Goths in A.D. 250, the city declined until Diocletian pushed the barbarians out and brought peace to the area. During the period of Megas Constantinos and the subsequent years of Byzantium, annual affairs were introduced. Salonika became a vital commercial and transportation center attracting traders not only from the Balkan area but from Alexandria, Beirut, Vienna, and such distant areas as Algiers and Paris. During the Turkish occupation (1430–1912) the city lost its vitality to other commercial and shipping centers, mainly Trieste. Only after the establishment, in 1871, of the railways connecting Salonika with Istanbul to the east and Monastir and Belgrade to the west and the north, the city started gaining its geographical and economic importance.

With the recent trend toward a closer cooperation among the Balkan countries and the European Union as well as the implementation of regional development programs in Macedonia and Thrace, Salonika is expected to be an important industrial and transportation center not only for northern Greece and the Balkans, but for the Aegean Sea and eastern Mediterranean in general. This would help further the development of the rich soil and subsoil resources of northern Greece and the neighboring areas. The exploitation of coal, petroleum, and other metal resources in eastern Macedonia and Thrace, the development of middle and large industries in Salonika and in other northern cities, and the spread of tourist activities in the area would help improve the commercial and cultural life of the city.

Further economic development in the Balkan countries is expected to take place through a new water transportation network, by connecting the rivers of the Danube-Morava-Vardar (Axios) to create a waterway from the Danube to the Aegean Sea. This would materialize through the establishment of a navigable canal of some 400 miles between Morava and Vardar. It is expected that the annual traffic of goods would increase from the present 3 million tons to more than 50 million tons after the eventual completion of the canal. The EU and the United Nations Development Program could finance part of the project. Such a project would facilitate transactions not only among the Balkan countries, but between them and other neighboring countries such as Austria, Slovakia, the Czech Republic, Germany, and Hungary, as well as between Europe and the Middle East. Already, river boats from Odessa and other parts of the Black Sea sail to Rotterdam by way of the Danube and the Rhine. Such a waterway would facilitate river traffic down to the Aegean Sea and reduce the cost of transportation between Belgrade and Salonika.

The economic advantages of such an important waterway are obvious. The present distance from Europe to Port Said by way of the Dardanelles or the Adriatic Sea would be reduced by one-third. Instead of 3,000 kilometers or more, it would be only 2,000 kilometers by way of Salonika. The city then would soon be an important Europort, a natural gateway from the Balkans and Eastern Europe to the promising markets of the Arab countries with their surplus petrodollars. From that point of view, the port should be organized to accommodate sea traffic as a result of trade expansion. The Greek Transit Zone in particular (operating since 1913), which handles about 300,000 tons annually, needs expansion and modernization to provide for loading-unloading facilities, container shipping, and storage places for commodities in transit. Other Balkan countries expressed interest in related meetings and even offered part of the expenses for a speedy modernization of the port. Other cities among the Morava River such as Skopje, Kumanovo, Vranje, Lescovac, Nis, Stalac, and Svetozarevo would get developmental benefits from this waterway connecting Salonika with Belgrade.

Improvement in land transportation may be another important contribution to the development of Salonika and the surrounding area. There is already heavy traffic on the road connecting Europe with the Mideast. Trucks and cargoes move from Europe through Belgrade, Sofia, Istanbul, and Ankara to take electronic equipment from France to Iran or machinery from Germany to Saudi Arabia and other Arab countries. The opening of the waterway to Salonika would reduce the burden of the heavy traffic in this rough central road and facilitate rapid and less costly transportation between central Europe, the Mideast, and North Africa. Furthermore, construction of the highway connecting Egoumenitsa with Salonika and Istanbul would help the development of agriculture (mainly the production and marketing of fruits, vegetables, and cereals in Epirus, Macedonia [mainly Vermion], and Thrace), as well as tourism, particularly in the attractive, picturesque areas of Halkidiki.

The use of Salonika as a transportation center would have beneficial side effects for commercial and industrial enterprises in the area. Shipping industries, manufacturing firms, trade stores, tourist offices, hotels, restaurants, and a host of other commercial and industrial activities would flourish in the city and the surrounding regions. This would have a multiple income and employment effect on the rapidly growing population of the city and the economy of Macedonia, in addition to the educational and cultural betterment resulting from improvement in communications and technological transformation. All these expected changes would contribute to mitigating the suspicions and conflicts so prevalent in the history of the Balkan Peninsula, which is considered the powder keg of Europe.

The Greek government, recognizing the importance of the area and the expected benefits to the entire economy, appointed a committee responsible for the organization and coordination of the work needed for the expansion and development of the port. The Committee for the Coordination of the Europort of Salonika (CCES) has the responsibility of hiring the scientific and technical personnel for designing and extending the port (possibly westward to the Axios estuary), improving related shipping and commercial activities of the area, and coordinating transportation from the Balkans and other European countries to the Middle East and to North Africa. This would include the development and utilization of a ferry-boat connecting Salonika and other Mediterranean ports. The projected transformation of Axios into an effective waterway would also free thousands of acres for cultivation and production of such agricultural products as cotton, fruits, corn, wheat, and tobacco.

From the viewpoint of sea transportation, the activities of the port of Salonika increased rapidly in the last twenty years. More than 50 percent of the cargo was for other countries. The rapid growth of the country's commercial fleet plays an important role in the increase of shipping activities of the port. In addition, the development of land and air transportation gives more and more importance to Salonika as a regional and international transit center. The railway station alone handles about half of the country's foreign trade (that is, about 2 million tons of merchandise annually), and about 3 million passengers. The airport, on the other hand, handles more than 5 million kilograms, in merchandise, and about 1 million passengers annually. These air operations, which account for around 30 percent of those of the entire country, help reduce the burden of Athens' airport, which is among the first in Europe in transit activities.

Other important activities in the area are the international annual fairs in which Greek and foreign goods are exhibited. Such fairs stimulate exports and improve the balance of payments of the country. Among the many countries and the United Nations that participate in the fair are all of the Balkan countries, including Albania, each with its own pavilion. Furthermore, the expansion of the University of Salonika, one of the largest in Europe, and the organized periodic international conferences give a new cultural flavor to the city.

However, while great emphasis is given to the positive and beneficial side effects of the development of Salonika as a shipping, industrial, and commercial center, little attention, if any at all, has been given to the negative side effects from pollution and environmental deterioration. The fact that the port of Salonika has been gradually polluted is largely ignored. The glut created at times from oil leaks and industrial dumping, and the air and land pollution from Esso-Papas refineries and similar neighboring industries, may transform Salonika, "the Bride of Thermaekos," into a sad and ugly city. (I observed the undesirable effects of pollution in the city, during my research trips to the Balkan countries.) Therefore, care should be taken to avoid turning the clean waters of Axios and the surrounding sea a dull, brown color from untreated effluents from the big cities and industries upstream, as well as oil leaks and other dumpings from boats and barges plying the rivers and the harbors. Also, protection of the area from air, land, and noise pollution should be considered in any future developmental programming.

The ancient monuments and natural beauty primarily in Macedonia and Greece, would attract even more tourists and researchers. The old and new discoveries of archaeological collections at Athens (Acropolis), Crete (Cnossus), Mycenae, Pilos, Tiryns, Macedonia (Vergina), and in other Greek places related to classical and Hellenistic periods, as well as Byzantine art objects, would attract waves of visitors throughout the year who wish to satisfy their curiosity about and expand their knowledge of ancient history. On the seashores of mainland Greece and on the Ionian and Aegean islands, tourists could dawdle over ancient sites and wine-dark water.

The natural beauty and dry climate of Greece and the other Balkan countries would also continue to attract large numbers of foreigners. The picturesque beaches and the rich history, as well as the innumerable archaeological monuments, would make the area one of the most popular destinations for international tourists.

FOREIGN TRADE

Immediately after World War II, the Socialist Balkan and Eastern European countries had little choice but to trade with one another, mainly because of the prevailing cold war between the East and the West. However, the gradual warming brought about a step-by-step increase in trade between East and West, and between the northern and southern Balkan countries. Thereafter, the increase in intra-Balkan trade has been remarkable, some of it at the expense of trade within the Socialist bloc.

Intrabloc trade may impose costs upon the Balkan countries insofar as it means trade diversion. Moreover, the grouping of a number of countries in a protective arrangement may make the poor poorer and the rich richer, unless the more advanced countries are willing to run the risk of slowing their own trade and growth in favor of their poorer partners. However, the beneficial effects of intrabloc trade on the balance of payments, terms of trade, industrialization, and economic growth of the countries involved may be expected to be higher than the detrimental effects of trade diversion. That is, trade creation will most probably exceed trade destruction as a result of closer cooperation.

The creation and strengthening of regional markets among the Balkan countries does not imply renouncing the development of trade with non-Balkan countries. There seems to be no contradiction between the two. On the contrary, the development of regional trade seems to be complementary to free trade in general.

In similar groupings of less developed countries the growth of mutual trade in manufactured goods has been slower than similar sales to the rest of the world. What we can expect in the Balkan countries, however, is a gradual increase of mutual overall trade, depending on the degree of specialization, economic cooperation, and customs accommodations. Historical, political, and nationalistic factors do not seem to favor rapid growth of trade in the area. What is definitely favorable to closer economic links is the geographical position of these countries, which facilitates land and sea transportation and joint investment ventures, as well as the differences in factor specialization.

A serious problem in the effort to achieve closer trade cooperation among these countries may be the degree of flexibility on the industrial location, possibilities for subsidization, and a fair distribution of gains or losses from investment and trade transactions. There is a danger that the more industrial northern Balkan countries would dominate Greece and Turkey in industrial production. The fact that half of the national product of former Yugoslavia, Romania, and Bulgaria comes from industry, compared with only about one-third in the case of Greece and Turkey, means that the latter may face difficult problems in their efforts to speed up industrialization. The increase in imports of machinery and other industrial products by Greece and Turkey from the EU and northern neighbors would prevent these countries from establishing their own industries in such products. This would mean less employment and income for them, as well as an increasingly unfavorable balance of trade. However, if the Balkan countries are complementary (in many aspects) in terms of production, close cooperation and the creation of customs unions would be beneficial for all of them, despite the differences in their degree of industrialization.

For the high rates of growth to continue and for closer cooperation to be achieved, disparities among the Balkan countries should be reduced and policies of regional balance adopted. However, one should not expect miracles, because it takes a considerable amount of time and effort for changes to be implemented in these countries with great differences.

The Balkan countries can create trading or export companies similar to those in Japan and (to some extent) in Germany. Established private enterprises can undertake such foreign-trade operations with other European countries. Some of the advantages of such companies might be the following:

1. They would promote better understanding and trade coordination with their counterparts in other countries.
2. They would provide an effective way of coordinating policies with the EU.
3. They would make possible a more effective bargaining position for trading products in which they specialize. From time to time they can negotiate mutual trading in products that could not be exchanged under free trade conditions.

A serious problem for Greece and Turkey in trading with their northern neighbors is the monopolistic nature of imports by these economies. There is a great disadvantage to abrupt changes in trade policy, mainly because of noneconomic considerations in the bargaining and trading process. As long as trading decisions ignore the demands of the consumers and arbitrarily change, the flow and the size of exports to one, or to a group of economies, is uncertain. Increase of trade with such countries seems to depend more on the promotion of friendly governmental relations than on marketing and sales promotion.

The total or partial abolition of clearings (where a certain portion of exchanges may be in kind) is expected to increase the economic, and decrease the noneconomic, considerations in foreign trade among these countries. Moreover, free trade and payments in hard currencies would make them first-class customers to each other, instead of keeping them in the unfavorable position wherein each country tries to dump its unwanted products on the other. Under such conditions the Balkan countries can play a more effective role in promoting trade between the EU and Russia and, more important, as a bridge between Europe and the Middle East.

Some big enterprises in Turkey and other Balkan countries are oligopolies or monopolies. They may enjoy comfortable rates of profit under protection imposed, in many cases, for the support of small companies. These firms may neglect innovative activities. Under these conditions such "sleeping" firms may face difficult problems when exposed to greater competition as a result of closer cooperation with the EU and other countries.

A large majority of enterprises in these Balkan countries are middle-size efficient companies, while the small ones must depend on overworked family members and are in operation mainly because of protection. In order to survive foreign competition, it would be advisable that they group themselves into larger economic units. Then, through better organization and production planning, they could achieve economies of scale and lower costs.

Such groups may take the form of holding companies or of production cooperatives, depending on the competitive organizations they are expected to face in international markets. An adjustment period of a few years may be required for these small companies to organize and prepare themselves for the expected challenge from other enterprises. Such companies are mainly in the canning, fats, glass, electrical, cosmetics, rubber, and ceramic industries.

Interregional Trade

Although interregional relations among Balkan countries are not yet ready for customs unions, closer trade ties are possible and desirable. It seems that the fears and suspicions that prevail among these nations, including Albania, which is usually overlooked in regional studies, are political or psychological rather than economic. Economic relations may be considered as the means of breaking such political and psychological barriers, which may be stronger among these nations than between them and other big international competitors. Furthermore, the size of the market is, and must be, a divisive factor in policy considerations for trade and investment expansion.

It should not be overlooked that there may be obstacles to closer trade cooperation because of fear of future competition resulting from techno- logical transformation and assimilation. Expected competition, especially in exported products, is an additional obstacle to closer ties among the Balkans. Already there is strong price and quality competition among Greece, Turkey, and (to some extent) Bulgaria in grapes, wine, and tobacco. It may be suggested that instead of working to establish a customs union, in the very near future it may be better for these countries to work to create a sound basis for economic integration, with emphasis on joint investment; later they can proceed toward economic unification. Joint investment ventures can proceed *pari passu* with closer trade cooperation in products that are complementary in the Balkan economies and eventually in the EU countries.

It seems that developed countries at more or less the same stage of development can successfully create customs unions and eventually inte- grate their economies. The Balkan countries, however, have neither devel- oped nor underdeveloped economies. They can be classified as being at the semideveloped level of the self-sustained stage of growth. Furthermore, the fact that these countries have had political and territorial differences in the past, and still have now, has prevented the fullest development of trade among them. The gradual abolition of such differences would show in what products each country has comparative cost advantages, so that greater regional specialization and higher levels of production can be obtained.

In the past, almost all Balkan countries have stressed outward trade instead of relying on inward or intra-Balkan trade. The main reasons for such an outward looking policy include the following:

1. Political and territorial differences and suspicions have prohibited expansion of trade among the Balkan nations.

2. Specialization in production and export to developed nations of mainly primary products by almost all the Balkan nations has not allowed a satisfactory growth of intra-Balkan transactions.

3. Geopolitical and structural differences have not permitted mutual investments and joint ventures.

However, a significant degree of differentiation and diversification in the production process has taken place in recent years. As a result, there is some degree of specialization in different products and emphasis in different sectors. An obvious difference, on a sectoral level, is the greater emphasis on industrialization by the northern Balkan economies, and emphasis on services by the southern economies of Greece and Turkey. Such differences in specialization offer fertile grounds for further increase in intra-Balkan trade. The fact that Bulgaria, Romania, and, to some extent, former Yugoslavia were, for a long time, exporting their products primarily to the former planned economies, and Greece and Turkey were exporting mainly to the Western market economies, suggests that some degree of specialization has been developed. Therefore, complementary trading and joint ventures may be expected to increase in the foreseeable future.

The establishment of an Intra-Balkan Chamber of Commerce and Industry would benefit all the countries involved. It could promote more trade and tourism, solve problems of tariffs and transportation, and arrange the establishment and operation of joint ventures among the member nations. Such joint investment ventures might include the production of bauxite, uranium, copper, and other metals. The promotion of more trade and investment among the Balkan countries, in turn, would make their exports more independent than relying on the economic conditions of one or of a few countries in the West or in the East. This would be particularly important for Greece, Turkey, and former Yugoslavia, whose exports depend heavily on the market conditions of Germany.

The expected abolition of "clearings," or bilateral agreements, between Balkan countries, and the introduction of multilateral trade, would bring about adjustment of production and trade toward complementary commodities. Greater efficiency, cheaper production, and a healthier basis for long-term trade would be created among the nations of that area. Such trade liberalization would eventually show in which fields and commodities each country has comparative advantages, so that production and intra-Balkan trade could be improved. This would indicate which factors are complementary, where closer cooperation might be fruitful, and whether eventual unification would be preferable as an alternative to free international trade or national isolation and autarky. The establishment of intra-Balkan institutions or cartels in sectors such as transportation, manufacturing, agriculture, tourism, and other services might then be needed to coordinate and promote trade and investment, thereby creating economic ties that would be difficult to break because of political or other differences.

Although the present trade among the Balkan countries is a small proportion (about 6 percent) of their total foreign trade, the trend is positive. Thus, Bulgaria has signed agreements with Turkey to export electricity, with the provision to increase such exports later. Similar agreements were concluded between Bulgaria and Greece on matters of trade, transportation, communications, electricity, and other infrastructural and cultural projects. Bulgaria produces relatively large amounts of electricity, mainly from hydroelectric projects and atomic reactors. However, environmental problems have appeared for these old-fashioned and dangerous reactors.

The former centrally planned economies of the northern Balkans realized that the policy of autarky is detrimental to technological modernization and long-term economic development. Opening their borders to more international trade and investment means not only selling more of their products to other countries but also importing new products, new techniques, and new methods of production. On the other hand, the economies of Greece and Turkey may import from their Balkan neighbors not only cheaper products but also some new methods of production. Such methods may include the construction of man-made lakes (useful for irrigation), the planting of new forests, and even the setting up of pilot cities so widespread in Bulgaria.

Growth of Foreign Trade

All Balkan countries used to export mostly primary commodities and import mainly machinery and fuel. As expected, therefore, their terms of trade—the price index of exports over the price index of imports—were not improving in the past. However, lately there is improvement, or no deterioration, as the terms-of-trade ratio was 101 (1987 = 100) for Greece; 100 for Romania; and 111 for Turkey in 1992. Balkan nations should try to achieve higher industrialization in order to further improve their terms of trade as well as their employment conditions. There seems to be a trend in that direction, as the percentage share of primary commodity exports (except fuels and metals) is declining and that of manufacturers is growing.[2]

A serious problem for some Balkan countries is the growing external debt. In Turkey, total external debt increased from $19.1 billion in 1980 to $54.8 billion in 1992, and in Bulgaria from $0.4 billion to $12.1 billion, for the same years. In former Yugoslavia, it declined from $18.5 billion in 1980 to $16.5 billion in 1991, and in Romania from $9.8 billion in 1980 to $3.5 billion in 1992. In Greece, the long-term public external debt increased from $4.5 billion in 1980 to $23.4 billion in 1992. A large portion of the export earnings of these countries is used to pay for the service of their foreign debt. In 1992 Turkey paid 32 percent of such earnings to service its external debt, Romania paid 9 percent, Bulgaria paid 7 percent, and former Yugoslavia paid 20 percent (in 1991).[3] Table 7.3 shows foreign trade, reserves, and external debt for the Balkan countries.

There is considerable evidence that sustained economic growth requires a structural transformation toward an increase in the share of industry and a shift away from primary to manufactured exports. There is also evidence that continued emphasis on import substitution ultimately leads to a slowing

Table 7.3
Foreign Trade, Current Account Balances, International Reserves, and Foreign Debt of the Balkan Countries, 1994 (billion current U.S. dollars)

	Bulgaria	Greece	Romania	Turkey	Yugoslavia
IMPORTS	3.50	23.41	5.81	22.87	18.91
In percentages from:					
European Union	31.40	60.30	25.20	43.90	44.30
USSR	43.20	1.90	17.50	5.20	13.00
U.S.A.	3.20	6.70	5.80	8.40	4.50
EXPORTS	3.50	9.84	4.30	14.71	14.36
In percentages to:					
European Union	13.00	63.50	34.30	51.70	45.70
Former USSR	49.80	1.00	21.60	4.50	10.70
U.S.A.	3.40	5.70	3.00	5.90	4.80
CURRENT ACC. BALANCE	0.45	-2.14	-1.51	-0.94	-1.20
GROSS INTERN. RESERVES	n.a.	5.94	1.60	7.51	3.40
TOTAL EXTERNAL DEBT	12.10	23.40	3.50	54.80	16.50
(as % of GDP)	124.50	34.80	14.00	47.80	30.10

Sources: World Bank, *World Development Report*; and United Nations, *Yearbook of International Trade Statistics*, both various issues.

Note: In some cases, earlier years' data were available. For Greece, public sector external debt. Former Yugoslavia's data.

of growth.[4] During the postwar years and until the collapse of communism, Bulgaria, Romania, and Yugoslavia seemed to follow the first growth prescription, emphasizing faster industrialization than Greece and Turkey, while Albania more or less followed an autarkic, balanced-growth approach. In recent years, however, all these countries pursued an export expansion that has been largely offset by import liberalization. However, Turkey has continued to stress an import substitution policy and has maintained high levels of protection.[5]

The adjustment of the domestic economic structure and growth pattern to long-run improvement of the terms of trade and the reduction of external deficits has become an important policy priority for all Balkan economies. This policy is aimed at the restraint or reduction of imports when exports cannot be expanded. This has hindered economic growth, reduced the supply of consumer and capital goods, and raised prices. As a means of easing import demand, policy makers have set moderate growth targets and projected a reduced pace of investment. A marked decline in economic growth has already taken place in the northern Balkan countries because of the unusually low rates of growth in industrial production that used to offset swings in agricultural production, as well as the difficulties of transformation from the planned to the market economy.

FOREIGN INVESTMENT AND MULTINATIONAL EXPANSION

One of the most important issues of economic development in recent years has been the growth of big corporate enterprises of an international character. The growth of such giant corporations requires expansion in many nations. Balkan nations cannot be excluded from this economic intercourse.

The rapid expansion of multinational corporations throughout the Balkan nations may create problems of economic and political influence. In this region of extensive prejudice and ethnic conflicts, it is difficult to predict the new trends and the repercussions of such an international corporate expansion. We live in a period of uncertainty, in which the supporters of state controls close their eyes when confronted with the real economic gains arising from the market mechanism. At the same time, supporters of free competition cannot see that large parts of production escape the laws of the market because of the effects created by the formation of monopolistic transnational companies.

In order to counteract the ever-increasing influence of large corporations, what may be needed is some form of regional cooperation among governments, acting as a unified power like the EU, against the growing corporate power. However, such multigovernment and regional policies should try to protect the public and not discourage multinational investment. Technology requires capital concentration and bigness, which in turn require market expansion and suggest a "multicountry" investment policy in the area.

The flow of foreign investment, mainly from industrial countries, provides overhead capital, jobs, and technology for the recipient Balkan countries in exchange for raw materials, as well as returns for the investing countries. In order to have the flow of foreign investment and the accompanying technological transfer continue, favorable conditions, including guarantees against administrative controls and the assurance of profitable opportunities, must prevail.

All the Balkan countries offer attractive terms to foreign investors and multinational corporations in return for the introduction of new technology and know-how. Despite criticism that such corporate "beasts" influence and even threaten the economic and political life of the host countries, they are considered, at the same time, agents of technological innovation that provide managerial expertise, capital investment, and employment.

Foreign investment is welcome in all Balkan countries and plays a vital role in their economies. In particular, Greece (since 1953, Law 2687) and Turkey offer many privileges to foreign investors, to the point of being criticized for making their economies too open to foreign economic and political influence. In addition to traditional investments from Western corporations, joint ventures and mutual investments from the Middle East are appearing in Greece and Turkey and gradually in other countries.

A number of foreign enterprises have established themselves in Balkan economies for trade and investment. This economic exchange has been intensified during recent years.[6] The Balkans are willing to forsake certain controls over incoming foreign investors in return for the hard currency so needed to pay for imported Western equipment and technology. The Intercontinental Hotels Corporation operates and continues to build new hotels in Eastern European cities, including Bucharest, Zagreb, and Belgrade. A Japanese consortium, which includes the Nippon Steel Corporation and the Mitsui and Mitsubishi groups, has created trade centers in a number of Eastern European countries, including Bulgaria.

Romania, to some degree following the example of Hungary, has introduced special legislation for joint ventures with the West, especially for investment involving new technology, in which provisions have been made for more protection and less control.

For the financing of exports and trade transactions among Eastern and Western European countries, a number of joint banks have been established in Eastern European countries. They include the French-Romanian Bank, the French-Yugoslavian Bank, and the International Bank of Central Europe in Budapest, in which Balkan economies share up to 50 percent.

Although joint investment ventures among the Balkan countries have been limited, a number of joint enterprises and investment projects have been established, primarily on a bilateral basis. Such joint ventures between Bulgaria and Greece include the Chemiport-Bilimport Company, in which Unifert Company, of Lebanon, participates, for the production of chemical products; the Machine Export Industry (MEVET); the DKW, which cans vegetables and fruits at Almyros (Greece), and in which the Bulgarian Plont Export, the Greek Kanaris Company, and Uink-Konk of Holland participate; and the Kopelouzos-Balkan Car Impex Company, which manufactures and repairs buses. More joint Greek-Bulgarian ventures are in the process of development for the production and trade of fish products, meat products and sausages, and the manufacturing of leather products.

Joint investment ventures can be planned and implemented on hydroelectric dams and irrigation projects, especially in border areas, such as Samoritz-Islaz, near the Danube, and the Iron Gate on the Yugoslavia-Romania border. Other joint investments may include mining enterprises for the extraction and processing of iron, lead, zinc, bauxite, petroleum, and other subsoil resources. Also, bilateral agreements may be concluded for transportation, communications, electricity, banking, tourism, and manufacturing. However, careful feasibility studies are needed to overcome the limited or nonexistent research and the lapses and lacunae of statistical information prevailing in this region. (Additional foreign investments are presented in chapters for individual countries.)

Since the end of World War II, all Balkan countries have received some form of aid, primarily from the United States and the former Soviet Union. Such aid was needed because of economic adversities immediately after the war. However, continuation of aid breeds unhealthy economic dependency. Moreover, aid is often given for political and security reasons, and hidden strings are customarily attached. It would be better for the Balkan, as well as other recipient countries to ask for more trade rather than aid. The transfer of needed technology may take place through trade and investment agreements or joint ventures with multinational corporations, which could stimulate economic development while respecting the economic and political independence of the area.

Loans have been provided by international institutions. Romania, Turkey, and Yugoslavia received loans from the World Bank for the construction of the Danube–Black Sea Canal, for irrigation for structural adjustments, and for highways and agricultural credit, respectively.

Their mutual needs for raw materials, capital, and technology will most likely force greater cooperation among the EU and Balkan countries. It is expected that more joint ventures and multinational cooperations between the EU and the Balkans, on financial, infrastructural, and other projects will take place. The European Currency Unit (or Euro) as a Europe-wide monetary unit, or another internationally accepted currency, probably will help improve economic and sociopolitical relations in the area.

In light of further trade and investment cooperation between the northern Balkan countries and the EU nations, the question remains: What problems may appear in the future? It would seem that the trend toward more economic transactions between these two groups of countries does not represent a new movement toward integration, but a policy of gradually abandoning autarky in favor of a more open trade among neighboring nations, particularly Austria and Greece. The aim is to avoid scarcities and eliminate trade obstacles among these countries. From that standpoint, trade with Greece, Turkey, and other EU members or associate members are expected to improve.

INTERNATIONAL INVOLVEMENT IN BALKAN CONFLICTS

United States' Relations with Greece and Turkey

Greece and Turkey are members of the North Atlantic Treaty Organization (NATO) and receive military and nonmilitary aid from the United States, which has a number of military bases in both Greece and Turkey. The most important bases in Greece are those in Souda Bay, Crete (for navy and submarine installations), and one near Kavala in northern Greece. Of the bases in Turkey, the most important are those of Korlou and Izmit, on both sides of the Dardanelles straits, Ortakoy and Insirlik (near Syria and Cyprus), and Erhak-Malatya (in southern Turkey). A number of bases have advanced weapons, and U.S. AWACS (planes of early warning), including that of Arta, Greece, have been stationed in both countries.

In October 1986, Greece and the United States signed the Defense and Industrial Cooperation Agreement (DICA). Although it does not list specific projects, it refers to future participation in technological research and know-how, so that the Greek armed forces can become self-sufficient in hardware development and eventually be able to sell spare parts and defense equipment to the United States. A similar agreement was made between Turkey and the United States in February 1987.

After the collapse of the Soviet Union, Turkey asked for greater U.S aid to modernize its 600,000-member army to match reduction and to eventually eliminate U.S. forces in Europe.

Both countries received some form of aid, mainly from the United States, and Turkey also received aid from the former Soviet Union. U.S. postwar aid (1946–77) amounted to $5.1 billion for Greece ($1.5 billion under the Marshall Plan in 1947–51) and $3.7 billion (1954–82) for Turkey. Also, Turkey received $4.2 billion in aid from the former Soviet Union and the Eastern Bloc. Technical assistance to Greece was terminated in 1962, and major economic aid ended in 1964; only military assistance under the auspices of NATO continued thereafter.[7]

To enjoy continuing use of bases and sites for listening posts in Turkey, the United States supplies Ankara with additional weapons from surplus stocks. Washington may also reduce Turkey's payments on the $1.6 billion it owes in military debt. This may take place through a buy-down feature; that is, by transferring Turkish military debt to the private banking sector with U.S. government guarantees. Similar supply measures and transfers may be considered between Greece and the United States as well.

In addition to the annual financial and military assistance for the American base rights, Turkey, along with Egypt, Israel, and other military debtors, was offered debt relief worth an estimated $800 million over a number of years. Also, Turkey will be able to purchase secondhand U.S. military equipment at bargain prices.

Because of complaints from Greece about Turkey over the occupation of northern Cyprus, the U.S. Congress has imposed a seven-to-ten ratio of aid to Greece versus Turkey since 1975.[8] Presently, Greece receives about $350 million in U.S. aid, and Turkey receives about $500 million annually.

In a number of European and non-European countries, including Greece and Turkey, the United States maintains the Voice of America (VOA) facilities. Such facilities on the island of Rhodes and outside Kavala (in northern Greece), as well as in eastern Turkey, are broadcasting American viewpoints to Eastern Europe, North Africa, and the Middle East. However, with the collapse of communism, they lost much of their importance.

United Nations Troops in Cyprus and Turkish Problems

For more than twenty years (since July 1974) Turkish troops have occupied northern Cyprus, and United Nations peacekeeping soldiers remain there. As a result, Greece and Turkey are constantly in conflict over the Cyprus problem. Future socioeconomic and political developments between Greece and Turkey depend primarily on the settlement of the problems over Cyprus. Although peace efforts by the UN secretary general have been frustrated so far, implementation of the UN resolutions seems to lead to a viable and lasting solution for Cyprus. Such resolutions call for the withdrawal of all foreign troops (notably the 35,000 Turkish soldiers), freedom of movement (including the return of some 200,000 Greek Cypriot refugees to their homes), and the setting up of the Federal Cypriot Republic to accommodate both the Greek Cypriot majority (80 percent) and the Turkish Cypriot minority (18 percent). This would ensure the rights of the Turkish Cypriot and the Greek Cypriot communities, and reduce or eliminate hatred and conflicts between Greece and Turkey.

The Cypriot government complains that the Turkish government transfers people from eastern Turkey to Cyprus to occupy the homes of the Greek Cypriot refugees. Populating northern Cyprus with peasants from other regions of Turkey has been a familiar policy since the time of the Ottoman expansion. After the Turks conquered Anatolia (1071–81), they slowly and surely uprooted and chased away the Greeks and the other inhabitants, or they converted them forcefully or persuasively to Islam. Newly conquered areas in the Balkan Peninsula, including Albania and Bosnia, were populated to a large extent by Turks, unemployed warriors, and collaborators from other regions. At the same time, the diabolic policy of taking Christian baby boys violently away from their parents and converting them into Muslim soldiers (*janissaries*) proved to be a crude and inhuman, yet effective, measure in keeping Ottoman control over Greece and other Balkan countries for more than four centuries. Perhaps such measures may be considered strange in modern societies, but the example of northern Cyprus is frightening. (For more information on this issue see chapter 4 of this book.)

From a political point of view, Greece and, more so, Turkey experienced uneasiness and disturbances during the postwar years. Although mostly under democratic regimes, Greece had a seven-year (1967–74) military dictatorship, and Turkey had more years under open or concealed military rule than democratic rule. For the first time after the military dictatorship in 1980, the third in less than thirty years, elections were conducted in 1983 in Turkey, but politicians of the previous major parties were barred from election.

Although the Turks are mostly Sunni Muslims, there is a sizeable minority of Shiites, about a quarter of the population. Power is held primarily by the western camp, but, from time to time, there appeared violent conflicts between the traditionalists, or fundamentalists, and power holders. The Sunni-Shiite rivalry and the struggle for independence by the Kurds are the two main internal problems of modern Turkey. The theocratic character of Islamic fundamentalism is at odds with secular Western values, and supports a return to religiopolitical fanaticism and the violent ethos of Islam in fulfillment of God's will.

While Greece and the rest of Europe face problems of depopulation, Turkey, a Muslim country, faces risks of demographic explosion and, therefore, slow or no growth in per capita income. However, Turkish leaders, boasting of population increases in their country, promise to rescue Europe from depopulation by flooding the EU countries, including Greece, with Turkish immigrants. There are already more than 5 million Muslims in Western Europe. Also, there are 1,334 EU companies in Turkey.

The geographical position of Greece and Turkey, between Europe and the oil producing countries of the Middle East, gives them some economic and strategic advantages. Because of the problems in Iran after the revolution against the Shah, the long Iran-Iraq war, and the U.S.–Iraq war of 1991 over Kuwait, a substantial amount of oil is transferred to the Western countries via land pipes. Because of the insecurity of the oil pipe network going to the Red Sea (through the desert of Saudi Arabia) and the troubles in the Persian Gulf, growing amounts of oil are transferred through Turkey and the eastern Mediterranean. Also, about 50 percent of Russian exports and imports travel through the Dardanelles straits and the Aegean Sea.

From a strategic point of view, there is the impression among U.S and other Western policy makers that Turkey is an important country because of its location. Turkey, as a NATO member, tries to keep good relations with the United States and Western Europe so that it can attract aid and increase trade. On the other hand, being an Islamic country, it tries to keep good relations with other neighboring Islamic countries. At the same time, however, it tends to occupy the Kirkuk oil wells of Iraq. Mainly because of U.S. military aid, Turkey has a strong army, the leaders of which have become aggressive, and they envision the revival of the tyrannical Ottoman rule.

Civil War in Bosnia and Herzegovina and Croatia

Sarajevo, where Garvrilo Princip, a Serbian nationalist, assassinated Archduke Ferdinand (heir to the Austro-Hungarian throne) on June 28, 1914, became the center of conflicts between the Serbs and the Muslims. Since March 1992, when Bosnia and Herzegovina declared the formation of a new state, the Bosnian Serbs (more than one-third of the population) objected, and a civil war began. From time to time, Serbian guns from the surrounding areas bombed Sarajevo and five other areas (Bihac, Tuzla, Gorazde, Zepa, and Srebrenica) designated as safe areas and protected by UN peacekeepers, whereas periodic battles were conducted throughout Bosnia, mainly between Serbs and Muslims. Srebrenica and Zepa fell to Bosnian Serbs in July 1995. Also, serious conflicts took place between the Serbs and Croats, currently allies (and former allies and former enemies) with Muslims, not only in Croatia (Krajina area) but in Bosnia, as well. Moreover, Muslims in the Bihac area fought against the Muslim-led government of Sarajevo and the civil war in Bosnia and Croatia continued for more than three years. The southern Slavs, known as the Serbs, felt that they were denationalized in their own ancestral territory and abducted into a new state they did not trust, but Western favoritism toward the Muslim-led government internationalized the war.

The United Nations Security Council imposed sanctions against Yugoslavia, because of their support of the Bosnian Serbs, and sent some 22,000 peacekeeping troops, mainly from France, into the area. About 1,450 Turkish troops joined the peacekeeping force in Bosnia, a movement which angered Serbia and other Balkan states because of fears that the Turkish involvement could restart centuries-old animosities. A number of times (from February 28, 1994, onward), the peacekeepers requested NATO flights for reconnaissance and air strikes (the most serious of which was that of May 25, 1995, near Sarajevo) against Serbian heavy guns. In retaliation, Bosnian Serbs detained hundreds of peacekeepers and shelled Tuzla and other cities. Moreover, Radovan Karadzic and other Bosnian Serb leaders used counteroffensive measures, which measures made the Atlantic unity look like an oxymoron scheme and put Western Europe, Russia, and the United States at odds.

Gradually, the civil war in Bosnia is becoming more and more a religious war. Turgut Ozal, the late president of Turkey, warned that the capitalist-communist balance of power would be replaced by a Christian-Muslim confrontation. All-Muslim elite attack units, such as the Black Swans, who bow toward Mecca in mosques for their success, are examples of the

Islamization of the Bosnian society. Muslim-led Bosnian troops threatened United Nations peacekeepers as well, placing mines outside their camps and blocking aid convoys to the 300,000 people in Sarajevo.

The ethnic and religious conflicts in the area might be avoided by arranging the split of former Yugoslavia through negotiations, as happened with the former Czechoslovakia and the former Soviet Union. However, the premature recognition of Croatia's breakaway from Yugoslavia and the pushing for the creation and recognition of an independent Bosnian state by the West, under German pressure, made the civil war inevitable. Alija Izetbegovic, the Muslim Bosnian leader, reached an accord with Bosnian Serb and Croat leaders in Geneva to divide peacefully Bosnia and Herzegovina, which was never a nation, but an administrative area in Yugoslavia, as it had been under the Hapsburgs and the Turks. As Henry Kissinger, former U.S. secretary of state, said, "I don't believe that Bosnia has ever in history been a nation."[9] Nevertheless, Izetbegovic later reneged after obtaining pledges of German and Western support for a unified multiethnic Bosnia under his rule.

Conflict of Greece with FYROM

As mentioned previously, after the split of former Yugoslavia, the Vardar region of southern Yugoslavia, which Tito named Republic of Macedonia for expansionary reasons, was formed into a new state by the Slavic leaders of Scopje and was named "Macedonia." The United Nations recognized it as the Former Yugoslav Republic of Macedonia (FYROM). Greece objected to the use of the name "Macedonia."

The Greeks claim that the name "Macedonia" was used for future expansion is justified because "during Greece's civil war, from 1946 to 1949, Greek Macedonia was the communist stronghold, and Tito had plans for a broader communist Macedonia that included at least the part of the region that now lies in Greece."[10] Even now there are nationalists in FYROM who believe that all the inhabitants in the region, including those in Greek Macedonia, should belong to one state. From that standpoint, "Greece fears, with reason, that recognizing a 'Macedonia' will stir these irredentist embers." Therefore, "not all of the Greek inflexibility over the name is rooted in antiquity and culture,"[11] Greek identity goes back several thousand years, even before Aristotle (from Stagera of Macedonia) and Alexander the Great, and continues until now. Although Greece is not afraid from the standpoint of security, small states like FYROM usually find larger champions, such as Turkey, creating alliances which undermine everyone's security. Moreover, in an analogy of what Henry Kissinger said about Bosnia, FYROM never in history has been a nation.

On February 16, 1994, Hellas (Greece) imposed a trade embargo on FYROM, which led to transportation problems, mainly from the port of Salonika, and shortages in gasoline and other commodities. However, food and medical products were exempted for humanitarian reasons. The embargo was to continue according to the Greek government, until FYROM changes its usurped name, "Macedonia," abandons the use of the Alexander the Great flag, and eliminates the expansionary statements from its constitution.[12]

Through the U.S.–brokered efforts, Hellas and FYROM reached a compromise in New York on September 13, 1995, which lifted the trade embargo Hellas had imposed against FYROM.

FYROM, a provisional name with which the republic was admitted to the United Nations, changed its flag with a sixteen-pointed star of Vergina used by Alexander the Great and the Hellenic Macedonians. Also, FYROM accepted the interpretation of some of its constitutional provisions so that they would not imply claims against Hellenic Macedonia.

Karolos Papoulias, the-then foreign minister of Hellas, and Stevo Crevenkovski, his FYROM counterpart, signed the agreement. Cyrus Vance, the UN mediator, and Richard Holbrooke, the U.S. assistant secretary of state, were instrumental in bringing the two parties together. However, the name "Macedonia," which was usurped by Tito in 1945 for expansionary reasons in Hellenic Macedonia and the Aegean Sea, would be the subject of later negotiations.

U.S. Policy in Bosnia and FYROM

The U.S. policy in former Yugoslavia, initially followed, to a large extent, the EU policy. First Germany rushed to recognize the split of Yugoslavia, then the other EU countries and the United States followed. After the civil war started in April 1992, the United States, along with the main EU countries, supported the United Nations' resolutions to send peacekeeper troops into Croatia and Bosnia, but no American soldiers. The U.S. support was mainly in aircraft, through NATO, for reconnaissance and for bombing places with heavy Bosnian Serb weapons, mainly around Sarajevo.

Lawrence Eagleberger, the undersecretary and later secretary of state under President George Bush, who was considered an expert on Yugoslavia, played a significant role in speeding up the split of former Yugoslavia and the following catastrophic civil war, particularly in Bosnia. Eagleberger encouraged Slovenia, in 1991, to split from Yugoslavia and fighting started, in spite of the six month moratorium suggested by the EU to cool off conflicts and arrange details of independence through negotiations. Also Warren Zimmermann, a former U.S. ambassador in Yugoslavia, was against the agreement of Lisbon in March 1992, under the aegis of the EU, which would have given 44 percent of the Bosnian land to the Bosnian Serbs, and which was accepted by all interested parties. Zimmermann influenced Alia Izetbegovic, the Bosnian leader, who changed his mind and rejected the agreement, leading to the beginning of the Bosnian tragedy a month later. The argument of Zimmermann was that the agreement would encourage Russia to demand land for the Russians who live in the former Soviet republics.[13]

In June 1995, an American F-16 plane (under NATO) was hit by a rocket, and the pilot was rescued six days later. The detained peacekeepers were released by the Serbs with the implicit understanding that no more bombing would be requested by the UN through NATO. After the Bosnian Serbs took hundreds of UN soldiers hostage because of a serious NATO bombing in Pale, near Sarajevo, the principle Western policies began to accept political and military realities, adjusted to the idea of allowing the Bosnian Serbs to form a federation with Bosnian Muslims and Bosnian Croats.

In order to avoid the spread of war in other neighboring nations, the United States initially sent 300 soldiers to FYROM. Later, more American marines were sent and, together with other UN troops, more than 1,000 peacekeepers were sent to the area, mainly to protect FYROM from Serbian expansion to the south.

The overall U.S. policy in the Balkans is to keep peace. Some 20,000 American troops and 40,000 other NATO troops, were committed to Bosnia for that reason. However, Iran and other Muslim countries are already smuggling arms into Bosnia, whereas Tansu Ciller, prime minister of Turkey, and Benazir Bhutto, prime minister of Pakistan, visited Sarajevo and expressed their support to the Muslim-led Bosnian government. If Iran or other Muslim countries become nuclear, then intimidation northward becomes obvious.[14]

Probably, some form of self-rule, and an eventual EU membership might be needed to steam-out ethnic conflicts in the area. America can provide assistance through Enterprise Funds, as it did for Central Europe since 1989 (totaled over $10 billion), during the transition period, and with technical advice, training, and investment capital. Already, in Bulgaria, U.S. advisors have helped to privatize state-owned businesses through innovative auctions. In Romania, U.S. assistance helped the National Federation of Mayors to present their local concerns to the attention of the national government. Also, training is provided for judicial procedure, rewriting commercial codes, environmental cleanup, and financial reforms to solidify democratic practices and free markets in the Balkans and other Eastern European countries. In addition, special U.S. presidential emissaries are working in Cyprus, FYROM, and other areas to improve relations and to deal with unresolved legacies, which Ottomans and Hapsburgs, czars, and commissars have left behind.[15] The goal is to have a free and democratic Europe, as Monnet and Marshall, Schumann and Spaak envisioned after World War II. The United States wants a stable and prosperous EU, with which it has more than $300 billion in annual trade and large amounts of mutual investments, for its security, interests, and growth.

The success of democratic and free market reforms in the Balkans is the proper answer to the ethnic hatreds and lack of security in the region. Such reforms and closer cooperation with the European Union (EU) and the United States make all more secure and prosperous. Nevertheless, the return of historic grievances, aggressive nationalism, religious conflicts, and social dislocations jeopardize the establishment of democratic institutions and the process of economic development.

For protective and humanitarian reasons, more than 8,000 U.S. Department of Defense personnel, as well as four ships and dozens of aircraft, provide support to NATO operations in the Balkans. Moreover, some 5,000 U.S. personnel provide medical services for UN peacekeepers in Zagrem, whereas about 800 American troops, together with about 700 other UN peacekeepers, have been deployed in the Former Yugoslav Republic of Macedonia (FYROM), to help stabilize that small land-locked country and prevent conflict spillover. More than 6,000 sorties of U.S. aircraft delivered over 50,000 tons of supplies (humanitarian aid) to Sarajevo. This is the largest program of air drops since the Berlin airlift. On the diplomatic front, the United States, through the five-nation Contact Group (Britain, France, Germany, Russia, and the United States), played a constructive role in resolving the problems of the former Yugoslavia.

In August 1995, the Croatian army moved into the Krajina region and after days of fighting it drove about 140,000 Serbs from their homes, reducing their number in Croatia to less than 3 percent. In addition, President Franjo Tudjman of Croatia made it clear that he would not allow 30,000 Muslims who fled from Bosnia to stay in Croatia. Tudjman went from fervent communism to ardent nationalism and, helped financially by Croatian emigres in Canada and the United States, managed to create a conservative mainly Roman Catholic state and to support the U.S. plan for a confederation of Croatia with Bosnia and Herzegovina. He criticized Tito, whom he once served as a general, and wrote a book, *Wastelands: Historical Truths* (1988), in which Tudjman argues that only 900,000 Jews, not 6 million, were killed by the Nazis and less than 70,000 Serbs died in the hands of the Ustashe Croats who collaborated with the Nazis. Tudjman regained most of the area lost to the Serbs in 1991 and vowed to recapture Eastern Slavonia.

From August 30 to September 14, 1995, NATO warplanes, mostly F-117 stealth bombers, attacked the Bosnian Serbs' heavy weapons and ammunition storage places around Sarajevo (mainly Pale, and other places), in order to force the removal of their tanks and heavy weapons and accept the U.S. peace plan. In addition, on September 11, NATO used thirteen Tomahawk missiles from ships offshore, which are guided by satellite and evade radar following the contours of the terrain only a few hundred feet above the ground. On September 8, 1995, under pressure of ongoing NATO bombing, the Croats and the Serbs agreed in Geneva to create a Serbian republic within Bosnia and to accept the legal existence of the Bosnian state. The peace plan, promoted by Richard Holbrooke ("Le Kissinger des Balkans," as the French daily *Le Figaro* called him), the assistant secretary of state, provides that 51 percent of Bosnia-Herzegovina would be ruled by the Muslim-Croat federation and the rest by the Bosnian Serbs. Because of the waves of NATO bombings against the Bosnian Serbs, with some civilian casualties and extensive property damages, the Bosnian Muslims, at times helped by Croat soldiers, push back the Serbs.

On September 26, 1995, peace talks started with the three parties in New York. It would seem that Croatia came out the big winner of the civil war, after the gains of the Krajina region and, together with Bosnian Muslims, large parts of Bosnia held previously by Bosnian Serbs. However, it is possible that the loose Bosnia-Croat federation may break later. Already Tudjman warned the West, which punished the Serbs with three-year economic sanctions and patted him on the back, that "a Muslim dominated state there could become a bridgehead for Islamic militancy in Europe."[16]

As a result of the U.S. peace efforts, three Balkan presidents—Slobodan Milosevic of Serbia, Alija Izetbegovic of Bosnia, and Franjo Tudjman of Croatia—gathered at an American military base in Dayton, Ohio, for peace talks in November 1995. Representatives of Britain, France, Germany, Russia, and the European Union also participated in the conference. (Further details in chapter 5.)

8

Balkan and European Cooperation

TRENDS FOR COOPERATION

The geographic position of the Balkan countries, at the hub of three continents—Europe, Asia, and Africa—attracts the competition of the big powers for political and economic influence and domination. As was indicated in the historical review, there have been many antagonistic efforts made by the big powers, especially the neighboring ones, to impose their policies and even to annex parts of the Balkan Peninsula. Such influence has been responsible for divisions among the Balkan peoples that have led to open conflicts and even to civil wars.

The common historical experience of the Balkan peoples, under long foreign occupations and periods of influence, has tended to create social and cultural similarities among them, such as common religion (mainly Christian Orthodox) and certain social customs (such as the drinking of raki). Because of these and other characteristics, some writers, mainly the Romanian historian Nicholae Iorga, have proposed a common Balkan type and common culture, "Balkanology."[1]

As the Ottoman Empire declined because of external wars and internal revolutions, the big powers of that time—Russia, Austria, France, and England—prepared schemes either for dividing the Balkan countries or for unifying them under their individual control or influence. These schemes, which at times were abandoned and at other times modified, aimed primarily to promote the political and economic interests of the big powers. For example, the increase of trade between England and Turkey, mainly through the Anglo-Levantine Company, forced England to support the status quo and to discourage any effort toward Balkan liberation from the Ottoman rule. What prevailed for centuries in the area can be described by the Balkan saying, "A few donkeys quarreled in someone else's barn," or, as they say in Africa, "When elephants quarrel, the grass is destroyed." In other words, the big powers quarreled over the Balkan Peninsula, and the result was its socioeconomic backwardness.

Efforts to achieve cooperation and eventual unification were made from time to time, but with limited results. During the struggle against the Ottoman yoke, a number of Greek revolutionaries urged the Balkan peoples to unite against their common enemy. Rhigas Pheraios (Valestinlis), Alexander Ypsilanti, the Poulios brothers (in Vienna), and Joannes Capodistrias (the Russian foreign minister of Greek descent) were the main supporters of closer cooperation. The "*thourios*" (war song) of Rhigas, which called for unification and revolution against the common enemy, was for years the "national anthem" of the oppressed Balkans, mainly the Greeks, Bulgarians, and Romanians. Influenced by the French Revolution, Rhigas not only agitated with such revolutionary slogans as "one hour of free life is better than forty years under slavery," but he also suggested the economic and political unification of all peoples of the Balkan Peninsula on an equal basis.

Other groups or individuals, such as Georgi Rakovski and Lyuben Karavelov (Bulgarian revolutionaries), Illya Garashanin (a Serbian), Charilos Tricoupis (a Greek premier), and Francesco Crispi (an Italian premier of Albanian decent), worked for a closer cooperation of the Balkan peoples and even proposed the creation of the United States of the Danube, a federation of the Danubian countries. In the 1860s a number of alliances were formed, usually between Serbia and one of its neighbors (Montenegro, Greece, Bulgaria, and Romania), with provisions that other neighbors would join later. Under the influence of the big powers and the regional disputes over annexation of certain territories, primarily in Macedonia, Epirus, and Transylvania, these efforts for closer cooperation, especially the federative ideas of the Christian Balkan states of 1912, were abandoned. Moreover, the constant suspicions and disputes led to the Balkan wars of 1912–13.

More intense efforts to achieve closer economic and sociopolitical cooperation began after the Balkan wars, and were particularly strong in 1924–31. Such efforts were supported by the agrarian parties of Croatia and Bulgaria, led by Stefan Radich and Alexander Stambuliski, respectively. Also, a number of writers advocated the creation of a Balkan Federation, and for this purpose published the journal *La federation balkanique*, which had a great influence in Balkania as well as abroad. During 1930–34 more concrete results were achieved through the Balkan conferences (Athens, October 1930; Istanbul, October 1931; Bucharest, October 1932; and Salonika, November 1933). The main supporters of these conferences were Alexander Papanastassiou (a former premier of Greece) and Nicolai Titulescu (foreign minister of Romania). At these conferences, resolutions calling for the improvement of communications and the construction of roads and railways from the Adriatic to the Black Sea, and from the Danube to the Aegean, were adopted. Moreover, for the development of inter-Balkan and foreign trade, the conferences urged economic collaboration in tourism, credit, tariffs, and protection of Balkan agricultural products.[2] Resolutions also were adopted for the establishment of the Balkan Chambers of Commerce and Industry, Agriculture, and International Commerce, as well as a Central Tobacco Office, a Center Cereal Office, an Inter-Balkan Grain Exchange, and a Central Union of Cooperative Societies.

In February 1934, Greece, Romania, Turkey, and Yugoslavia initiated a Balkan pact that was signed at Athens. It was hoped that Bulgaria would join them later. In October of that year, those four states created the Balkan Entente, which replaced the fifth Balkan Conference, scheduled to take place at Istanbul. The entente, which was designed to make decisions and take actions on both economic and legislative matters, met at Belgrade in May 1936, and signed a treaty of friendship with Bulgaria at Salonika in July 1938. However, its importance was overshadowed by the expansionary policies of Italy and Germany.

The dependence of all Balkan countries on German markets for their exports was another factor in contributing to a strong German influence in the area. This economic dependence increased during the international economic depression, when prices of Balkan agricultural products decreased by about 50 percent, and the exports to Germany increased from 16 percent in 1933 to 27 percent in 1937 for Bulgaria, Greece, Romania, and Yugoslavia, and from 19 to 51 percent for Turkey. In addition to engaging in economic competition over exports, the Balkan countries considered proposals for bilateral agreements, such as the federation of Greece and Turkey (by Venizelos and Ataturk) and the closer ties of the Slavs of Bulgaria and Yugoslavia, promoted by France against Italy. England tried to exert influence over Greece and Turkey in order to steer them away from the Soviet sphere of influence. All these factors had a repressive effect on the efforts to set out a pan-Balkan federation.

Interventions or influence of foreign powers frequently resulted in divisions and conflicts among the Balkan peoples. The big powers frequently used the principle of "divide and rule" to enhance their own interests. Thus, efforts by the Balkan countries to establish closer cooperation among themselves, independent of the desires of their "patrons," were frustrated.

There seems to be a desire for closer cooperation, and even federation, among the Balkan nations. In addition to the efforts to achieve unity of the people in the Balkan Peninsula for political reasons, moves toward a Balkan federation took place in the postwar years. Yugoslavia, under Tito, was desirous of such a federation or a wider union.[3]

Bulgaria, under Dimitrov, proposed a Balkan Customs Union in 1948. In 1954, Greece, Turkey, and Yugoslavia signed an alliance agreement. Although this alliance faded into obscurity, good relations among these countries continued for years thereafter. In 1957, Romania's prime minister, Chivu Stoica, proposed a Balkan conference that would include Albania, Bulgaria, Greece, Romania, Turkey, and Yugoslavia. This proposal, which was renewed in 1959 and was accepted by all the others except Greece and Turkey, was aimed at gathering the Balkan leaders to consider economic and security problems of the region.

Regardless of which big power was behind some of these proposals (presumably Russia for those of Bulgaria and Romania), the idea of an association of Balkan nations seemed to acquire a life of its own. On its own initiative, Bulgaria had assumed a more active role in settling regional disputes with Greece and Yugoslavia, in order to prepare the ground for future economic and cultural cooperation. New Balkan conferences, broader than that of Athens in 1976, were those in Belgrade in 1988, and in Tirana in 1990. Statements and appeals for further cooperation have been made by almost all the leaders of the region.[4] Activities including scholarly conferences, music festivals, athletic games, and tourist and trade agreements have taken place frequently. These efforts which have been intensified in recent times, are expected to continue after conflicts, mainly in Bosnia, are over.

National individualism and the imperialism of other countries have always been the main obstacles to closer cooperation among the Balkan countries. A working association of the previously hostile Balkan peoples requires the downgrading of the hatred and emotionalism that have promoted ethnic and territorial disputes. The recent worldwide trends of cooling fiery nationalism and of instituting closer communications may provide new impetus for the improvement of the economic and social relations of the Balkan peoples. In such a peaceful and progressive environment, agitation by minorities in these countries may cease and more energy may be devoted to the common goal of improving the economic conditions of all the peoples in the area. Although nationalism should be treated with respect, partisan indoctrination should be avoided if some form of federation or closer economic cooperation is to be realized. In order for a new federative venture to succeed, a nobler human purpose, with an international outlook, should replace the hates and rivalries that have devastated the Balkan people for centuries.

On many occasions the agreements and disagreements over closer cooperation among the Balkan countries have depended on the personalities or the ambitions of the leaders. Recent visits of these leaders to their neighbors have helped to iron out differences among them and to prepare the ground for closer economic and sociopolitical relations. Emphasis should be given to commercial and economic exchanges, and sooner or later improvements in the sociopolitical arena will follow. Then all the Balkan people will be able to visit and work in any of the areas of the peninsula in which, in addition to so many differences and conflicts, they share many common interests.

There is always the possibility of regional or political disputes and frictions. But these probably would lead to greater isolation, restrictions on resource movements, loss of potential economies from large-scale production, and less economic and cultural development. Similar nationalistic differences existed among almost all the EU countries, but the need for a common economic policy and development subordinated them to a considerable extent. On the other hand, contemporary technological advancements in transportation and communications have helped to liquidate national and territorial differences, and to support trends toward closer friendship and even regional unification. The improvement of economic and political relations among the Balkan countries would induce a reduction in military spending, not only among these countries, but also among the big powers that have alliances with them.

After the drastic changes in Eastern Europe and the former Soviet Union in 1989, the winds of freedom and democracy were blowing through the Balkan region as well. Although ethnic rivalries, which were suppressed under communism, surfaced again, gradual and painful efforts are being made toward democracy and a market economy similar to that of the European Union with which they pursue closer relations. All the Balkan countries started moving rapidly toward privatization and free market reforms. However, Albania, Bulgaria, Romania, and former Yugoslavia, without democratic traditions and under government-controlled, or command, economies for a long time, move slowly and painfully toward economic and political reforms.

DANUBE BASIN OR EUXENE COMMON MARKET?

The establishment of a Danube basin common market, including the old Hapsburg countries, as a buffer against a reunited strong Germany seems impractical in present-day Europe. Such a group that may include Austria, Hungary, the Czech and Slovak republics, Romania, and the former Yugoslavia may be useful to the security interests of the European Union and particularly to a rejuvenated Germany for some time to come. However, an economic association and eventual integration with the EU is more effective and beneficial to all European countries, instead of departmentalizing the old continent in different fortress groups.

A similar intra-bloc common market for the Balkan countries (Albania, Bulgaria, Greece, Romania, Turkey, and the former Yugoslavia) is also impractical and not beneficial to the countries concerned. Intra-Balkan trade may impose costs upon the countries involved insofar as it means trade diversion. The beneficial effects of intrabloc trade on balance of payments, industrialization, and economic growth may not exceed the detrimental effects of trade diversion of a Balkan common market. This may be so because the Balkan countries produce mainly competitive primary products, not so much complementary products, and a formation of a common market may make them poorer instead.

The neighboring countries of the Black Sea—primarily Turkey, Romania, Greece, Bulgaria, Armenia, and Georgia—agreed to create "the union of Euxene countries." Aristotle, in his writings about wonderful hearings, named a similar formation at that time (fifth century B.C.) the common market of Euxene.[5] From an economic point of view, this infant union is not expected to have impressive results, mainly because these countries produce primarily competitive products. However, from a sociopolitical standpoint, such a union may prove to be beneficial for further cooperation, as a pioneering movement toward an eventual pan-European union, under the auspices of the EU. Already Greece is a full member and Turkey an associate member of EU, while the other neighboring nations are also expected to become associate members in the near future. Again, a closer cooperation with the EU may be more beneficial, although painful, for a transitional period of adjustment. In the meeting in Athens in April 1995, the Euxene countries pledged further cooperation.

THE EUROPEAN UNION AND THE BALKANS

The European Union: Formation and Expansion

The European Union (EU), which initially was named the European Economic Community (EEC) and for some time later the European Community (EC), was established in 1957 at Rome with six members—Belgium, Luxembourg, the Netherlands, France, West Germany, and Italy—commonly known as the "Inner Six." It was formed to gradually reduce internal tariffs. Because the group was successful, the United Kingdom and Denmark, as well as Ireland, joined the EU in 1973. Greece and Turkey became associate members of the EU in 1962 and 1964, respectively, and were allowed to export many of their products to the community free of duty, while retaining tariffs during a transition period. Special arrangements and association agreements have been negotiated or signed with a number of countries in Africa, the Middle East, Asia, and Latin America, as well as Spain and Portugal. Greece became the tenth full member of the EU in 1981, and Spain and Portugal became the eleventh and twelfth full members, respectively, in 1986.[6]

For Spain and Portugal a ten-year transitional period was provided for agricultural products and a seven-year period for fish, for which tariffs would be reduced by the EU. For industrial products, the transitional period was three years for Spain and seven years for Portugal. No time interval was provided for the introduction of the value added tax for Spain, and only three years was given to Portugal, compared to five years for Greece (extended for another two years, later). Also, a seven-year period was provided for the free movement of the Spanish and Portuguese workers in the EU, as was initially provided for Greece.

Austria, Finland, and Sweden became members of the EU in January 1995. Table 8.1 shows the main economic indicators of the EU countries.

To promote a better monetary system, the EU put into operation, on March 13, 1979, the European Currency Unit (ECU), as Article 107 of the Treaty of Rome enunciated. This new monetary unit is defined as the weighted average of member currencies. It was also agreed that in case of fluctuations of member currencies beyond a certain margin (2.25 percent, with some exceptions), the EU would intervene to preserve stability.

Perhaps the most important and difficult problem of the EU is that of the agricultural policy regarding subsidy payments from the northern to the southern (Mediterranean) member nations. This is one of the main functions of the Common Agricultural Policy (CAP), which deals with the determination of price support of the Mediterranean agricultural products, includ-

Table 8.1

Economic Indicators of the EU (European Union) Countries, 1994

Country	Population (millions)	Per Capita GNP (current dollars)	Average Annual Inflation 1980–92	Current Account Balance ($bill.)
Austria	7.9	22,380	3.6	-0.7
Belgium	10.0	20,880	4.1	5.4
Britain	57.8	17,790	5.7	-20.7
Denmark	5.2	26,000	4.9	4.7
Finland	5.0	21,970	6.0	-4.9
France	57.4	22,260	5.4	3.5
Germany	80.6	23,030	2.7	-25.6
Greece	10.3	7,290	17.7	-2.1
Ireland	3.5	12,210	5.3	2.6
Italy	57.8	20,460	9.1	-25.4
Luxembourg	0.4	22,895	4.2	-0.1
Netherlands	15.2	20,480	1.7	6.6
Portugal	9.8	7,450	17.4	-0.2
Spain	39.1	13,970	8.7	-18.5
Sweden	8.7	27,010	7.2	-5.2

Sources: World Bank, *World Development Report*; and International Monetary Fund, *International Financial Statistics*, both various issues.

Note: In some cases, earlier years' data were available.

ing those of Greece, southern Italy, and France, as well as those of the new members, Spain and Portugal. The southern European regions press for better prices while northern countries, particularly Germany and Britain, press for low prices of these products. Northern countries producing large amounts of meat and dairy products, such as Denmark, Belgium, and the Netherlands, collect sizable subsidies. For milk only, subsidies amount to about 30 percent of the total agricultural subsidies. Italy, Spain, Ireland, Greece, and Portugal also receive substantial subsidies for their agricultural products. Germany and Britain are the major contributors to such subsidy payment.

Nevertheless, Britain wants to reduce its net cost on EU membership, and Germany wants its share on union expenditures to be kept under control in the future.

The main decision-making bodies of the EU, that is, the Commission, the Council of Ministers, and the Europarliament, determine budgetary revenues and appropriations in accordance with the Treaty of Rome of 1957 and the consequent agreements and directives of the Union.

The treaty establishing the European Union (Treaty of 1957) guarantees free movement of persons within the member states. According to Article 7 of this treaty, "Within the scope of application of the Treaty, and without prejudice to any special provisions contained therein, and discrimination on grounds of nationality shall be prohibited." Therefore, workers can move freely and establish themselves, while self-employed persons can set up and manage undertakings in other member nations. The main goals of this provision and the open-door policy are to facilitate a supranational labor market, to enhance an integrated economic growth, and to promote a closer sociopolitical cooperation.

The EU, through the Competition Directorate, began to enforce ceilings on the value of regional incentives in order to prevent distortions in trade among members and to emphasize continentwide priorities. However, its actions supplant rather than supplement national efforts. The EU policies seem to favor imports of labor-intensive goods from less-developed countries and tend to defend old industries by recruiting temporary, migrant workers from less-developed parts of Europe, such as former Yugoslavia, Greece, and Turkey.

The EU has been successful in almost all fields. Labor, capital, entrepreneurs, and consumers are free to move and to compete in the markets of all member nations. Common agricultural, transportation, and other economic policies, uniform external tariffs, and coordinated monetary and fiscal measures are rapidly being advanced. Even political cooperation is being successfully promoted, in spite of differences in languages, cultures, and other areas. Both internal and external trade has increased, primarily because of the reduction in tariffs by high-duty countries during the creation of a common tariff policy.[7]

Moreover, the countries of the EU hold elections every five years for a European Parliament. This political movement is another milestone on the road to closer cooperation and eventual unification. The members of the parliament are elected directly by the people of each member country, instead of being selected from members of national parliaments, as was done before. This process is expected to strengthen the ideals of democracy and the principles of human rights among the members and, indirectly, among the countries associated with the EU. From an economic point of view, this trend would eliminate dangers from speculation, stabilize the

European currencies, and would reduce the possibility of severe recessions and high rates of unemployment.

About 50 percent of total EU revenue comes from the value added tax (VAT) which is 1 percent of those collected by the member countries, 33 percent from custom duties, and 13 percent from levies on certain agricultural products, such as sugar. For member nations that have not introduced the VAT as yet, GDP is used as the basis of VAT calculation.

Net budgetary allotments from the EU are received primarily by poorer member countries, whereas richer member countries usually have net payments. As a result of their demand for budget cuts in farm spending, EU meetings end, at times, in deadlock, leaving the fifteen-nation common market on the brink of bankruptcy. On the other hand, it is argued that, in terms of investment and new technology, Japan and the United States are leaving Europe behind.

On the international financial sector, the rapid development of the EU and world money markets cannot leave the monetary policies of the Balkan countries unaffected. The recent divergence of a rapidly growing "symbolic" economy of money, credit, and capital and a slowing "real" economy of goods and services has repercussions upon the determination of exchange rates, interest rates, and related policy measures in all Balkan countries. These countries borrow large amounts of money from the international capital market and are affected by interests and amortizations they have to pay. The epidemic of too much trading of money, bonds, and stocks, representing commercial assets, and not enough operation of the real assets in the production process, presents dangers not only for the more-developed EU and other countries but also for the less-developed economies of the Balkans.

The new trend of creating homogeneous money market services in the EU and expanding the role of the financial institutions on a worldwide basis requires significant reforms and innovations in the largely stagnating Balkan banking systems. Also, international competition in banking and money markets will, sooner or later, force deregulation, more effective operations, and aggressive marketing in all the Balkan nations. With the gradual shift of more financial activities to the money markets of the EU, innovative reforms in the Balkan banks, with perhaps less emphasis on their intermediate role and more on financial investment activities, become imperative.

Realignments of the currencies of the EU nations, linked under the European Monetary System (EMS), and currency speculations affect exchange rates and monetary policies in all Balkan nations. Interest rate differentials, trade performance, differences in productivities, strikes, and other disturbances force down the values of weak currencies and may drain the reserves of the respective central banks. All these events put pressure on the EMS, where currencies are permitted to fluctuate (by +2.25 percent against one another) and are expected to affect more and more future monetary decisions in the Balkan countries.

According to the regulations of the EU, all the trade and capital barriers within the EU states would be eliminated. In addition to free movement of commodities and investments, current account operations, short-term securities, and financial loans and credit would be covered. Also, the European Parliament endorsed a proposal by the EU Commission to abolish taxes on stock market transactions. These measures are expected to promote trade in securities and to improve the competitiveness of the EU as an international financial center. The less-developed Balkan economies, however, need far more time to introduce free movement of capital and to adjust to related EU rules.

Economic development and closer cooperation of the EU nations lead to their gradual currency unification. The introduction of the European Currency Unit (ECU), although weak at the beginning, slowly and steadily gains ground among the member nations and eventually in international financial markets. Because of low inflation and the growing, stable economies of Germany, Britain, and France, their currencies, especially the German mark, are among the soundest currencies in the world, making the ECU also an important monetary unit.

The European Currency Unit is based on a currency basket that includes the currencies of the EU member nations, but with different weights. The German mark carries the most weight (30 percent), followed by the French franc (19 percent), the British pound (13 percent), and the Italian lira (10 percent). Less weight has been assigned to the currencies of smaller member nations. Every five years, the ECU (recently named Euro) is adjusted to new weights, according to the share of every member to the gross domestic product (GDP) of the EU.

In cases of serious problems with the balance of payments of an EU member nation, articles 108 and 109 of the Rome Treaty of 1957 provide for a special committee that suggests measures of mutual support and possible deviations from certain obligations of the member states in question.

The Maastricht Treaty of 1991 provides that nations can qualify to enter the single European currency only if they reduce their budget deficits to less than 3 percent of GDP and their government debt to below 60 percent of GDP; inflation should be no more than 1.5 percent and long-term interest rates no more than 2 percent of the average of the three best-performing members, whereas exchange rate fluctuations should be no more than 2.25 percent, by 1999.

Greece as a Member of the EU

In order to retain and augment trade with Western European countries, Greece has pursued a policy of closer economic ties with the EU. As a result, an association agreement was signed on July 9, 1961, which became effective November 1, 1962. A transitional period of twenty-two years was allowed for gradual tariff reduction and preparation for full membership.

With the agreement of May 28, 1979, Greece became the tenth member of the EU, effective January 1, 1981. Despite the country's full membership, there were provisions for a five-year transitional period for agricultural products, in general, and a seven-year period for tomatoes and peaches, for which tariffs would be generally reduced by the, then, EEC and, now, EU. A similar five-year period was provided initially for Denmark, Ireland, and the United Kingdom. Another seven-year transitional period was provided for the free movement of Greek workers into other EU countries.

There was and still are, pro and con arguments concerning Greece's membership to the EU. Some economists and politicians argue that it will bring significant economic and political advantages in the foreseeable future. Others feel that the EU membership makes Greece a "provincial backwater," and it may not prove to be as beneficial as others believe; instead, the fascination with the EU membership may lead to serious hardships, at least with respect to some sensitive and protected industries.

It would seem that the joining of Greece with the EU would not entail a catastrophe for the country's economy, nor would it provide an answer for all its problems. From an economic, and especially from a sociopolitical, point of view, there would seem to be no better alternatives.

For protected small-scale and old-fashioned industries producing such goods as footwear, cloth, leather, and metal products, there is heavy pressure. Complete elimination of tariffs on imports from the EU and tariff reduction on imports from non-EU countries (in harmony with those of the EU) forced a number of industries and handicrafts operations to close. An example is the closing of Pitsos Company, producing refrigerators, which was taken over by a German concern.

Given that a large number of the Greek enterprises employ fewer than 10 persons, it is obvious what the EU membership means for such family-owned firms. Many of these protected small enterprises have been or would be wiped out. Moreover, the high elasticity of imports for their products or close substitutes (around two) would make things worse. In order to survive EU competition, such small enterprises should merge with larger ones that are able to apply the modern technology of mass production. However, the fact that labor cost is lower (about half) in Greece compared to that of the EU gives an advantage to these labor-intensive industries over their EU counterparts.

Nevertheless, Greece's entry into the EU has generated enthusiasm among many people, and may have stimulated modernization of the Greek economy and some dash of beaucratic inertia. Perhaps the intensive competition from the EU firms may have forced Greek entrepreneurs and middlemen earning high profits to reduce their luxurious and conspicuous consumption in favor of productive investment. But in the future such EU competition may prove detrimental to the economy as unemployment may be expected to increase, emigration of skilled persons to intensify, and the balance of trade to deteriorate.

In the near future there may be greater opportunities for Greece to increase exports to its Balkan neighbors and the Middle East than to the EU countries. EU duties for Greek industrial products have been eliminated since 1974, and no large thrust for these products is still expected.

Total Greek exports to the EU (about $6 billion in 1992, compared with about $199 million in 1960) are less than half of imports. This means that the EU is equally or more interested in keeping Greece in its economic sphere of influence, because it sells far more to Greece than it buys. Moreover, with the incorporation of the sizable Greek merchant fleet, representing 14 percent of the world tonnage, the EU would enhance its maritime power. At the same time, Greece needs the market of the EU, where it sells about half of its exports.

It is expected that Greek exports to the EU countries will rise, but not as much as imports, which are more than double the amount of exports. The increase in exports will take place primarily in agricultural products. However, exports of industrial products, for which EU duties have already been eliminated, are not expected to increase much. Another reason for low expectations for increases in industrial exports is the elimination of government subsidies and other tax privileges for such products as a result of Greece's accession to the EU. Therefore, the gap in the balance of trade would, most probably, continue to be large. From that point of view, EU membership should not frustrate efforts for further economic cooperation with other Balkan and Mediterranean countries.

Transportation is a sector in which membership to the EU has beneficial effects. It should continue to play its traditional favorable role in the economy, in general, and in the country's balance of payments, in particular. However, earnings from shipping depend primarily on changes in world trade. Empirical research indicates that Greek shipping earnings are affected by changes in the value of world exports and, to a lesser extent, by the number of seamen.

Greece receives support payments from the EU (Fond Europeen d'Orientation et de Garantie Agricole, or FEOGA), as a result of the implementation of EU regulations, for investment in storage facilities for wheat and corn and for the processing of fruits and vegetables, as well as for standardization of olives and olive oil. Moreover, there are annual payments for the price support of olive oil, sugar, tobacco, wheat, wine, peaches, tomatoes, and other fruits and vegetables, as well as for support of the fishing industry and cattle raising.

There seems to be no disagreement between the supporters and the critics of accession that the value of future business transactions of Greece with the EU is expected to further increase the gap in the balance of trade, since imports are expected to increase more than exports. Moreover, exports consist mostly of raw materials or semimanufactured products which do not greatly help to improve labor conditions. There is some improvement in the balance of payments as a result of incoming investment capital introduced by foreign multinationals, mainly from the EU. However, the inflow is not great, because foreign firms generally use host-country sources for financing, making it difficult for local enterprises to use domestic savings for investment. This has been the recent experience of foreign firms investing in developing countries. However, the inflow of capital for speculation and for the purchase of land is intensified, driving real estate prices further up.

Nevertheless, the "invisible" sources, especially tourism, shipping, and emigrant remittances, continue to play their traditional favorable role. But these sources and, even more, deposits from abroad, especially from emigrants, are the subject of international political and economic changes, and therefore are unstable and unpredictable. However, there is nothing wrong with Greece or any other country searching simultaneously for trade expansion and, possibly, other regional associations to the north, the east, or elsewhere. Such trade expansions would make the country a more independent and less subservient partner in the EU or in any other group. This policy would raise its prestige and improve its bargaining position in the future, instead of remaining a poor satellite of the EU. Therefore, Greece should explore the possibility of entering other economic groups or signing trade agreements with other nations, mainly the Balkan and other Mediterranean and Black Sea nations that import large amounts of Greek products. Accession to the EU should not discourage efforts for more cooperation among the Balkan countries. These pioneering efforts might be instrumental and helpful toward closer cooperation between the EU and Russia or the CIS nations.

In sector terms, the entry of Greece into the EU would mean more specialization and expansion in such agricultural lines as peaches, raisins, grapes, lemons, oranges, and olives. In general, agriculture is in an advantageous position when the EU subsidies for it are considered. In addition, many Greek farmers will be forced to modernize their production through mechanization, and will probably have to form larger farm units for cheaper production and distribution of their products. This is particularly important for Greek agriculture because of the fragmentation of land into small, inefficient lots (stamps). Similar favorable effects are expected in mining products, particularly bauxite, lignite, and aluminum.

As mentioned previously, another sector which benefits from the membership is transportation, especially shipping, mainly because of the country's geographic position and its large commercial fleet. The EU uses oil to cover 55 percent of its energy needs, and 90 percent of it is imported, mainly from the Middle East. Greek ships can transport oil as well as other products to and/or from the EU. The Greeks, then, can continue to make their fortunes from Homer's "wine-dark sea."

Tourism, already a flourishing sector, would not only keep its importance but expand further, mainly because of Greece's excellent climate and archaeological remains. It may be expected that this sector would continue to play a vital role in covering a large part of the country's balance-of-trade deficit.

Most difficulties occur in the industrial sector, mainly manufacturing, in which certain firms may expand, but most of them will be suppressed or wiped out. More important, the establishment of new ones would be difficult. It is not only that most European industries are more advanced and can produce cheaper and better products, but also that they will continue innovating and modernizing, making it difficult for old or new Greek industries to compete or even to survive.

From a sociopolitical point of view, as an integral part of the EU, Greece can expect to enjoy more protection and more respect from other countries. Moreover, the social structure of the country may improve, and its democratic institutions may be strengthened.

As an outpost on the European frontier, Greece would become the eastern Mediterranean balcony of the EU. As long as free movement of population and unrestricted property acquisition are allowed, rich Europeans, primarily Germans who exhibit a strong fondness for Greek touristic and archaeological centers, would settle permanently in the country, a process that has already begun, primarily in the islands. Such an economic "invasion" will be intensified when another EU candidate, Turkey, with many unemployed or underemployed workers, becomes a full member of the EU and enjoys the same freedom of movement and settlement in other member countries. *Mutatis mutandis*, similar results would be expected for other countries entering the EU, particularly the other Balkan countries.

Turkey's Relationship with the EU

In July 1959, Turkey applied for association with the EU. However, both parties were hesitant. Turkey's industry was too weak to face free competition, and the EU feared that Turkey would require significant economic assistance and that its cheap agricultural exports would present problems in the community. Nevertheless, Turkey became an associate member of the EU in September 1963. By the end of the summer of 1970, the EU concurred on Turkey's entry into the second stage of the development plan. In September 1980, the EU imposed a protocol freezing the association agreement with Turkey because of the abolishment of democracy and human rights by the then-established military dictatorship.

In order to prepare the ground for unfreezing the protocol that the EU imposed, Turkey promised a number of investments and trade opportunities to the EU member nations, particularly to Germany.

There is serious skepticism in Western Europe regarding the impact on the EU of the eventual acceptance of Turkey's petition for admission. The rapid population growth and the high rates of unemployment and underemployment would present severe problems in the EU countries with already high unemployment. Another problem would be the millions of Turkish peasant farmers and the millions of tons of produce expected to be brought under the community subsidies umbrella. The high cost of subsidizing and storing grain stocks, which absorbs a large portion of the total community budget, is expected to rise substantially. With Turkey, EU unsalable grain stocks are expected to rise significantly whereas the Common Agricultural Policy (CAP), already in serious difficulties, would be in jeopardy.

From a political standpoint, full membership of Turkey in the EU would bring a large number of delegates, more than 100, to the European Parliament. This number would increase year after year with the rapidly growing Turkish population. When the Turkish population reaches 70 to 80 million in the near future, Turkey, with some 150 members, would control about one-fourth of the total seats of the EU Parliament. Moreover, all the problems of Turkey, with so many troubled neighboring countries, would become, to some extent, problems for the European Defense Community that may gradually supplant NATO. Other difficulties the EU would encounter with Turkey's admission are the Turkish problems regarding human rights, the Kurdish and Armenian issues, and the occupation of 40 percent of Cyprus by Turkish troops.

From a demographic point of view, a serious problem may appear if Turkey becomes a full member of the EU and enjoys freedom of workers' movement and settlement in other member countries. In such a case, it would be expected that Greece, with relatively higher wages, would be flooded by unemployed or underemployed Turkish workers with the possibility of changing the largely homogeneous nature of the Greek population.

However, the free movement guarantees are not absolute and Articles 48(3) and 56(1) permit member states to control the influx of workers on grounds of "public policy," public security, or public health. The term "public policy" is broad, and its interpretation has been left largely to the national authorities. From that point of view, Greece may prohibit Turkish workers and entrepreneurs from entering freely and establishing themselves in the country. In the long run, though, such a discrimination on the basis of nationality is expected gradually to be reduced and eventually to be abolished in all EU states. Presently, Greece objects to granting the right of free movement within the EU to Turkish workers on economic and sociopolitical grounds, according to the accession agreement. Also, longstanding practices of discrimination and oppression against minority populations by Turkey should be stopped.

For Turkey's accession to the EU, adjustments are needed as rapidly as possible to the economic conditions required by the EU market and production technology. As long as it accepted that it is advantageous to enter the EU, Turkey must also accept that its domestic policies should change accordingly. This means that it has to operate under conditions of an open economy without any consideration of resorting to protective measures, even for infant and moribund industries. Advances in communications and transportation and the rapid diffusion of technology require that not only Turkey, but eventually all countries, including those of Western Europe and the Balkans, have to adjust their policies toward a global economy. The increased globalization of the world economy creates a spider's web of interdependent interest that no country can ignore without facing dire consequences. The lessons from the British economic policies, during the last quarter of the nineteenth century, suggest that protectionism and retaliation lead to marasmus and decay. As Alfred Marshall stated a century ago, such measures would eventually harm the countries involved. From that point of view, reduction in trade barriers by such groups as the EU would enhance free trade.

Although Turkey's association with the EU presents long-term economic and political advantages, in the short run, difficult conditions and even social disturbances may appear. Already, Turkey is expected to face serious problems in the near future. As it was expected, more efficient large industries in the more advanced EU nations can apply modern capital-intensive technology and produce cheaper and higher-quality products than their Turkish counterparts. The elimination of tariffs and other protective measures in Turkey may result, in many cases, in bankrupt or "problematic" industries and enterprises, in both the private and public sectors.

In order to have the support of the other EU nations, Turkey offers advantages for the establishment of large industrial projects, hotels and other tourist resorts, banks and other financial companies, and transportation and trade facilities, so that the EU can expand to the markets of Islamic nations. To the EU's southern members, Turkey would offer eventual support for favorable treatment of their agricultural and other Mediterranean products by the other EU nations.

Nevertheless, objections to the entrance of Turkey into the EU are advanced by Greece (according to the Treaty of Rome), mainly because of the bad treatment of the Greek populations in Istanbul (Constantinople) and the islands of Tenedos and Imvros in the Aegean. The confiscation of the properties of the Greeks in Turkey, illegal occupation of part of Cyprus by Turkish troops, and the harassment in the Aegean Sea are all additional reasons for such Greek objections. Nevertheless, Greece lifted its objections and in December 1995 Turkey was accepted in the customs union of the EU, effective January 1, 1996.

More than one-third of Turkish exports are absorbed by the EU (a slight increase from 1960), 3 percent by the United States (a decline from 24 percent in 1960 and 10 percent in 1970), and only 3 percent by the former Comecon countries (a decline from 9 percent in 1960 and 1970). The largest part (45 percent) is absorbed by the Middle East and North Africa (an increase from 22 percent in 1980).

During the first five years after the association, concessions were given by the EU to four basic agricultural exports, while the Protocol of 1970 provided for free access of all Turkish industrial products to the EU, except textiles and petroleum. In addition, a loan of $175 million was given by the EU over the first five years and additional amounts later.

After the military coup on September 12, 1980, the EU governments became critical of the loss of human rights and freedoms in Turkey. Particularly, the European Parliament and the Council of Europe expressed concern about the dissolution of trade unions and political parties and the imprisonment of their leaders and other people who disagreed with the regime.

Although Britain, Germany, and Belgium have been sympathetic to Turkey, following the U.S. foreign policy, other EU members are reluctant to admit Turkey to the EU until democracy has been fully restored and not implicitly or explicitly directed by the military.

Because of weak Turkish industry and the expected economic burden on other members from Turkey's cheap agricultural products, mainly cotton, and related EU subsidies, full membership is not predicted to take place in the near future.

Another serious problem is that of the free movement of labor provided by the above protocol. It would seem that it is impossible for the community, and especially for Germany, to absorb the large and growing numbers of unemployed Turks. Germany, with 1.6 million Turks, out of more than 2 million in the EU, faces problems of integration and possible repatriation of the Turkish workers. This is a sensitive issue for Ankara because of the substantial remittances received every year that are so valuable for closing the gap in the trade balance.

As an associate member, Turkey was allowed to export many products to the EU countries duty free, while gradually reducing tariffs on imports from the EU during the transition period of association. Turkish agricultural products would enjoy preferential treatment compared to those of other Third World countries. The EU would be expected to absorb surpluses at guaranteed prices, subsidize agricultural exports, and support regional development and structural adjustment in the Turkish economy.

The complete elimination of Turkish tariffs on imports from the EU leads not only to the reduction of customs revenue, but also to losses of income and employment. This is so because of the replacement of domestically produced industrial, as well as agricultural, goods (for which productivity is less of that in the EU) with imported goods. Special treatment of the Turkish products, along with similar Mediterranean products, seems to be needed for some time to come. In that case, the negative effects of the accession could be reduced through redistribution of taxes and EU grants for regional and social development, especially for the poor areas.

Turkish agriculture is inferior to that of the other EU countries. The average size of each farm in Turkey is smaller in comparison to those of the EU nations, farms are scattered over large distances, and the level of agricultural equipment is very low. Furthermore, agricultural population is more than 50 percent, compared to less than 10 percent, on the average, for the EU. As a result, farm productivity in Turkey is far lower than in the EU countries, and average income is even lower. The policy of the EU, which favors large agricultural units with modern equipment, leads to higher productivity in the long run, but to more unemployment and misery for the owners of small- and medium-size farms in the short run. Turkish farmers, with limited or no proper training, may try in vain to find jobs in the industrial sector, which is already under heavy pressure from EU competition. Therefore, pressure for migration of young farmers to European industries will continue.

Close relations between Turkey and the EU means that the economy is more open to international and EU competition. This means that if Turkey is unable to achieve the desired structural changes and improve its industrial position, it might be forced to specialize even more in the primary sector. Competition is expected to be more intensive after the reduction of tariffs on imports from the EU for such protected products as clothing, footwear, and metals. Moreover, the reduction of Turkish tariffs on similar imports from third countries to the levels of the EU would make things worse.

The government and the financial institutions, in exercising their fiscal and credit policies, should emphasize productive investment, mainly in the manufacturing and the exporting sectors. The fact that labor is relatively cheaper in Turkey than in the other EU countries should make such investment successful in reducing inflation and improving the balance of trade. Perhaps investment in entrepreneurial and technical training is the most promising endeavor to be pursued by public policy, both for long-term employment and high productivity.

Turkey wants full EU membership, but serious obstacles lie in its path that may delay actual membership until the end of the century and even longer. In addition to the Greek objections for economic reasons and for the conflict over Cyprus, doubts are expressed about Turkey's fitness for membership by other EU members as well. As mentioned previously, there are fears that Western Europe would be flooded with Turkish immigrant workers, while large subsidies would be paid by the EU to the agricultural sector, which absorbs about half of the work force and accounts for only one-fifth of the gross domestic product. Also, there is an ambiguity in Turkey's claim to be considered European at all, despite its recognition in the Treaty of Paris in 1856 and its associate membership in the EU since 1964. Moreover, there are fears that EU membership could provoke an Iran-style Islamic fundamentalist backlash among the poor classes, although most Turks adhere to Sunni rather than Shiite Islam.

RELATIONS OF FORMER YUGOSLAVIA WITH THE EU

Since 1970, when an EU–Yugoslavia Joint Committee was established, a number of trade and investment agreements have been signed. Also, a joint declaration of economic cooperation in Belgrade was signed on December 2, 1976, that marked a turning point in EU–Yugoslavia relations.

A few days later, the European Investment Bank granted loans of $68.5 million (50 million ECUs or 1.25 billion dinars) for such projects of mutual interest as the extension of the high-tension electricity network and its connection with Greece, Italy, and other European countries, as well as the construction and widening of the trans-Yugoslavian motorway, which provides a direct link between the community on the one hand and Greece, Turkey, and the Middle East on the other.

The former Yugoslav republics enjoy many benefits from the community's generalized system of preferences. Some 310 agricultural products and all manufactures and semimanufactures are covered by this system, which provides complete freedom from customs duties. However, certain ceilings or quotas have been laid down for different industrial products.

From the viewpoint of foreign trade, the former Yugoslavian republics depend more and more on the EU. One-fourth of their exports go to and close to half of their imports come from the EU. Former Yugoslavia was in the twelfth position among the community's customers and twenty-sixth among its suppliers until 1990. About half of the trade deficit was and still is with the EU.

The Multifibre Arrangement of 1976, which has been renewed repeatedly, provided that Yugoslavia would exercise voluntary restraint in its exports of a number of textile products, such as cotton yarn, knitted undergarments, pullovers, and trousers. Other agreements provided for closer cooperation in the fields of telecommunications, air and water pollution, metallurgy, and research projects.

In the 1980s, Yugoslavia and the EU signed new agreements that permit gradual reduction of tariffs for Yugoslav exports of large quantities of wine, fruits, beef, textiles, metals, and other industrial products and extended investment loans.

In the EU–Yugoslavia cooperation agreements, provisions were made for specific tariff concessions on products of particular interest to Yugoslavia. For a number of industrial products, tariffs would be reduced in stages. However, Yugoslavia would introduce or increase tariffs or quantitative restrictions insofar as such measures would be necessary for the protection of certain industries and the workers associated with them. Special attention was to be given to the fields of energy, transportation, tourism, and fishing because of their importance to both parties, as well as to the Yugoslav workers in the EU member countries. Moreover, further cooperation to promote the free trade zone established between Italy and Yugoslavia by the Osimo agreement were stipulated.

In the long run, all these economic activities aimed not only at the actual increase in trade, but also at closer sociocultural and political cooperation of the EU and Yugoslavia. Furthermore, former Yugoslavia, together with Greece, constitutes a natural bridge between Central Europe and the oil-producing Middle East countries that is of vital importance to the EU for its energy needs. One can speculate that even the negotiations and the timing of Greece's entrance into the EU were affected, to a large extent, by such considerations. Therefore, EU concessions to Yugoslavia may be justified on those grounds. In the future it would seem desirable for the EU to admit the former Yugoslav republics. This would not only facilitate traffic and stimulate trade, but it would also increase the EU's political influence in the Balkan and eastern Mediterranean regions.

Unfavorable weather conditions, mainly during the winter, and ethnic and other disturbances in the former Yugoslavia and other Balkan nations make transportation of passengers and products from the central and northern European countries to Greece and the Middle East, and vice versa, problematic. From that standpoint, other routes and transportation means, such as shipping from the western ports of Greece to Italy and other EU countries, play a vital role for the development of trade and tourism. Thus, the Greek ports of Patras and Igoumenitsa-Corfu facilitate a growing number of shipping routes to Brindisi, Agona, and other ports of Italy. Not only is the number of cargo ships growing, but new cruise-ferry boats are being built to facilitate fast transportation of passengers. Patras then can become an important gateway to Europe. Also, improvement of the Egnatia highway (initially built during the period of the Roman Empire), connecting the Adriatic coast-Salonika-Istanbul is expected to increase EU–Middle

East trade and investment. Moreover, further widening of the Athens-Patras highway will improve internal and external transportation in the area.

EU RELATIONS WITH OTHER BALKAN COUNTRIES

In 1949, Bulgaria and Romania joined the former Soviet Union and other Eastern European countries to create the Council of Mutual Economic Assistance (CMEA), or Comecon. Albania joined Comecon in 1949, and Yugoslavia became an observer.

Initially Comecon was not too effective, mainly because of the lack of raw materials and labor. Its longevity and expansion have made it more effective on matters of regional cooperation and economic development. However, transactions between the member nations remained mostly bilateral and, to a limited extent, multilateral. In contrast with the EU, where market integration was stressed, Comecon emphasized production integration and long-term economic development. Comecon was dissolved in 1990.

The mutual needs for raw materials, capital, and technology will probably force greater cooperation between the Balkans and the EU. It is expected that more multinational corporations and joint ventures on financial, infrastructural, and other projects will take place. The special drawing rights of IMF or other internationally accepted currency probably will help improve economic and sociopolitical relations in the area.

The trend toward more foreign trade in Albania, Bulgaria, Romania, and former Yugoslavia makes them not fully immune to stagflation emanating from abroad. In spite of their largely controlled economies, they are affected by world economic changes.

In light of further trade and investment cooperation, it would seem that the trend toward more economic transactions does not represent a new movement toward integration, but a policy of gradually abandoning autarky in favor of a more open trade among neighboring nations. The aim is to avoid scarcities, eliminate trade obstacles, and improve economic and political relations.

Special trade agreements have been enacted between the EU and the Balkan countries. In March 1980, Romania signed an agreement with the EU to reduce restrictions and increase mutual trade in industrial and other products, whereas negotiations for the EU association of Albania, Bulgaria, and Romania continue.

A serious cause of high trade deficits and the huge debts of the Balkan nations is the low level of investment. The low level of private investment, in turn, is due primarily to the lack of confidence, bureaucratic inertia, lack of innovative entrepreneurship and modern management, and strong competition from well-established firms in the EU and other advanced countries. Capital owners prefer short-run financial investment in stocks, bonds, and other instruments, or deposits with financial institutions, with quick returns, at the neglect of long-term real investment in plant and equipment.

It can be argued that association or membership with the EU would be beneficial in the long run from both an economic and a political point of view. However, for some years to come, severe problems of unemployment, high trade deficits, and reduction in the real per capita income may be the result, especially for Albania, Bulgaria, and Romania.

The value of future business transactions of the Balkan countries with the EU is expected to widen the gap in the balance of trade, since imports are expected to increase more than exports. There would be some improvement in the balance of payments as a result of incoming investment capital introduced by EU and American companies. Another sector expected to benefit from the accession is transportation, mainly because of the geographical position of the Balkans in relation to Europe and the Middle East.

The Albanian, Bulgarian, Romanian, and other Balkan economies need structural changes toward industrialization and improvements in their tax system. Close relations with the EU are expected to speed up such structural changes and bring some limitations on matters of policy making, not only on tariffs and foreign trade in general, but also on a number of domestic economic policies, such as adjustment of taxes, elimination of export subsidies, budgetary appropriations, exchange rate fluctuations, and the like. For the Balkans, a transitional period may be provided initially for the review and application of the value added tax and other reforms that were badly needed, independent of the EU membership. The Balkans, though, may be provided with enough time to implement tax reforms that are expected to reduce bureaucracy and increase the productivity of the public sector. Moreover, there will be less confusion over tax legislation in the long run.

FUTURE EXPECTATIONS

Currently the break of the former Yugoslavia into independent republics presents problems to the EU and even some deaths to the EU peace mission in the fighting among Serbs, Croats, and Muslims. A proper policy for the EU may be to accept them as associate members. The same policy may be followed for the other Balkan states, primarily Albania, Bulgaria, and

Romania. Such a plan of enlarging the EU, by incorporating the Balkan Peninsula, can induce the peoples of the region to work hard, have high hopes for the future, and adopt rapid economic and political adjustments to EU policies and directives, including adaptation of democratic principles.

It seems that closer relations with the European Union would reduce or eliminate disturbances and improve the socioeconomic conditions of these countries. In a letter to the leaders of the major EU and Balkan nations, I suggested that they pursue vigorously the entrance of the Balkan countries in the EU at the present time. The cost from tariff reduction and other assistance would be less than the ongoing military involvements through the United Nations, NATO, and other groups or countries. Membership of the Balkan countries in the EU would steam out ethnic and religious conflicts, increase the EU–Middle East trade and investment, and give hope for economic and sociopolitical improvement to the peoples involved.

The office of the British prime minister answered that "Mr. Major has asked that your letter and the closure be passed to the Department with particular responsibility for the matter you raise so that they, too, are aware of your views." The office of the president of France answered that "[President] Francois Mitterrand has always stated that in time, the central and eastern European countries would become part of the union, in an integral way and without shortcuts or compromises" (translated from French). However, President Mitterrand emphasized that probationary periods can be introduced, as in the case of Britain and Spain, for the Balkans and other European countries, including Cyprus and Malta, which are little prepared to be thrown into this grand union without borders. In that way, enlargement would not be contradictory to deepening, so that to avoid emptying, little by little, the existing European Union, regarding its content, structure, and strength. At the same time, the other countries must share objectives and respect the guidelines of the EU.[8]

The main problem for the EU to incorporate the Balkan countries is the price support of farmers, which already cost $60 billion a year paid mainly to Portugal, Spain, and Greece primarily by Germany, Britain, Belgium, and the Netherlands. But such subsidies can be converted to income supplements instead.

The expectations of Poland, the Czech and Slovak republics, and Hungary to join the EU create favorable conditions for the inclusion of the Balkan states in the EU. Moreover, such an enlargement would be advantageous geographically, not only for the Balkans through more efficient transportation networks, but for all EU members that would use the Balkan

Peninsula as a natural bridge for mutual trade and investment with the Middle Eastern countries.

Rapid improvements in transportation and communications, the spread of multinational companies, and twenty-four–hour access to stock markets in a global economy liquidate nationalism and the notion of sovereignty. From that standpoint, the EU should consider further enlargement, incorporating Eastern European and Balkan countries and introducing a domestic and free market system, without frontiers, all over Europe. Although there are growing pains from domestic economic, religious, and political feuds, the EU has to overcome borders and the emotion of virginity of sovereignty. Ethnic conflicts in the former Yugoslav republics show that movements to the opposite direction are far more painful economically, politically, and in terms of human lives. Market expansion and sociopolitical tranquility need to overcome borders and to introduce a new concept of transnational democracy.

Although quotation mongers may try to show the opposite, the increasing integration of Western Europe, moving toward united states of Europe, proves that the argument of the inevitability of war among capitalist countries is weak. The parallel integration process in the former Soviet republics (through the Commonwealth of Independent States, or CIS) and the increasing cooperation between the two groups (the EU and the CIS) indicate that some form of transition, and probably the genesis of a new common market, is in the process.

Nevertheless, Greece and Turkey spend large amounts of money for defense to protect themselves from each other. The paradox is that both nations belong to NATO. They are "presumably" allies. Also, they are related economically, because Greece is a member and Turkey an associate member of the EU. Their needs for further economic cooperation might be so important that eventually they might be forced to reduce their mutual mistrust and look for ways and means to improve the standards of living of their people, instead of spending large amounts of foreign exchange to buy rapidly depreciating military hardware.

From that point of view, Greece, which spends 7.2 percent of the GNP for defense (the highest in the NATO alliance) and keeps 2.35 percent of its population on active duty, could ask the EU creditors to press Turkey, economically and politically, to stop its old-fashioned expansionary policies in the Aegean and withdraw its occupation troops from Cyprus. Then, Greece would be able to use a part of foreign exchange, now spent for defense, for interest and principal debt payments to foreign banks. It would be in the interest of the creditor banks and the other EU countries to see

Greece and Turkey eliminate their fundamental imbalances between export earnings and interest payments and move to higher development plateaus.

Deep-rooted nationalistic differences between Greece and Turkey have been and still are exploited by major powers for their own interests. The European Union offers a good opportunity to reduce and even eliminate such differences and possible conflicts that proved to be so destructive in the past. Closer economic and, eventually, political ties with the EU would make them partners in a common cause, that of socioeconomic development, as happened with other EU nations, such as France and Germany.

Instead of fortifying their borders and preparing for further conflicts and wars, their EU membership could bring them together in lasting economic and technological progress. This is the way to improve the standard of living of their peoples and to move forward to new cultural, political, and economic cooperative ventures. Such a cooperation would reduce payments to other countries for army supplies and save resources for domestic investment. Then, unemployment would be reduced and production and income would increase many times over the initial investment (through the domestic multipliers).

Military expenditures constitute a large part of the budget and an even greater portion of foreign trade deficits. Both countries have to buy planes, tanks, rockets, and other armaments from other countries. Their disputes over Cyprus locked them into a mutual military buildup, because when one side's strength is comparable to another's, their mutual strength is a deterrent to war. As a result, defense spending drains their economies and deprives them of domestic investment and per capita income. Instead of spending on domestic projects to create jobs and increase per capita income, they spend their limited resources to buy more and more weapons that depreciate and rapidly become obsolete.

To keep up with new military technology, they have to buy new and more expensive war material, squeezing their economies further and tightening the belts of their people so that new resources can be saved for more payments for armaments and so on, ad infinitum. In that way, they create jobs and stimulate the economies of other countries that may have an economic interest in feuding and perpetuating regional conflicts in this strategic area. The EU membership, therefore, may be considered as a panacea for their mistrust and enormous military spending. Moreover, closer economic relations and eventual accession of Cyprus to the EU would make things easier for further cooperation of the three countries involved.

In our nuclear age, closer cooperation between neighbor nations becomes imperative. As a result of the fallout from Chernobyl near Kiev, Ukraine, in April 1986, large areas of Europe have been contaminated. Grass, grain, and fruits have been affected and demand for agricultural and dairy products has largely declined, particularly in Germany and other neighboring countries. This event indicated that political differences among European or other countries should be subordinated to the common efforts of avoiding nuclear or other similar dangers. It shows that all nations must look for the best in each other, not the worst. National conflicts should give way to common human causes. Economic and political convergence should be emphasized, on regional as well as international levels. Although we cannot undo technology, cooperation to improve it for the protection of humanity becomes urgent, even in nations with a history of mistrust and conflict such as the Balkans.

TRADE DEFICITS AND DEBT PROBLEMS

A common problem for the Balkan countries is the sizable deficit in the balance of foreign trade. More revenue from exports of goods and services is required to pay for growing imports, the value of the currency is under pressure of depreciation, and the credit position deteriorates. However, the geographical location of the countries in relation to the markets of Europe and the Middle East makes them important for trade and investment opportunities. All Balkan countries have introduced laws that encourage foreign investments, so that new technology can be acquired and hard currency can be earned.

Modest fiscal and monetary policies may be designed to spur growth, control inflation, and improve the balance of payments. However, in the effort to reduce trade deficits, care should be taken to avoid reduction of such imports as the machinery and raw materials needed for further development. Moreover, distributional and regional investment policies should not discourage technological innovations and long-run growth to the extent of severely impairing the international trade position of these countries.

Policies to reduce economic growth and moderate imports and price increases may make exports more competitive because of declining inflation. As a result of such policies, projections are that, even if the deficits of the balance of payments are eliminated, debt-servicing expenses would increase because of the previous debt obligations already undertaken. It is expected, therefore, that interest and amortization (domestic and foreign) would rise in the near future.

However, real debt would be substantially lower if inflation in creditors' currencies, mainly the dollar, occurs. Thus, a 5 percent annual inflation in such currencies would reduce real debt to less than half in ten years, while a 10 percent annual inflation would reduce it by more than 50 percent in only five years.

The policy of liberalization of the economies of the Balkan states and the emphasis on the free market forces of supply and demand is expected to lead to an increase of imports and high trade deficits. And this in spite of the favorable trade conditions with the nations of the Middle East and the EU countries. In order to reduce budget and trade deficits, Balkan and other European governments have imposed high taxes on gasoline. As a result, the price of gasoline remains high ($4 to $5, compared to about $1 to $1.50 in the United States, per gallon) despite the fact that petroleum prices are sometimes reduced. This makes public transportation attractive, reduces accidents and pollution, increases governmental revenue, and improves the balance of foreign trade.

A number of firms in all Balkan countries encounter financial difficulties because they cannot service their debt obligations. Managerial shortcomings and inefficient marketing techniques to promote products at home and abroad may be considered responsible for these difficulties. Moreover, many products are under official price control, and in many instances they cannot cover their costs from increased wages, raw material prices, and high interest rates.[9]

Commercial banks, which are, more or less, controlled by the Balkan governments, continue to finance such inefficient or "problematic" firms without requesting or enforcing improvement in organization, innovation, and competitiveness at home and abroad. The main reasons are that abandoning such moribund firms financially can lead to bankruptcy, the loss of the money already lent to these firms, and higher unemployment. As a result, the unorthodox and dangerous practice of short-term loans to such weak firms continues; short-term lending is rolled over to long-term financing, debts pile up, and the inflationary pressures are permanently looming behind these economies.

The Balkan countries are rich in mineral resources. Large amounts of minerals such as bauxite, lignite, and aluminum are exported in the form of raw materials primarily to the EU countries, while a good deal of finished metal products are imported from these countries. It would be proper, then for the Balkan countries to utilize fiscal and monetary policy incentives to develop their metal industries. Such a policy would help domestic employment and improve the balance of trade by reducing imports of metal products, the raw materials of which are produced in these countries.

Moreover, more value added taxes would be levied from the multistage process of manufacturing these products domestically.

Many enterprises are family owned and small in size and, as such, are unable to apply the modern technology of mass production. Nevertheless, labor costs are far less than those of the EU, and this gives a comparative advantage to the labor-intensive Balkan industries. It would seem that small enterprises need to merge into larger ones to be able to implement capital-intensive production techniques and advanced managerial know-how so that they can be efficient and competitive in domestic and foreign markets.

Loose taxing/spending policies significantly contribute to operating budget and foreign trade deficits as well as to rising prices and interest rates. Empirically, there is a close relationship between budget deficits and foreign trade deficits for the Balkans and for other countries. This means that government expenditures should be reduced, so that, depending on the income elasticity of demand, imports be reduced. The policy of reducing economic growth, for purposes of moderating inflation, would mean higher unemployment and perhaps reduction in per capita income, which leads to political costs for the governments in power.

As mentioned earlier, a major reason for the debts of the Balkan countries is their trade deficits. Imports are always higher than exports. The gap is so large that the earnings from tourism and other invisibles are not sufficient to cover the difference. As a result, deficits appear in current accounts, particularly with the EU. These deficits, in turn, usually lead to foreign borrowing and higher foreign debt.

Efforts to reduce imports of consumer or semiluxurious goods are expected to have better results in the short-run than aggressive strategies to increase exports. Exported products of the Balkan countries, such as fruits, vegetables, and other agricultural or semimanufacturing products, face strong competition in the EU and other markets, primarily from Spain, Portugal, Italy, and, to some extent, France. For some products, there is severe competition even among these countries.

Although exports are increasing year after year, the rise in imports is so high that it is difficult to reduce the huge trade deficits. As long as the world and, particularly, the EU economies are growing, austerity measures in one country, say Bulgaria or Romania, would not have a noticeable impact on the EU economic growth rates. Similarly, additional exports of the Balkan nations would not generate deterioration in everyone else's terms of trade. Therefore, additional exports of these deficit countries could be absorbed by other growing economies without much pain and dislocation in the more developed EU member nations, such as Germany, France, Britain, Italy, Belgium, and the Netherlands.

Hellas made many efforts to bring the Balkan countries together for closer cooperation, especially in the 1930s and 1970s. However, since the collapse of communism, she had more opportunities to play a decisive role for economic and geopolitical developments in the area. As a more advanced country, economically, democratically, and culturally, with strong connections to Western nations and as a member of the EU, she was expected to take stronger initiatives in the Balkan Peninsula. There were many economic opportunities in trade and investment after the reforms in the former socialist countries in 1991 and later. However, emphasis was given to domestic policy and consumption, financed through foreign and domestic public sector borrowing, leading to a total debt of more than dr 30 trillion or about $130 billion (around 120 percent of GDP).

The culmination of ethnic and religious conflicts in the Balkan region is expected to reduce hatred and stimulate cooperation. As a result of economic stabilization and geopolitical normalization in their relations, investment and trade among the Balkan countries, as well as between them, the EU and other countries, would grow rapidly. Already, scores of European and American companies are moving into the dynamic and profitable Balkan markets, either alone or in joint adventures with local enterprises.

Notes

CHAPTER 1

1. More information in Terrot Glover, *The Challenge of the Greeks and Other Essays* (New York: Macmillan, 1942), chaps. 1–3; and Nicholas V. Gianaris, *The Economies of the Balkan Countries: Albania, Bulgaria, Greece, Romania, and Yugoslavia* (New York: Praeger, 1982), chap. 1.

2. General Secretariat of the Region of East Macedonia-Thrace, *Thrace* (Athens: Idea Advertising-Marketing SA, 1994), 48–52; and Pausanias (Attica I, IX, 5).

3. C. Stanley, *Roots of the Tree* (London: Oxford University Press, 1936), 24.

4. Further review in W. Tarn and G. Griffith, *Hellenistic Civilization*, 3d ed., rev. (London: Edward Arnold, 1952), chaps. 4, 7.

5. For the early history of Slavs, see B. Grekov, *Kiev Rus* (Moscow: Foreign Languages Publishing House, 1959), chaps, 2, 8; and Nicholas V. Gianaris, *Greece and Yugoslavia: An Economic Comparison* (New York: Praeger, 1984), chap. 1.

6. More details in Hugh Poulton, *The Balkans: Minorities and States in Conflict*, foreword by Milovan Djilas (London: Minority Rights Publications, 1991), 39, 57, 76. Also, Raymond Bonner, "Albanians in Kosovo Fearful of U.S. Deal with Yugoslavia," *New York Times*, April 9, 1995, A13.

7. Henry Camm, "Conflict With Greece Leaves Some in Albania Perplexed," *New York Times*, December 19, 1994, A13; and Poulton, *The Balkans: Minorities and States in Conflict*, 198–201.

8. Poulton, *The Balkans: Minorities and States in Conflict*, 182–83.

9. Ernest Barker, *The Political Thought of Plato and Aristotle* (New York: Dover Publications, 1959), 391.

CHAPTER 2

1. There were regular routes and established freight and passenger rates between Athens and other Balkan cities. "For example, one could go from Athens . . . to the Black Sea for two drachmas, that is for four days' pay for a rower, which seems convenient." C. Stanley, *Roots of the Tree* (London: Oxford University Press, 1936), 24.

2. Loans for shipping trips from Piraeus to the Black Sea, mainly carrying wheat, were granted with an interest rate of 3 percent per round trip. T. Glover, *The Challenge of the Greeks and Other Essays* (New York: Macmillan, 1942), 59.

3. H. Schonfield, *The Suez Canal in Peace and War, 1869–1969* (Miami: University of Miami Press, 1969), 4.

4. For comments on Plato's and Xenophon's writings on the division of labor and productivity, see T. Lowry, "Recent Literature on Ancient Greek Economic Thought," *Journal of Economic Literature* 17 (March 1979): 65–86.

5. W. Tarn and G. Griffith, *Hellenistic Civilization*, 3d ed., rev. (London: Edward Arnold, 1952), chaps. 4, 7.

6. For a penetrating and well-documented historical review, see L. S. Stavrianos, *The Balkans Since 1453* (New York: Holt, Rinehart and Winston, 1958), pt. I; and F. Schevill, *The History of the Balkan Peninsula*, rev. ed. (New York: Harcourt Brace, 1933), chaps. 1, 2.

7. J. Toutain, *The Economic Life of the Ancient World* (New York: Alfred A. Knopf, 1930), 232.

8. A thorough review of the early history of the Slavs is provided by B. Grekov, *Kiev Rus* (Moscow: Foreign Languages Publishing House, 1959), chaps. 2, 8.

9. This primitive communistic system of the early Slavs maintained a substantial economic and political equality among the pastoral and agricultural people who produced "an abundance of cattle and grain, chiefly millet and rye," as Emperor Maurice said. Schevill, *The History of the Balkan Peninsula*, 74–75. It is also argued that Romanian society, with its communal villages, did not pass through a feudal stage, but moved from something like egalitarian communalism to capitalism. H. Stahl, *Traditional Romanian Village Communities*, trans. D. Chirot and H. Chirot (New York: Cambridge University Press, 1980).

10. For more on the administrative problems of Byzantium, see R. Wolff, *The Balkans in Our Time* (New York: W. W. Norton, 1967), chap. 4.

11. Schevill, *The History of the Balkan Peninsula*, 10. For more detailed accounts, see L. Kirnoss, *The Ottoman Centuries, The Rise and Fall of the Turkish Empire* (New York: Morrow, 1977); S. Shaw, *History of the Ottoman Empire and Modern Turkey* (London: Cambridge University Press, 1976–77).

12. K. Paparrhegopoulos, *Historia tou Hellinikou Ethnous: Apo ton Arnchaiotaton Chronon Mechri ton Neoteron* (History of the Greek Nation: From the Ancient Years until the Recent Years) (Athens: S. Pavlidou, 1874), pt. A, 538.

13. The Ottoman Empire established the Phanariot regime in Moldavia (1711) and in Walachia (1716). The Phanariot rulers, chosen by the Porte from among the Greek aristocracy in Constantinople, used political oppression and economic exploitation until 1821. *Romania: Yearbook, 1976* (Bucharest: Scientific and Encyclopedic Publishing House, 1976).

14. For a short survey see E. Foster, *A Short History of Modern Greece, 1821–1956* (New York: Praeger, 1957), chap. 1.

15. From 1833 to 1863, Prince Otto of Bavaria ruled Greece. From then until 1967, Prince George of the Danish Glucksberg Dynasty and his descendants were enthroned with a few interruptions (mainly 1924–35 and 1941–46).

16. For further details see G. Hoffman, *The Balkans in Transition* (Princeton, N.J.: Van Nostrand, 1963), 52; A. Pepelasis, "The Legal System and Economic Development of Greece, *Journal of Economic History* 19, no. 2 (June 1959): 174–76.

17. Leadership was feeble among the Slavs in the centuries of their unchanging and relatively protected life. J. Schumpeter, *The Theory of Economic Development* (New York: Oxford University Press, 1961), 88.

18. Stavrianos, *The Balkans Since 1453*, 275.

19. Ibid., 299.

20. Ottoman exports of cotton and thread increased from 2.8 million *okas* in 1750 to 8.1 million *okas* in 1787 (one *oka* equals 1.28 kilograms or 2.82 pounds), while export tariffs declined from 5 percent to around 1 percent of the value of exports. Ibid., 286–88. The pattern of production of silk, cotton and raw material was dictated by European economic conditions. M. Czakca, "Price History of Bursa Silk Industry: A Study in Ottoman Industrial Decline, 1550–1650," *Journal of Economic History* (September 1980), 533–50.

21. For further information see W. Gewehr, *The Rise of Nationalism in the Balkans, 1800–1930* (Hamden, Conn.: Archon Books, 1967), chap. 2.

22. Clyde Farnsworth, "The Rise and Fall of Civilization According to Tax Collection," *New York Times*, October 3, 1993, E7. More details in Stavrianos, *The Balkans Since 1453*, 82–85; and Schevill, *The History of the Balkan Peninsula*, 10.

23. For an extensive bibliography see G. Torrey, "Some Recent Literature on Romania's Role in the First World War," *East European Quarterly* 14, no. 2 (Summer 1980): 189–206.

24. For these estimates, see W. E. Moore, *Economic Demography of Eastern and Southern Europe* (Geneva: League of Nations, 1945), 26; D. Kirk, *Europe's Population in the Interwar Years* (Geneva: League of Nations, 1946), 263ff.

25. Winston Churchill, *Memoirs of the Second World War* (Boston: Houghton Mifflin, 1959), 885–86.

CHAPTER 3

1. G. Botsford and E. Sihelr, eds., *Hellenic Civilizations* (New York: Columbia University Press, 1915), chaps. 1, 2; and G. Botsford and C. Robinson, Jr., *Hellenic History*, 5th ed. rev. D. Kagan (London: Macmillan, 1971), chaps. 1–3. For the period of Minoan (Cretan) civilization see Adam Hopkins, *Crete: Its Past, Present and People* (London: Faber, 1977), chap. 2. For the years 800–500 B.C. see C. Strarr, *The Economic and Social Growth of Early Greece: 800–500* B.C. (New York: Oxford University Press, 1977).

2. The first coins appeared in Lydia (Asia Minor) and in the Aegina island (near Athens), during the sixth century B.C. By that time, the Greek merchants managed to prevail over the Phoenicians in seabound trade. For more details, see Norman Angell, *The Story of Money* (New York: F. A. Stokes, 1929), chap. 4. Further valuable information is provided in T. Glover, *The Challenge of the Greeks and Other Essays* (New York: Macmillan, 1942), 78; and C. Stanley, *Roots of the Tree* (London: Oxford University Press, 1936), 24. For related philosophical discussions see E. Barker, *The Political Thought of Plato and Aristotle* (New York: Dover, 1959), chap. 9; and T. Lowry, "Recent Literature on Ancient Greek Economic Thought," *Journal of Economic Literature* 17 (March 1979), 65–86.

3. For more details see Andreas Andreades, *A History of Public Finance in Greece* (Cambridge, Mass.: Harvard University Press, 1933), 53–59; Augustus Boeckh, *The Public Economy of Athens* (New York: Arno Press, 1976), chap. 5, 494–510; and Nicholas V. Gianaris, "Greeks Had a Word for Reagan Tax Plan," *New York Times*, January 1, 1985, A26.

4. *Xenophon's Works*, trans. C. Ashley et al. (Philadelphia: Thomas Wardle, 1843), 681–91. Aslo M. Austin, *Economic and Social History of Ancient Greece: An Introduction* (Berkeley: University of California Press, 1977).

5. J. P. Mahaffy, *Rambles and Studies in Greece*, 2d ed. (London: Macmillan, 1878), chap. 6; and Arnold Toynbee, *Some Problems of Greek History* (London: Oxford University Press, 1969), pt. III.

6. J. Carey and A. Carey, *The Web of Modern Greek Politics* (New York: Columbia University Press, 1968), 31–33.

7. During the Roman period, Greece (Achaea) abounded in learning, but she was not self-sufficient in grain. J. Day, *An Economic History of Athens under Roman Domination* (New York: Arno Press, 1973), chap. 7; and W. Tarn and G. Griffith, *Hellenistic Civilization*, 3d ed., rev. (London: Edward Arnold, 1952), 266.

8. Byzantium was the name of the city given by the Dorians of Megara (a city on the Greek mainland west of Athens) who had established colonies at the eastern end of the Propontis (Sea of Marmara) in the Dardanelles during the seventh century B.C.

9. There, monks continue to follow the Byzantine tradition and even to live "isolated from all female life, whether hens, nanny goats, or women." Carey and

Carey, *The Web of Modern Greek Politics*, 36. See also D. Nicol, *The End of the Byzantine Empire* (New York: Holmes and Meier, 1979), chap. 4.

10. Arnold Toynbee, *Constantine Porphyrogenitus and His World* (London: Oxford University Press, 1973), 176–84; and J. Bury, *A History of the Eastern Roman Empire* (New York: Russell and Russell, 1966), chap. 7. Also, Moses Finley, *The Ancient Economy* (Berkeley: University of California Press, 1973), chap. 6.

11. Carey and Carey, *The Web of Modern Greek Politics*, 35.

12. B. Ward, *The Interplay of East and West* (London: Allen and Unwin, 1957), 22.

13. John Lampe and Martin Jackson, *Balkan Economic History, 1550–1950* (Bloomington: Indiana University Press, 1982), chap. 1; and D. Zakynthinos, *The Making of Modern Greece: From Byzantium to Independence*, trans. K. Johnstone (London: Basil Blackwell, 1976), chap. 6. For the Russian involvement, see Richard Clogg, *A Short History of Modern Greece* (New York: Cambridge University Press, 1979), 30–31; and George V. Giannaris, *Fititika Kinimata kai Elliniki Pedia* (Students' Movements and Hellenic Education), vol. I (Athens: Pontiki Press, 1993), 35.

14. L. S. Stavrianos, *The Balkans Since 1453* (New York: Holt, Rinehart and Winston, 1958), 276, 298–99.

15. For the cooperative nature of Ampelakia industries see J. Kordatos, *T'Ampelakia Ki'o Mythos Gia To Syneterismo Tous* (Athens: K. Strate, 1955), chaps. 4, 8. For the support of the Greek mercantile diaspora, see the valuable articles in R. Clogg, ed., *The Movement for Greek Independence, 1770–1821* (London: Macmillan, 1976).

16. Nicholas Kaltchas, *Introduction to the Constitutional History of Modern Greece* (New York: Columbia University Press, 1940), 11.

17. More details in Nicholas Gianaris, *The Province of Kalavryta: A Historical and Socioeconomic Review* (New York: National Herald, 1983), chap. 3.

18. William McGrew, *Land and Revolution in Modern Greece, 1800–1881* (Kent, Ohio: Kent State University Press, 1985), chap. 10; and C. Crawley, "Modern Greece, 1821–1930," in W. Heurtley et al., *A Short History of Modern Greece* (Cambridge: Cambridge University Press, 1965), 101.

19. Peloponnesus and the poverty-stricken Cyclades islands, particularly Delos (the great shrine of Apollo), Mykonos, Naxos, and Syros, with their barren soil and overfished seas, had a better cultural and economic life under Venetian than Ottoman control, primarily in artistic and tourist activities. Carey and Carey, *The Web of Modern Greek Politics*.

20. Loan sharks, thieves, and the power of the strong prevailed in many regions. Dominant classes and political elites with oligarchic clienteles exercised decisive influence upon the people. At the same time, the growing commercial bourgeoisie failed to exercise its political power.

21. Stavrianos, *The Balkans Since 1453*, 296–99.

22. Ibid.

23. For more details of this revolt and the formation of a new constitution in 1911, see Victor Papacosma, *The Military in Greek Politics: The 1909 Coup d'Etat* (Kent, Ohio: Kent State University Press, 1977).

24. Aurel Braun, *Small-State Security in the Balkans* (Totowa, N.J.: Barnes and Noble Books, 1983), 40–44.

25. Edward Foster, *A Short History of Modern Greece, 1821–1956* (New York: Praeger, 1957), 160.

26. H. Richter, *1933–1946: Dio Epanastasis kai Antepanastasis Stin Ellada* (Two Revolutions and Counterrevolutions in Greece), 2 vols. (Athens: Exantas, 1975), trans. from German; and J. Koliopoulos, *Greece and the British Connection, 1935–1941* (Oxford: Clarendon Press, 1977), chaps. 4, 6.

27. For a detailed review, see Gianaris, *The Province of Kalavryta*, chap. 4.

28. For further comments, see C. Woodhouse, *Apple of Discord: A Survey of Recent Greek Politics in Their International Setting* (London: Hutchinson, 1948), 146–47; and C. Myers, *Greek Entanglement* (London: Rupert Hart-Davis, 1955), chaps. 10, 18.

29. Winston Churchill, *Triumph and Tragedy: The Second World War*, vol. 6 (Boston: Houghton Mifflin, 1953), 325.

30. For more details, see Clogg, *A Short History of Modern Greece*, chap. 6.

31. For more detailed events see George V. Giannaris, *Mikis Theodorakis: Music and Social Change* (New York: Praeger, 1972), chap. 2; S. Xydis, *Greece and the Great Powers, 1944–1947* (Thessaloniki: Institute for Balkan Studies, 1963), chap. 2; E. O'Ballance, *The Greek Civil War, 1944–1949* (London: Faber and Faber, 1966), chaps. 4, 5.

32. For a detailed review see C. Munkman, *American Aid to Greece* (New York: Praeger, 1978), chap. 4; H. Psomiades, "The Economic and Social Transformation of Modern Greece," *Journal of International Affairs* 19 (1965): 194–205; Theodore Couloumbis, *The United States, Greece and Turkey* (New York: Praeger, 1983), chap. 1; and articles in Theodore Couloumbis and John Iatrides, eds., *Greek American Relations: A Critical Review* (New York: Pella, 1980).

33. Walter Lippmann in the *Herald Tribune*, April 1, 1947, reprinted in S. Rousseas, *The Death of a Democracy: Greece and the American Conscience* (New York: Grove Press, 1967), 84.

34. Rousseas, *The Death of a Democracy*, 83. See also W. McNeill, *The Greek Dilemma* (London: Victor Gollancz, 1947), 75–76; and Carey and Carey, *The Web of Modern Greek Politics*, 164–68.

35. For more details on U.S. involvement in Greek political affairs, see A. Papandreou, *Democracy at Gunpoint* (New York: Doubleday, 1970), chaps. 1, 2. Also, Kostas Athanasiades, *Diethnis Oikonomikes Sygrousis, 1945–1990* (International Economic Conflicts, 1945–1990) (New York: Kampana, 1990), 70–72, 115; and Athanasios Strigas, *Pagosmii Entolodohi* (Global Agents) (Athens: Nea Thesis, 1994), chaps. 8–11.

36. Carey and Carey, *The Web of Modern Greek Politics*, 164, 213.

37. Post–World War II governments came and went one after another in Greece with the following Prime Ministers: P. Tsaldaris, 1946–47; J. Sophoulis, 1947–49; N. Plastiras, 1950; S. Venizelos, 1951; A. Papagos, 1952–55; C. Caramanlis, 1955–63; G. Papandreou, 1963–65; (after G. Athanasiades-Novas and E. Tsirimokos failed to form a government) S. Stephanopoulos, 1965–66; Ioannis Paraskevopoulos, 1966–67; P. Kanellopoulos, 1967; military dictatorship, controlled by Col. G. Papadopoulos, 1967–73, and Maj. D. Ioannides, 1973–74; C. Caramanlis, 1974–80; G. Rhallis, 1980–81; A. Papandreou, 1981–89; S. Tzanetakis, 1989–90; X. Zolotas, 1990–91; C. Mitsotakis, 1991–93; A. Papandreou, 1993–96; Costas Simitis, January 22, 1996–present.

38. Kerin Hope, "Greece to Float 8% of State Telecoms Monopoly," *Financial Times*, May 30, 1995, 14.

CHAPTER 4

1. The shift from private to public enterprises (statism), in which the government owned at least 50 percent, presented serious problems of efficiency, especially in mining, wood and paper, oil refining, basic metals, and chemical industries. OECD and IMF economists have been critical of such subsidized inefficient SEEs. Richard Nyrop, ed., *Turkey: A Country Study* (Washington, D.C.: American University Press, 1980), chap. 3.

2. Morris Singer sees reverse trend of westernization promoted by Kemal Ataturk and the Islamic revival. See his *Economic Developments in the Context of the Short-Term Public Policies: The Economic Advance of Turkey, 1938–1960* (Ankara: Turkish Economic Society, 1978).

3. The two main parties before the dictatorship were the Justice Party under Suleiman Demirel, who was prime minister in 1965–71, 1975–78, and 1979–80; and the Republican People's Party under Bulent Ecevit, prime minister in 1974 and 1978–79. Nyrop, *Turkey: A Country Study*, chap. 4 and 303–4.

4. C. W. Ceram (pseud. for Kurt Marek), *The Secret of the Hittites: The Discovery of an Ancient Empire* (New York: Alfred A. Knopf, 1956); Nyrop, *Turkey: A Country Study*, chap. 1.

5. M. J. Cook, *Greeks in Ionia and the East* (London: Thames and Hudson, 1962).

6. Emperor Augustus, Julius Caesar's adopted son and heir (first century B.C.), selected Aphrodisias, a site in southwest Turkey, with Aphrodite's temple and other monuments, as his city, granting it autonomy and tax-free status. More details in Kenan Erim, *Aphrodisias* (New York: Facts on File, 1986). Also Jules Toutain, *The Economic Life of the Ancient World* (New York: Alfred A. Knopf, 1930), 232; and John E. Day, *An Economic History of Athens under Roman Domination* (New York: Arno Press, 1973), chap. 7.

7. Claude Cahen, *Pre-Ottoman Turkey* (New York: Tabbinger, 1968), 318–35; and William Davis, *A Short History of the Near East* (New York: Macmillan, 1937).

8. A serious attack by the Venetians took place in 1687 when they bombarded and partially damaged the Parthenon, which was used as a powder magazine by the Muslims.

9. Under the timar system, "Ottoman onslaught . . . destroyed peasant villages and generally disrupted settlement in the grain-growing lowlands." John Lampe and Martin Jackson, *Balkan Economic History, 1550–1950* (Bloomington: Indiana University Press, 1982), 33.

10. Lefteris S. Stavrianos, *The Balkans Since 1453* (New York: Holt, Rinehart and Winston, 1958), 276, 298–99.

11. More on taxation under the Ottoman rule in William McGrew, *Land and Revolution in Modern Greece, 1800–1881* (Kent, Ohio: Kent State University Press, 1985), chap. 2; and Lefteris Stavrianos, *The Ottoman Empire: Was It the Sick Man of Europe?* (New York: Holt, Rinehart and Winston, 1959), 49.

12. Ferdinand Schevill, *The History of the Balkan Peninsula*, rev. ed. (New York: Harcourt Brace, 1933), 10. Similar arguments in George W. Hoffman, *The Balkans in Transition* (New York: D. Van Nostrand, 1963), chap. 3.

13. Stanford Shaw, *History of the Ottoman Empire and Modern Turkey* (London: Cambridge University Press, 1976–77), chap. 6. For the argument that many of the Young Turks, including Djavid Bey and Mustafa Kemal (Ataturk), were hidden Jews, *doenmehs* (*the renegades*), see Joachim Prinz, *The Secret Jews* (New York: Random House, 1973), 118–22.

14. Philip Price, *A History of Turkey: From Empire to Republic* (London: Allen and Unwin, 1965), chap. 7.

15. Wayne Vucinich, *The Ottoman Empire: Its Record and Legacy* (New York: D. Van Nostrand, 1965), 178–79.

16. Vahan Kurkjian, *A History of Armenia* (New York: Armenian General Benevolent Union of America, 1964), 299. See also Gerard Chaliand, *The Armenians, From Genocide to Resistance*, trans. Tony Berrett (London: Zed Press, 1983); and Moses Khorenatsi, *History of the Armenians*, trans. R. Thomson (Cambridge, Mass.: Harvard University Press, 1978).

17. Kevork Bardkjian, *Hitler and the Armenian Genocide* (Cambridge, Mass.: Zoryan Institute, 1985), chap. 4. Also Doris Cross, "The Unanswered Armenian Question," *New York Times*, March 26, 1980, sec. A.

18. Kurkjian, *A History of Armenia*, 302. See also International League for the Rights and Liberation of Peoples, *A Crime of Silence: The Armenian Genocide* (London: Zed Books, 1985), chaps. 1–3.

19. For more details, see Marvine Howe, "Turks, Angry at 'Passivity,' Mourn Slain Diplomats," *New York Times*, March 13, 1981, sec. A.

20. Xenophon, the historian in ancient Greece, in his Anabasis, mentioned that "the Greeks . . . had been seven days passing through the country of the Kurds, fighting all the time . . . " and that they suffered more than from the king of Persia.

Edgar O'Ballance, *The Kurdish Revolt: 1961–1970* (Hamden, Conn.: Archon Books, 1973), 15.

21. Derk Kinnane, *The Kurds and Kurdistan* (London: Oxford University Press, 1964), chap. 4.

22. Marvine Howe, "Turks Imprison Former Minister Who Spoke up on Kurd's Behalf," *New York Times*, March 27, 1981; also, Fredirick Barth, *Principles of Social Organization in Southern Kurdistan* (Oslo: Universitets Ethnografiske Museum, 1953), chap. 1.

23. For example, on November 1980 some 200 Kurds were arrested and prosecuted by the Turkish military. Also, 2,331 Kurds were arrested and 447 were tried in April 1981, while 97 of them were punished by severe penalties or death; Marvine Howe, "Turkey Opens Campaign Against Kurdish Rebels," *New York Times*, April 1, 1981, sec. A.

24. Skirmishes near Diyarbakir, between Kurdish separatists and Turkish soldiers, are reported from time to time. At least 700 people, 200 security members, have been killed since mid-1984. Alan Cowell, "Turkey Admits Inroads by Kurdish Guerrillas," *New York Times*, October 22, 1987, sec. A.

25. "Spring in Turkey, and Kurds' Insurgency Revised," *New York Times*, May 17, 1987, sec. A.

26. More details in William Safire, "Stop the Turks," *New York Times*, March 30, 1995, A23; Alan Cowell, "War on Kurds Hurts Turks in U.S. Eyes," *New York Times*, November 17, 1994, A3; and "Turks and Kurds: Bash, then Talk?" *Economist*, March 25, 1995, 55–58. Washington provides 85 percent of Turkey's arms imports and 90 percent of its military aid. "American Arms Turkey's Repression," *New York Times*, October 17, 1995, A26.

27. Yasar Kemal, "Turkey's War of Words," *New York Times*, May 6, 1995, A19.

28. Celestine Bohlen, "A Sect of Muslims Feels Fundamentalist Threat," *New York Times*, June 3, 1995, L2. In the local elections of 1994, the Welfare Party, the Islamic party of Necmettin Erbakan, won Istanbul, Ankara, and twenty-two other cities, whereas in the general elections of 1995 it came first. This was a surprise in Turkey's seventy-two-year history as a secular republic, inspite of the aid from the West, mainly the United States (including $7.8 billion military aid in grants and loans). In 1996, the Motherland Party of Mesut Yilmaz formed the new government with the suppport of the True Path Party of former Prime Minister Tansu Ciller, who was later accused of economic scandals.

29. The word Turk was considered derogatory by the Ottomans. Also, the Byzantines did not want to be called *Hellenes* because of the pagan connotation. For Turkey's support, see Dankward Rustow, *Turkey: America's Forgotten Ally* (New York: Council on Foreign Relations, 1987).

30. Some 4,000 stores, 2,000 houses, and 29 Greek and some Armenian and Catholic churches, as well as a number of schools, were destroyed. Also, the funerals in Tsisli and Paloukli were profaned. More details in the reports of the

British Counselor Michael Steward, Istanbul, September 22, 1955, in the Archives of Foreign Office. Also *ELEFTHEROTYPIA*, January 8–13, 1985.

31. For the independence agreement, signed in Zurich, and its aftermath, see Stanley Kyriakides, *Cyprus: Constitutionalism and Crisis in Government* (Philadelphia: University of Pennsylvania Press, 1968); and Lawrence Stern, *Wrong Horse* (New York: New York Times Publishing Co., 1980).

32. For the rule of the Greek junta and its effects on Cyprus, see Andreas Papandreou, *Democracy at Gunpoint: The Greek Front* (New York: Doubleday, 1970); and Chris Woodhouse, *Karamanlis: The Restorer of Greek Democracy* (Oxford: Clarendon Press, 1982), chaps. 8–9.

33. On January 4, 1932, Turkey signed an agreement with Italy (Protocol of Italy–Turkey) that the Dodecanese islands, including the Imia islets, belonged to Italy. In 1947, they were ceded to Greece by Italy (Treaty of Paris).

CHAPTER 5

1. For a comprehensive review, see Stephen Clissold, ed., *A Short History of Yugoslavia: From Early Times to 1966* (New York: Cambridge University Press, 1966), chap. 1.

2. The importance of agriculture was very much recognized throughout the Roman period. Richard Duncan-Jones, *The Economy of the Roman Empire: Quantitative Studies* (London: Cambridge University Press, 1974), chap. 2.

3. For a brief historical review, see Fred Singleton and Bernard Carter, *The Economy of Yugoslavia* (New York: St. Martin's Press, 1982), chap. 2.

4. For such first-hand observations, see H. Brailsford, *Macedonia: Its Races and Their Future* (London: Methuen and Co., 1906), 102.

5. For more details, see J. Tomasevich, *Peasants, Politics and Economic Change in Yugoslavia* (Stanford, Calif.: Stanford University Press, 1955), 206.

6. At that time, and since 1878, Serbia has had its own national government. For detailed historical developments, see L. Stavrianos, *The Balkans Since 1453*, chap. 24.

7. M. G. Zaninovich, *The Development of Socialist Yugoslavia* (Baltimore: Johns Hopkins University Press, 1968), 33.

8. Occupation authorities were responsible for expulsion and forced migration of many Yugoslavs. Some 220,000 to 260,000 persons were deported or transferred to various camps to work in German factories. Leszek Kosinski, "International Migration of Yugoslavs During and Immediately After World War II," *East European Quarterly* (June 1982): 183–98. Bosnia-Herzegovina was part of wartime Croatia and Bosnian Muslim (Handjar) units of the SS were particularly effective in atrocities. Some 350,000 people (according to German reports) or 750,000 (according to Serbian historians) were exterminated by the Croats and the Bosnian Muslims, primarily in the Jasenovac camp. Nils Horner, "World War II Holocaust No Fiction," *New York Times*, May 12, 1994, A26.

9. Phyllis Auty, "The Postwar Period," in Stephen Clissold, ed., *A Short History of Yugoslavia: From Early Times to 1966* (New York: Cambridge University Press, 1966), 236–40.

10. Zaninovich, *The Development of Socialist Yugoslavia*, 171.

11. In the early 1960s, more than 90 percent of the peasants belonged to such cooperatives. Auty, "The Postwar Period," 247, 250.

12. Although criticism of governmental policies was permitted, the advocacy of other forms of government was not allowed. This can be inferred from the arguments of Milovan Djilas, for which he was sentenced to seven years in prison.

13. Marvine Howe, "Greece Joins Soviets in Urging Deep Arms Cuts," *New York Times*, February 25, 1983.

14. Further review in Jaroslav Vanek, *Participatory Economy* (Ithaca, N.Y.: Cornell University Press, 1971); and idem, *The General Theory of Labor-Managed Market Economies* (Ithaca, N.Y.: Cornell University Press, 1970), Also, L. Sire, *The Yugoslav Economy under Self-Management* (London: Macmillan, 1979), chap. 8.

15. For new problems of ethnicities and the principle of self-determinations, see Daniel P. Moynihan, *Pandemonium: Ethnicity in International Politics* (New York: Oxford University Press, 1993). More information in W. Gewehr, *The Rise of Nationalism in the Balkans, 1800–1930* (Hamden, Conn.: Archon Books, 1967), chap. 2.

16. "Croatia's Risky Offensive," *New York Times*, May 4, 1995, A24.

17. Hugh Poulton, *The Balkans: Minorities and States in Conflict* (London: Minority Rights Publications, 1991), 41–43. For the support of Bosnia by the Arab countries, see Roger Cohen, "Out of the Mad, Into the Morass," *New York Times*, April 16, 1995, A6.

18. Nicholas V. Gianaris, "Recognizing Macedonia Can Only Fuel Conflict," *New York Times*, May 21, 1992, A28.

CHAPTER 6

1. For more details see L. Stavrianos, *The Balkans Since 1453* (New York: Holt, Rinehart and Winston, 1958), 709–31. W. Gewehr, *The Rise of Nationalism in the Balkans, 1800–1930* (Hamden, Conn.: Archon Books, 1967), 116–17.

2. Faik Lama, "The Balance Sheet of the National Liberation War," *New Albania*, vol. IV (Tirana: N. Librit, 1979), 16.

3. In 1978, China broke definitely with Albania, and Tirana was deprived of Chinese trade and aid (at least $5 billion over the previous twenty years).

4. More detailed figures on Albanian emigration are provided by Mahir Domi, "Albanian Settlements in the World," *New Albania*, vol. V (Tirana: N. Librit, 1979), 20.

5. For details on reforms in Albania compared with other Eastern European countries, see M. Kaser, "Albania," in H. Hohmann et al., eds., *The New Economic*

Systems of Eastern Europe (Berkeley: University of California Press, 1975), chap. 9; Ramadan Marmullaku, *Albania and the Albanians* (London: C. Hurst, 1975), chap. 8. Also, Jurg Steiner, *European Democracies*, 3d ed. (New York: Longman, 1995), 294–95.

6. Andelman, "Albania Dips a Wary Toe." A trade agreement with Greece in 1980 provided for $50 million, compared with only $4 million in 1975. In 1980, trade ministers from Greece, Turkey, and Romania scheduled visits to Albania.

7. "Drug Smuggling: The Albanian Connection," *Economist*, October 29, 1994, 61.

8. Stambuliski was then captured and handed to IMRO terrorists, who tortured him and made him dig the grave in which he was buried. For the political success and the downfall of Stambuliski and the Agrarians, see Stavrianos, *The Balkans Since 1453*, 646–50; F. Schevill, *The History of the Balkan Peninsula*, rev. ed. (New York: Harcourt Brace, 1933), 509–11.

9. For a survey of technical progress, planometrics, and incentives, see G. Feiwei, *Growth and Reforms in Centrally Planned Economies: The Lessons of the Bulgarian Experience* (New York: Praeger, 1977), chaps. 4, 7, 9.

10. The reform "theses" of decentralization, suggested by Professors Angel Miloshevski and Petro Kunin, included the use of an incentive portion of wages in addition to the guaranteed portion. J. Brown, "Economic Reforms in Bulgaria," *Problems of Communism* (May–June 1966), 17–21.

11. For the reduced interest in self-management in Bulgaria, see Derek C. Jones and Micke Meures, "Worker Participation and Worker Self-Management in Bulgaria," *Comparative Economic Studies*, 33, no. 4 (Winter 1991), 47–81.

12. "Kathisteroun i Idiotikopiisis" (Privatizations are Delayed), *TO VIMA*, Athens, June 12, 1994, 35.

13. Kerin Hope, "Fund to Invest in Bulgaria," *Financial Times*, October 10, 1994, 19.

14. Stephen Kinzer, "Bulgaria Not Sure Whether It Should Turn East or West," *New York Times*, April 28, 1995, A11.

15. "I Ellada Pemti Stis Ependisis Sti Vulgaria" (Greece Fifth in Investment in Bulgaria), *TO VIMA*, Athens, April 30, 1995, D13.

16. For oil statistics see C. Jordan, *The Romanian Oil Industry* (New York: New York University Press, 1955). In 1975 crude oil production reached 14,590,000 tons.

17. For more statistical data see H. Roberts, *Romania: Political Problems of an Agrarian State* (New Haven: Yale University Press, 1951), 177.

18. For Romania's decentralization reforms and trade increase with the West, see John Montias, *Development in Communist Romania* (Cambridge, Mass.: M.I.T. Press, 1967), chaps. 4 and 7.

19. For additional sociopolitical considerations, see A. Damianakos, "Romania: In Search of Identity," *The Balkan Observer* 1 (New York) (1980): 7–9.

20. Kevin Done and Virginia Marsh, "Peugeot May Assemble Cars in Romania," *Financial Times*, May 8, 1995, 2.

21. "Romania Sell-Off Bill Passed," *Financial Times*, March 22, 1995, 2.

CHAPTER 7

1. The expected rate of economic growth (g) may be determined by the average propensity to save (s), the expected difference in foreign trade (exports–imports) as a percentage of national income (f), and the capital/output ratio (v):
$g = (s + f)/v$
Assuming $s = 0.15$, $f = 0.03$, and $v = 3$, the rate of economic growth would be 6 percent of the national income: $g = (0.15 + 0.03)/3 = 0.18/3 = 0.06$.
More in Nicholas V. Gianaris, "International Differences in Capital-Output Ratios," *American Economic Review* 60, no. 3 (June 1970), 465–77.

2. World Bank, *World Development Report, 1994* (New York: Oxford University Press, for the World Bank, 1994), 186–91.

3. World Bank, *World Development Report*, various issues; and Nicholas V. Gianaris, *Greece and Turkey: Economic and Geopolitical Perspectives* (New York: Praeger, 1988), 143.

4. Hollis Chenery presented data on semi-industrial countries, in which Turkey and Yugoslavia were included, that support these findings. See his "Interactions Between Industrialization and Exports," *American Economic Review, Proceedings*, May 1980, 381–92.

5. Although imports by Greece from the United States have been limited, about 5 percent of an estimated $17 billion import bill, the actual value of American sales to Greece started rising. Many Greek industries, large and small, look across the Atlantic for capital, equipment, and know-how with which they can improve their competitiveness against their EU counterparts.

6. Profits from joint ventures are taxed at rates up to around 34 percent.

7. Ron Ayres, "Turkish Foreign Relations," in Khamsim Collective, *Modern Turkey: Development and Crisis* (London: Ithaca Press, 1984), 117–27.

8. For the postwar policy of the United States, see Theodore Couloumbis, *The United States, Greece and Turkey: The Troubled Triangle* (New York: Praeger, 1983); and Harry N. Howard, *Turkey, The Straits and U.S. Policy* (Baltimore: Johns Hopkins University Press, 1974).

9. Lar-Erik Nelson, "The World According to Kissinger," *New York Newsday*, April 123, 1994. Also, A. M. Rosenthal, "Lighting Bosnia's Fire," *New York Times*, December 23, 1994, A35. For the Islamization of Bosnian society, see Chuck Sudetic, "Bosnia's Elite Force: Fed, Fit, Muslim," *New York Times*, June 16, 1995, A12.

10. Raymond Bonner, "The Land That Can't Be Named," *New York Times*, May 14, 1995, E6.

11. Ibid. Also, Ronald I. Friedman, "To Greeks Macedonia's Not Just a Name," *New York Times*, May 19, 1995, A30; and Nicholas V. Gianaris, "Recognizing Macedonia Can Only Fuel Conflict," *New York Times*, May 21, 1992, A28.

12. George Soros, the international financier who supported FYROM with millions of dollars, suggested the name "Slavo-Macedonia" and that Scopja's flag with the sun of Vergina (the symbol of Alexander the Great) be changed. "Piesis sta Skopia yia Allagi Simeas, Onomatos apo ton Soros" (Pressures on Skopja for Change in Flag, Name from Soros), (New York), *National Herald,* May 30, 1995, 7.

13. Nicholas Stavrou, "Lost Chances for Balkan Peace," *Washington Post*, June 28, 1995, A20.

14. Further analysis in William Safire, "War on the World," *New York Times*, June 1, 1995, A25; and A. M. Rosenthal, "Why Only Bosnia? " *New York Times*, May 30, 1995, A17.

15. More details in the statement by Richard C. Holbrooke, U.S. Assistant Secretary of State for European and Canadian Affairs, before the North Atlantic Assembly in Budapest, May 29, 1995, 4–6 and 18–19. Also, his statement before the International Relations Committee, U.S. House of Representatives, March 9, 1995, 10–30.

16. Misha Glenny, "And the Winner Is . . . Croatia," *New York Times*, September 26, 1995, A23. For the main reasons of conflict, see Susan L. Woodward, *Balkan Tragedy* (Washington, D.C.: Brookings Institution, 1995); Roger Cohen, "Taming the Bullies of Bosnia," *New York Times Magazine*, December 17, 1995, 58–63, 76–78, 90, 95, and "The Balkan End-Game," *Economist*, January 20, 1996, 19–21.

CHAPTER 8

1. In the countryside there are many physical similarities and numerous common characteristics, especially in music and peasant dances such as the Slav *kolo*, the Romanian *hora*, and the Greek *choria*. Lefteris Stavrianos, *Balkan Federation* (Hamden, Conn.: Archon Books, 1964), 2–4.

2. For a thorough review, see R. Kerner, *The Balkan Conferences and the Balkan Entente* (Berkeley: University of California Press, 1940), chaps. 5–8.

3. The members of the ruling presidium, elected in rotation for one-year terms after Tito's death, expressed also desires for closer Balkan ties.

4. Constantine Caramanlis, who was prime minister of Greece in 1955–63 and 1974–80, was instrumental in promoting Balkan cooperation, as were Prime Minister George Rhallis (1980–81) and Prime Minister Andreas Papandreou (1981–89 and 1993–January 1996).

5. Athanasios Kanellopoulos (Euvoulos), "I Evropi kai o Horos tou Mellontos mas," (Europe and the Place of Our Future), *TO VIMA*, Athens, July 5, 1992, A14.

6. For growth limits of the EU, see Paul Taylor, *The Limits of European Integration* (New York: Columbia University Press, 1980). Also, Nicholas V. Gianaris, "The Limits of the European Union: The Question of Enlargement," in George Kourvetaris and Andreas Moschonas, eds., *Political Sociology of European Integration* (Westport, Conn.: Praeger, 1996), chap. 13.

7. Sociopolitical and environmental aspects of the EU are in C. Pinkele and Adamantia Polis, eds., *The Contemporary Mediterranean World* (New York: Praeger, 1983), chap. 5; Richard Pomfret, *Mediterranean Policy of the European Community* (New York: Macmillan, 1986).

8. As they stated in their letters, Prime Minister John Major and President Francois Mitterrand (July 11 and July 27, 1994, respectively) considered my proposal seriously, although with some reservations regarding the time of Balkan membership in the EU.

9. For privatization in the Balkan and other countries, see Nicholas V. Gianaris, *Modern Capitalism: Privatization, Employee Ownership, and Industrial Democracy* (Westport, Conn.: Praeger, 1996), chaps. 4–6.

Bibliography

"America Arms Turkey's Repression." *New York Times*, October 17, 1995, A26.

Andreades, Andreas. *A History of Public Finance in Greece*. Cambridge, Mass.: Harvard University Press, 1933.

Angell, Norman. *The Story of Money*. New York: F. A. Stokes, 1929.

Athanasiades, Kostas. *Diethnis Oikonomikes Sygrousis, 1945–1990* (International Economic Conflicts, 1945–90). New York: Kampana, 1990.

Austin, M. *Economic and Social History of Ancient Greece: An Introduction*. Berkeley: University of California Press, 1977.

Ayres, Ron. "Turkish Foreign Relations." In Khamsin Collective, *Modern Turkey: Development and Crisis*. London: Ithaca Press, 1984.

"The Balkan End-Game." *Economist*, January 20, 1996, 19–21.

Bardkjian, Kevork. *Hitler and the Armenian Genocide*. Cambridge, Mass.: Zoryan Institute, 1985.

Barker, Ernest. *The Political Thought of Plato and Aristotle*. New York: Dover Publications, 1959.

Barth, Frederick. *Principles of Social Organization in Southern Kurdistan*. Oslo: Universitets Ethnografiske Museum, 1953.

Boeckh, Augustus. *The Public Economy of Athens*. New York: Arno Press, 1976.

Bohlen, Celestine. "A Sect of Muslims Feels Fundamentalist Threat." *New York Times*, June 3, 1995, L2.

Bonner, Raymond. "Albanians in Kosovo Fearful of U.S. Deal with Yugoslavia." *New York Times*, April 9, 1995, A13.

———. "The Land That Can't Be Named." *New York Times*, May 14, 1995, E6.

Botsford, George and E. Sihelr, eds. *Hellenic Civilizations*. New York: Columbia University Press, 1915.

———— and C. Robinson, Jr. *Hellenic History*, 5th ed. rev. D. Kagan. London: Macmillan, 1971.

Brailsford, H. *Macedonia: Its Races and Their Future*. London: Methuen and Co., 1906.

Braun, Aurel. *Small-State Security in the Balkans*. Totowa, N.J.: Barnes and Noble Books, 1983.

Brown, J. "Economic Reforms in Bulgaria." *Problems of Communism* (May–June 1966).

Bury, J. *A History of the Eastern Roman Empire*. New York: Russell and Russell, 1966.

Cahen, Claude. *Pre-Ottoman Turkey*. New York: Tabbinger, 1968.

Camm, Henry. "Conflict with Greece Leaves Some in Albania Perplexed." *New York Times*, December 19, 1994, A13.

Carey, J. and A. Carey. *The Web of Modern Greek Politics*. New York: Columbia University Press, 1968.

Ceram, C. W. *The Secret of the Hittites: The Discovery of the Ancient Empire*. New York: Alfred A. Knopf, 1956.

Chaliand, Gerard. *The Armenians, From Genocide to Resistance*. Trans. Tony Berrett. London: Zed Press, 1983.

Chenery, Hollis. "Interactions Between Industrialization and Exports." *American Economic Review, Proceedings*, May 1980.

Churchill, Winston. *Memoirs of the Second World War*. Boston: Houghton Mifflin, 1959.

————. *Triumph and Tragedy: The Second World War*, vol. 6. Boston: Houghton Mifflin, 1953.

Clissold, Stephen, ed. *A Short History of Yugoslavia: From Early Times to 1966*. New York: Cambridge University Press, 1966.

Clogg, Richard. *A Short History of Modern Greece*. New York: Cambridge University Press, 1979.

————, ed. *The Movement for Greek Independence, 1770–1821*. London: Macmillan, 1976.

Cohen, Roger. "Out of the Mad, Into the Morass." *New York Times*, April 16, 1995, A6.

————. "Taming the Bullies of Bosnia." *New York Times Magazine*, December 17, 1995, 58–63, 76–78, 90, 95.

Cook, M. J. *Greeks in Ionia and the East*. London: Thames and Hudson, 1962.

Couloumbis, Theodore. *The United States, Greece and Turkey: The Troubled Triangle*. New York: Praeger, 1983.

———— and John Iatrides, eds. *Greek American Relations: A Critical Review*. New York: Pella, 1980.

Cowell, Alan. "Turkey Admits Inroads by Kurdish Guerrillas." *New York Times*, October 22, 1987, sec. A.

———. "War on Kurds Hurts Turks in U.S. Eyes." *New York Times*, November 17, 1994, A3.

Crawley, C. "Modern Greece, 1821–1930." In W. Heurtley et al., *A Short History of Modern Greece*. Cambridge: Cambridge University Press, 1965.

"Croatia's Risky Offensive." *New York Times*, May 4, 1995, A24.

Cross, Doris. "The Unanswered Armenian Question." *New York Times*, March 26, 1980, sec. A.

Czakca, M. "Price History of Bursa Silk Industry: A Study of Ottoman Decline, 1550–1650." *Journal of Economic History*, September 1980.

Damianakos, A. "Romania: In Search of Identity." *The Balkan Observer* 1 (New York), 1980.

Daulas, Dimitris. "I Ethnikes Mionotites Kata To B' Pagosmio Polemo." (Ethnic Minorities in World War II). *Logos*, Athens, August 11, 1995.

Davis, William. *A Short History of the Near East*. New York: Macmillan, 1937.

Day, John. *An Economic History of Athens under Roman Domination*. New York: Arno Press, 1973.

Dochia, A. "Privatization and Foreign Investment Potential in Romania." In Hellenic Center for European Studies, *The European Community and the Balkans*. Athens: Ant. N. Sakkoulas Publishers, 1955.

Domi, Mahir. "Albanian Settlements in the World." *New Albania*. Tirana: N. Librit, 1979.

Done, Kevin and Virginia Marsh. "Peugeot May Assemble Cars in Romania." *Financial Times*, May 8, 1995, 2.

"Drug Smuggling: The Albanian Connection." *Economist*, October 29, 1994.

Duncan-Jones, Richard. *The Economy of the Roman Empire: Quantitative Studies*. London: Cambridge University Press, 1974.

ELEFTHEROTYPIA, January 8–13, 1985.

Erim, Kenan. *Aphrodisias*. New York: Facts on File, 1986.

Farnsworth, Clyde. "The Rise and Fall of Civilization According to Tax Collection." *New York Times*, October 3, 1993, E7.

Feiwei, G. *Growth and Reforms in Centrally Planned Economies: The Lessons of the Bulgarian Experience*. New York: Praeger, 1977.

Finley, Moses. *The Ancient Economy*. Berkeley: University of California Press, 1973.

Foster, Edward. *A Short History of Modern Greece, 1821–1956*. New York: Praeger, 1957.

Friedman, Ronald I. "To Greeks Macedonia's Not Just a Name." *New York Times*, May 19, 1995, A30.

General Secretariat of the Region of East Macedonia-Thrace. *Thrace*. Athens: Idea Advertising-Marketing SA, 1994.

Gewehr, W. *The Rise of Nationalism in the Balkans, 1800–1930*. Hamden, Conn.: Archon Books, 1967.

Gianaris, Nicholas V. *The Economies of the Balkan Countries: Albania, Bulgaria, Greece, Romania, and Yugoslavia*. New York: Praeger, 1982.

————. *The European Community and the United States: Economic Relations*. New York: Praeger, 1991.

————. *The European Community, Eastern Europe, and Russia: Economic and Political Changes*. Westport, Conn.: Praeger, 1994.

————. *Greece and Turkey: Economic and Geopolitical Perspectives*. New York: Praeger, 1988.

————. *Greece and Yugoslavia: An Economic Comparison*. New York: Praeger, 1984.

————. "Greeks Had a Word for Reagan Tax Plan." *New York Times*, January 1, 1985, A26.

————. "International Differences in Capital-Output Ratios." *American Economic Review* 60, no. 3 (June 1970).

————. "The Limits of the European Union: The Question of Enlargement." In George Kourvetaris and Andreas Moschonas, eds., *Political Sociology of European Integration*. Westport, Conn.: Praeger, 1995.

————. *Modern Capitalism: Privatization, Employee Ownership, and Industrial Democracy*. Westport, Conn.: Praeger, 1996.

————. *The Province of Kalavryta: A Historical and Socioeconomic Review*. New York: National Herald, 1983.

————. "Recognizing Macedonia Can Only Fuel Conflict." *New York Times*, May 21, 1992, A28.

Giannaris, George V. *Fititika Kinimata kai Elliniki Pedia* (Students' Movements and Greek Education), vol. 1. Athens: Pontiki Press, 1993.

————. *Mikis Theodorakis: Music and Social Change*. New York: Praeger, 1972.

Glenny, Misha. "And the Winner Is . . . Croatia." *New York Times*, September 26, 1995, A23.

Glover, Terrot, *The Challenge of the Greeks and Other Essays*. New York: Macmillan, 1942.

Grekov, B. *Kiev Rus*. Moscow: Foreign Languages Publishing House, 1959.

Herodotus. IV, 3.

Hoffman, George. *The Balkans in Transition*. New York: D. Van Nostrand, 1963.

Holbrooke, Richard C. *Statement Before the International Relations Committee*, U.S. House of Representatives (March 9, 1995): 10–30.

————. *Statement Before the North Atlantic Assembly in Budapest* (May 29, 1995): 4–6.

Hope, Kerin. "Fund to Invest in Bulgaria." *Financial Times*, October 10, 1994, 19.

————. "Greece to Float 8% of State Telecoms Monopoly." *Financial Times*, May 30, 1995.

Hopkins, Adam. *Crete: Its Past, Present and People*. London: Faber, 1977.

Horner, Nils. "World War II Holocaust No Fiction." *New York Times*, May 12, 1994, A26.

Howard, Harry N. *Turkey, The Straits and U.S. Policy*. Baltimore: Johns Hopkins University Press, 1974.

Howe, Marvine. "Greece Joins Soviets in Urging Deep Arms Cuts." *New York Times*, February 25, 1983.

————. "Turkey Opens Campaign Against Kurdish Rebels." *New York Times*, April 1, 1981, sec. A.

————. "Turks, Angry at 'Passivity,' Morn Slain Diplomats." *New York Times*, March 13, 1981, sec. A.

————. "Turks Imprison Former Minister Who Spoke up on Kurd's Behalf." *New York Times*, March 27, 1981.

"I Ellada Pemti Stis Ependisis Sti Vulgaria" (Greece Fifth in Investment in Bulgaria). *TO VIMA*, Athens, April 30, 1995, D13.

International League for the Rights and Liberation of Peoples. *A Crime of Silence: The Armenian Genocide*. London: Zed Books, 1985.

Jones, Derek C. and Micke Meures. "Worker Participation and Worker Self-Management in Bulgaria." *Comparative Economic Studies* 33, no. 4 (Winter 1991): 47–81.

Jordan, C. *The Romanian Oil Industry*. New York: New York University Press, 1955.

Kaltchas, Nicholas. *Introduction to the Constitutional History of Modern Greece*. New York: Columbia University Press, 1940.

Kanellopoulos, Athanasios (Euvoulos). "I Evropi kai o Horos tou Mellontos mas." (Europe and the Place of Our Future). *TO VIMA*, Athens, July 5, 1992, A14.

"Kathisteroun i Idiotikopiisis" (Privatizations are Delayed). *TO VIMA*, Athens, June 12, 1994, 35.

Kaser, M. "Albania." In H. Hohmann et al., eds., *The New Economic Systems of Eastern Europe*. Berkeley: University of California Press, 1975.

Kemal, Yasar. "Turkey's War of Words." *New York Times*, May 6, 1995, A19.

Kerner, R. *The Balkan Conferences and the Balkan Entente*. Berkeley: University of California Press, 1940.

Khorenatsi, Moses. *History of the Armenians*. Trans. R. Thomson. Cambridge, Mass.: Harvard University Press, 1978.

Kinnane, Derk. *The Kurds and Kurdistan*. London: Oxford University Press, 1964.

Kinzer, Stephen. "Bulgaria Not Sure Whether It Should Turn East or West." *New York Times*, April 28, 1995, A11.

Kirk, D. *Europe's Population in the Interwar Years*. Geneva: League of Nations, 1946.

Kirnoss, L. *The Ottoman Centuries, The Rise and Fall of the Turkish Empire*. New York: Morrow, 1977.

Koliopoulos J. *Greece and the British Connection, 1935–1941*. Oxford: Clarendon Press, 1977.

Kollintzas, Trifon and George Bitros. *Anazitontas tin Elpida Gia tin Elliniki Oikonomia* (Pursuing the Hope for the Greek Economy). Athens: Institute for Economic Policy Studies, 1992.

Kordatos, J. *T'Ampelakia Ki'o Mythos Gia To Syneterismo Tous* (The Ampelakia and the Myth of their Partnership). Athens: K. Strate, 1955.

Kosinski, Leszek. "International Migration of Yugoslavs During and Immediately After World War II." *East European Quarterly* (June 1982): 183–198.

Kurkjian, Vahan. *A History of Armenia*. New York: Armenian General Benevolent Union of America, 1964.

Kyriakides, Stanley. *Cyprus: Constitutionalism and Crisis in Government*. Philadelphia: University of Pennsylvania Press, 1968.

Lama, Faik. "The Balance Sheet of the National Liberation War." *New Albania*, vol. IV. Tirana: N. Librit, 1979, 16.

Lampe, John and Martin Jackson. *Balkan Economic History, 1550–1950*. Bloomington: Indiana University Press, 1982.

Lowry, Todd. "Recent Literature on Ancient Greek Economic Thought." *Journal of Economic Literature* 17 (March 1979): 65–86.

Mahaffy, J. P. *Rambles and Studies in Greece*, 2d ed. London: Macmillan, 1878.

Marmullaku, Ramadan. *Albania and the Albanians*. London: C. Hurst, 1975.

McGrew, William. *Land and Revolution in Modern Greece, 1800–1881*. Kent, Ohio: Kent State University Press, 1985.

McNeill, William. *The Greek Dilemma*. London: Victor Gollancz, 1947.

Montias, John. *Development in Communist Romania*. Cambridge, Mass.: M.I.T. Press, 1967.

Moore, W. E. *Economic Demography in Eastern and Southern Europe*. Geneva: League of Nations, 1945.

Moynihan, Daniel P. *Pandemonium: Ethnicity in International Politics*. New York: Oxford University Press, 1993.

Munkman, C. *American Aid to Greece*. New York: Praeger, 1978.

Myers, C. *Greek Entanglement*. London: Rupert Hart-Davis, 1955.

Nelson, Lar-Erik. "The World According to Kissinger." *New York Newsday*, April 12, 1994.

Nicol, D. *The End of the Byzantine Empire*. New York: Holmes and Meier, 1979.

Nyrop, Richard, ed. *Turkey: A Country Study*. Washington, D.C.: American University Press, 1980.

O'Ballance, Edgar. *The Greek Civil War, 1944–1949*. London: Faber and Faber, 1966.

————. *The Kurdish Revolt: 1961–1970*. Hamden, Conn.: Archon Books, 1973.

Papacosma, Victor. *The Military in Greek Politics: The 1909 Coup d'Etat.* Kent, Ohio: Kent State University Press, 1977.

Panandreou, Andreas. *Democracy at Gunpoint: The Greek Front.* New York: Doubleday, 1970.

Paparrhegopoulos, K. *Historia tou Hellinikou Ethnous: Apo ton Archaiotaton Chronon Mechri ton Neoteron* (History of the Greek Nation: From the Ancient Years until the Recent Years). Athens: S. Pavlidou, 1874.

Pausanias. *Attica* I, IX, 5.

Pepelasis, Adamantios. "The Legal System and Economic Development of Greece." *Journal of Economic History* 19, no. 2 (June 1959): 174–76.

"Piesis sta Skopia yia Allagi Simeas, Onomatos apo ton Soros" (Pressures on Skopja for Change in Flag, Name from Soros). New York: *National Herald,* May 30, 1995, 7.

Pinkele, C. and Adamantia Polis, eds., *The Contemporary Mediterranean World.* New York: Praeger, 1983.

Pomfret, Richard. *Mediterranean Policy of the European Community.* New York: Macmillan, 1986.

Poulton, Hugh. *The Balkans: Minorities and States in Conflict.* London: Minority Rights Publications, 1991.

Price, Philip. *A History of Turkey: From Empire to Republic.* London: Allen and Unwin, 1965.

Prinz, Joachim. *The Secret Jews.* New York: Random House, 1973.

Psomiades, Harry. "The Economic and Social Transformation of Modern Greece." *Journal of International Affairs* 19 (1965): 194–205.

Richter, Heinz. *1933–1946: Dio Epanastasis kai Antepanastasis Stin Ellada* (Two Revolutions and Counterrevolutions in Greece). Trans. from German. 2 vols. Athens: Exantas, 1975.

Roberts, H. *Romania: Political Problems of an Agrarian State.* New Haven: Yale University Press, 1951.

"Romania Sell-Off Bill Passed." *Financial Times,* March 22, 1995, 2.

Romania: Yearbook, 1976. Bucharest: Scientific and Encyclopedic Publishing House, 1976.

Rosenthal, A. M. "Lighting Bosnia's Fire." *New York Times,* December 23, 1994, A35.

———. "Why Only Bosnia?" *New York Times,* May 30, 1995, A17.

Rousseas, Stephen. *The Death of a Democracy: Greece and the American Conscience.* New York: Grove Press, 1967.

Rustow, Dankward. *Turkey: America's Forgotten Ally.* New York: Council on Foreign Relations, 1987.

Safire, William. "Stop the Turks." *New York Times,* March 30, 1995, A23.

———. "War on the World." *New York Times,* June 1, 1995, A25.

Schevill, Ferdinand. *The History of the Balkan Peninsula,* rev. ed. New York: Harcourt Brace, 1933.

Schonfield, H. *The Suez Canal in Peace and War, 1869–1969*. Miami: University of Miami Press, 1969.

Schumpeter, Joseph. *The Theory of Economic Development*. New York: Oxford University Press, 1961.

Shaw, Stanford. *History of the Ottoman Empire and Modern Turkey*. London: Cambridge University Press, 1976–77.

Singer, Morris. *Economic Developments in the Context of the Short-Term Public Policies: The Economic Advance of Turkey, 1930–1960*. Ankara: Turkish Economic Society, 1978.

Singleton, Fred and Bernard Carter. *The Economy of Yugoslavia*. New York: St. Martin's Press, 1982.

Sire, L. *The Yugoslav Economy under Self-Management*. London: Macmillan, 1979.

"Spring in Turkey, and Kurds' Insurgency Revised." *New York Times*, May 17, 1987, sec. A.

Stahl, H. *Traditional Romanian Village Communities*. Trans. D. Chirot and H. Chirot. New York: Cambridge University Press, 1980.

Stanley, C. *Roots of the Tree*. London: Oxford University Press, 1936.

Stavrianos, Lefteris. *Balkan Federation*. Hamden, Conn.: Archon Books, 1964.

———. *The Balkans Since 1453*. New York: Holt, Rinehart and Winston, 1958.

———. *The Ottoman Empire: Was It the Sick Man of Europe?* New York: Holt, Rinehart and Winston, 1959.

Stavrou, Nicholas. "Lost Chances for Balkan Peace." *Washington Post*, June 28, 1995, A20.

Steiner, Jurg. *European Democracies*, 3d ed. New York: Longman, 1995.

Stern, Lawrence. *Wrong Horse*. New York: New York Times Publishing Co., 1980.

Strarr, C. *The Economic and Social Growth of Early Greece: 800–500* B.C. New York: Oxford University Press, 1977.

Strigas, Athanasios. *Pagosmii Entolodohi* (Global Agents). Athens: Nea Thesis, 1994, chaps. 8–11.

Sudetic, Chuck. "Bosnia's Elite Force: Fed, Fit, Muslim." *New York Times*, June 16, 1995, A12.

Tarn, W. and G. Griffith. *Hellenistic Civilization*, 3d ed. rev. London: Edward Arnold, 1952.

Taylor, Paul. *The Limits of the European Integration*. New York: Columbia University Press, 1980.

Tomasevich, J. *Peasants, Politics and Economic Change in Yugoslavia*. Stanford, Calif.: Stanford University Press, 1955.

Torrey, G. "Some Recent Literature on Romania's Role in the First World War." *East European Quarterly* 14, no. 2 (Summer 1980): 189–206.

Toutain, Jules. *The Economic Life of the Ancient World*. New York: Alfred A. Knopf, 1930.

Toynbee Arnold. *Constantine Porphyrogenitus and His World*. London: Oxford University Press, 1973.

———. *Some Problems of Greek History*. London: Oxford University Press, 1969.

"Turks and Kurds: Bash, then Talk?" *Economist*, March 25, 1995, 55–58.

Vanek, Jaroslav. *The General Theory of Labor-Managed Market Economies*. Ithaca, N.Y.: Cornell University Press, 1970.

———. *Participatory Economy*. Ithaca, N.Y.: Cornell University Press, 1971.

Vucinich, Wayne. *The Ottoman Empire: Its Record and Legacy*. New York: D. Van Nostrand, 1965.

Ward, B. *The Interplay of East and West*. London: Allen and Unwin, 1957.

Wolff, Robert. *The Balkans in Our Time*. New York: W. W. Norton, 1967.

Woodhouse, C. *Apple of Discord: A Survey of Recent Greek Politics in Their International Setting*. London: Hutchinson, 1948.

———. *Karamanlis: The Restorer of Greek Democracy*. Oxford: Clarendon Press, 1982.

Woodward, Susan L. *Balkan Tragedy*. Washington, D.C.: Brookings Institution, 1995.

World Bank. *World Development Report*. New York: Oxford University Press, for the World Bank, annual.

Xenophon's Works. Trans. C. Ashley et al. Philadelphia: Thomas Wardle, 1843.

Xydis, S. *Greece and the Great Powers, 1944–1947*. Thessaloniki: Institute for Balkan Studies, 1963.

Zakynthinos, D. *The Making of Modern Greece: From Byzantium to Independence*, trans. K. Johnstone. London: Basil Blackwell, 1976.

Zaninovich, M. G. *The Development of Socialist Yugoslavia*. Baltimore: Johns Hopkins University Press, 1968.

Index

Abdul Hamid II, Sultan, 28–29, 73
Achaean League, 2, 14, 16
Achaeans, 2, 13, 14, 35
Adrianople, Greece, 68
Aegean Islands, 17, 38, 39
Aegean Sea, 134
Aegina, 14
Aeoleans, 1, 35
Agapiou AE, 58
Agno, 58
Agrarian Party, 113
Alaric I, King, 18
Alawites, 78–79
Albania: Balkan cooperation and,
    160; Comecom and, 179; drug traf-
    fic and, 111; early inhabitants of,
    19–20; economic history of, 109–
    10; economic model of, 127; eco-
    nomic reforms by, 7; European
    Union and, 179, 180, 181; foreign
    trade and, 58, 110–11, 131, 179;
    GNP and, 131; Greece and, 4, 58;
    highway construction and, 59; Ital-
    ian investment in, 108; Kosovo

and, 100; minorities in, 3; Muslim
    conversions and, 103; Ottoman
    rule and, 21, 27, 107; political his-
    tory of, 107–9; privatization and,
    111; World War II and, 32, 89, 90,
    108–9
Albania Labor Party (ALP), 109
Albanian League, 107
Albkrom state enterprise, 111
Albpunndimpeks, 58
Alexander, King, 88
Alexander of Battenburg, King, 28
Alexander the Great, 2–3, 14, 15–16,
    38, 66, 105, 133
Alexandroupolis, Greece, 58, 59
Algiers, 29
Alia, Ramiz, 110
Alpha Finance, 59–60
Alps, 5
Aluminium de Greece, 54
Ambelakia enterprise, 41
American International Group, 116
Amoco Romania Petroleum Com-
    pany, 123

About the Author

NICHOLAS V. GIANARIS is Professor of Economics at Fordham University. Dr. Gianaris is the author of nine books with Praeger, including *Modern Capitalism*: *Privatization, Employee Ownership, and Industrial Democracy* (1996), *The European Community, Eastern Europe, and Russia*: *Economic and Political Changes* (1994), *Contemporary Economic Systems*: *A Regional and Country Approach* (1993), and *The European Community and the United States*: *Economic Relations* (1991). Three other books deal with Greece and the Balkan area.

ISBN 0-275-95541-9

9 780275 955410

HARDCOVER BAR CODE